Folk Music and the New
Left in the Sixties

Folk Music and the New Left in the Sixties

MICHAEL SCOTT CAIN

McFarland & Company, Inc., Publishers
Jefferson, North Carolina

The author died on January 30, 2018, after completing the manuscript for this book.

LIBRARY OF CONGRESS CATALOGUING-IN-PUBLICATION DATA

Names: Cain, Michael Scott, author.
Title: Folk music and the new left in the sixties / Michael Scott Cain.
Description: Jefferson, North Carolina : McFarland & Company, 2019 | Includes bibliographical references and index.
Identifiers: LCCN 2019018006 | ISBN 9781476674728 (paperback : acid free paper) ∞
Subjects: LCSH: Folk music—Political aspects—United States—History—20th century. | Protest songs—United States—20th century—History and criticism. | Social movements—United States—History—20th century. | Nineteen sixties.
Classification: LCC ML3917.U6 C3 2019 | DDC 781.62/13009046—dc23
LC record available at https://lccn.loc.gov/2019018006

BRITISH LIBRARY CATALOGUING DATA ARE AVAILABLE

ISBN (print) 978-1-4766-7472-8
ISBN (ebook) 978-1-4766-3595-8

© 2019 Helene Toney Cain. All rights reserved

No part of this book may be reproduced or transmitted in any form or by any means, electronic or mechanical, including photocopying or recording, or by any information storage and retrieval system, without permission in writing from the publisher.

Front cover: Joan Baez and Bob Dylan performing at the Civil Rights March in Washington, D.C., on August 28, 1963 (National Archives)

Printed in the United States of America

McFarland & Company, Inc., Publishers
  Box 611, Jefferson, North Carolina 28640
    www.mcfarlandpub.com

To the memory of Jack Hartfield,
who was there.

We were young, we were reckless, arrogant, silly, headstrong … but we were right.—Abbie Hoffman

Folk music has pretty powerful medicine for changing your heart.—Peter Yarrow

Table of Contents

Preface	1
Introduction	5

Part I. Mississippi Needs Folk Singers

1. Background	16
2. Senator Keating Discovers a Crack in the Nation's Foundation	25
3. The Schizophrenic World of the Protest Song	31
4. Bob Moses Attacks Mississippi	34
5. Here's to the State of Mississippi	40
6. Carolyn Hester Goes to Mississippi	46
7. Joan Baez Boards the Mississippi Train	52
8. Peter, Paul and Mary	59
9. Bob Dylan: The Reluctant Spokesman	64
10. After the Summer Comes the Fall	72

Part II. "Hey, Hey, LBJ, How May Kids Did You Kill Today?"

11. The Radicalizing of Tom Hayden	76
12. Lyndon Johnson Fights a War on Two Fronts: In Vietnam and in the Streets	83
13. The Music of the People	91
14. Music and the Prefigurative Culture	99
15. Rise of the Prefigurative Culture	104
16. "Lyndon Johnson Told the Nation"	111

17. Impatience Leads to Escalation — 116
18. The Chicago Seven Get Famous — 124
19. The New Left Loses Its Credibility — 127
20. The Shift in Academia: What Is Relevant? — 133

Part III. Burn, Baby, Burn

21. Radicalism in Both Politics and Music Dies — 140
22. The Death of Music as Revolution — 152
23. You Don't Need a Weatherman… — 159

Conclusion — 166
Chapter Notes — 177
Bibliography — 184
Index — 189

Preface

In January of 2017, as the Trump administration was getting started and the nation was erupting in reaction to his actions, the *Washington Post* published a column by Richard Just arguing that the music of the sixties folk singer Phil Ochs is more important today than ever. In the column Just stated, "[A]s we enter the Trump era, and as a new mass protest movement begins to take shape, his music would be worthy of a revival."[1] Ochs' songs are directly relevant to the situation America faced under Trump, Just wrote, because they deal with the "deepest questions about democracy, dissent and human decency in a grim political age." He cited Lady Gaga's singing of Ochs' "The War Is Over" as an example, pointing out the way the song "suggests how political resistance in any age can be enlivened, refreshed and perhaps even galvanized by jarring notes of artistic creativity."[2] He also cited "There but for Fortune" as a "succinct reminder of the ethical basis of modern liberalism: that in a world with no level playing field, we have sizable obligations to those who are less lucky."[3]

At the time Just wrote, Trump had been president for only a few weeks and already there had been daily protests all across the nation. The University of California at Berkeley was once again exploding with protestors, with reports of violence and riots on campus. As the *New York Times* reported, the triggering action was the university Republican Club's scheduling of a speech by Milo Yiannopoulis, a reporter for the right-wing website *Breitbart* and a white supremacist provocateur. Yiannopoulis is no ordinary conservative. His speeches frequently take a hard turn toward hate speech (in a talk at the University of Wisconsin he ridiculed a transgender student by name) and he often attacks other races. Controversy tracks him like a heat-seeking missile.

At Berkeley he planned to publicly "out" transgender students.[4] Because of his history, Berkeley students and more than 100 faculty members petitioned the administration to cancel the speech. Citing free speech, the university's chancellor refused to do so. Protestors turned out and before long the protests turned violent. The speech was canceled.[5] A complicated situation quickly turned into a two-sided argument. Protestors on both the right and the left engaged each other, each blaming the other for the riots and the cancelation of the speech. Representatives for both sides said that peaceful demonstrations would not have shut down Yiannopoulis's speech; therefore the escalation was either, depending on your viewpoint, necessary or the most extreme form of censorship.[6]

Berkeley students claimed that the violent people were not students but community members who came to the campus to run wild. On CNN, former United States secretary of labor and current Berkeley professor Robert Reich repeated a never-confirmed rumor that the rioters were bought and paid for right-wing activists—hired to come to the event and stir up trouble.[7] Whoever they were and wherever they came from, school or community, they were there and the campus found itself divided and fighting, just as it had been back in the "Free Speech" days of the early sixties.

It was then that the calls like the one Richard Just issued for a revival of Phil Ochs' music began going out. Many writers published pieces declaring that Phil Ochs was needed again. Peter Stone Brown published an article in *Counterpunch* asking, "Where Is Phil Ochs When We Really Need Him?" In it, Brown says, "Considering the state of America in the 21st Century, I think about Phil Ochs a lot and what he might've written and sung about what's going on now. Where is Phil Ochs when we need him?"[8] David Hinkey, in his article "Forty Years Later, We Still Need Phil Ochs," discusses how Ochs could distill the essence of a situation or an event into a song then goes on to say, "I can't count the number of times during those years when I've been talking with someone about the events of the world and one of us would say, 'We really could use Phil Ochs.'" Yes, we could. When he was on his game, in the middle 1960s, Phil Ochs could turn a situation into a song that distilled it to exactly what mattered.[9]

So, why is the music of Phil Ochs—and, I would argue, folk music in general—so badly needed today? Rob Young explains it this way:

> Interest in folk music and other buried aspects of national culture tends to be reawakened at moments when there's a perceived danger of things being lost for ever. Successive folk revivals of the 20th century drew their impetus equally from the two historical landmarks that most permeate the British collective unconscious: the industrial revolution and the first world war. In the late 1960s and early 70s, fear of annihilation, technological progress and a vision of alternative societies filtered through popular and underground culture, conspiring to promote the ideal of "getting back to the garden."[10]

Preface

Among a large segment of the population, Trump's election meant a dramatic move away from the garden that was the Obama administration. Folk music is a means of understanding these seismic cultural shifts that are continually happening and helping to create an alternative. These are songs that explain the tenor of the times to their audiences.

Why Folk Music and Why Now?

To explain why people perceive a fresh need for folk music in our political realm we should probably understand the circumstances that brought our present situation into existence. Like so much of our culture today the phenomenon has its roots in the sixties. At that time, drawing on the roots their forerunners planted in the union movements of the thirties and forties, folk singers—following in the path of Woody Guthrie, Pete Seeger and the Almanac Singers, and the Weavers—artists of a new generation, stepped forward and created their own response to the world in which they found themselves. Foremost among these artists who mixed music and radical politics were Phil Ochs, Joan Baez, Peter, Paul and Mary, Carolyn Hester, and Bob Dylan. Although the work of other artists will be considered, this book will primarily utilize those five as examples. These are the singer-songwriters who stepped forward and helped change America. This book aims to show why and how it happened and what that early activism means to us as we go forward.

Introduction

My own few attempts at activism were centered around folk music. If I attended a rally chances are a major reason was to see the artists performing, and while I had a mental image of myself as an activist I was never truly comfortable in that role. My own few pitiful efforts at creating radical change began when I was living in Fort Lauderdale, going to college at Florida Atlantic University. One morning I drove over to see a friend, Barry, a redheaded, freckled-faced classmate of mine—another English major in love with Elizabethan drama. We often got together to swap notes. Barry was the only white kid I knew who was rooming with an African-American guy in a minority neighborhood.

To get to the apartment they shared you had to drive down Sunrise Boulevard, beyond the huge, booming new shopping mall that housed Jordan Marsh, Burdine's, and all the other upscale department stores and past Hugh Taylor Birch State Park. Then you kept driving, on beyond Holiday Park, where Chris Evert's father was the tennis pro and the officials displayed a completely restored World War II fighter plane on the playground. You could crawl around on the plane and even climb into it. The cockpit was a popular makeout spot. Before she fell in love with cats and began populating her novels with them, Rita Mae Brown described in *Rubyfruit Jungle* how she'd lost her virginity in that airplane.

You'd keep on going down Sunrise until you came to the Sunrise Drive-in with its attached permanent flea market, billed as the biggest in the world and with its own circus and drive-in movie. There were country music concerts on the stage, with stars like Johnny Cash and Merle Haggard playing there when they toured south Florida. Kevin Welch did a TV special from that stage. Beyond the world's largest flea market you turned north and drove a couple of blocks until you ran out of paved road. When you came to the dirt roads you had entered the black section of the city. It was like going back in time to the Dust Bowl days. The dirt roads, the rust on the foundation

Introduction

blocks of the concrete and stucco structures—CBS houses, they were called—the clothes drying in the sun in the yards, the corner food shops featuring old stock and inflated prices. It was all reminiscent of bad movies. It was *Tobacco Road*.

On TV not even minority characters were permitted to live like this; audiences would not have been comfortable watching it. Whenever I went over there I wondered how the city could let their people live in conditions like this. I also wondered why the people put up it. Not for the first time, but certainly in a strong way, the fact of injustice registered. Until I met Barry and his roommate, Mason, institutional racism was an abstract concept, like justice and truth. I hadn't really encountered it since I left Atlanta, where as a white kid in a segregated society I'd been largely immune to it, ignorant of its effects.

Parking in Barry's front yard—there were no driveways—I walked into the first-floor apartment, and Barry greeted me with, "You're just in time. We're going down to Miami to integrate Woolworth's lunch counter. How 'bout coming along?" The look in Mason's eyes said entirely too much. It went in many directions at once, from curiosity to mocking to alternately pleading and challenging. I could not refuse to go. Like the modern equivalent of a Native American I decided today was a good day to get my head bashed in—by cops, rednecks, John Birchers, or some combination of the three.

In those days, Woolworth's was a major shopping destination for working-class people. Originally known as Woolworth's five-and-ten-cent stores, they offered discounted prices on everything from clothing to live birds. The chain spread across the United States. At least one store could be found in every city and suburb, all of them crowded with shoppers picking up kitchenware, bedding, small appliances, shirts and blouses, even suits, all imported from Japan. Even the record albums were foreign pressings. About the only thing American in the stores were the racks of comic books and paperbacks. Those stores over the decades had become a symbol of America. Now we were learning they were a symbol of white, segregated America; only whites could eat at the lunch counters. Oddly enough those whites could be served by black employees and their food could be prepared by black cooks, but only whites could eat there.

On February 1, 1960, the chain's policy of closing off the lunch counter to the majority of its shoppers was challenged. In Greensboro, North Carolina, four African-American college kids—Franklin McCain, Joseph O'Neil, David

Introduction

Richmond, and Ezell Blair—took their lives into their own hands and climbed onto stools at the lunch counter of the local Woolworth's and tried to order. They were refused, of course, and directed to leave. They declined and sat politely and peacefully. Their resistance attracted supporters and within six months the Greensboro Woolworth's was serving lunch to anyone who sat down at the counter.[1] The movement spread and a couple of years later, when I met Barry and Mason that day, throughout the country Woolworth stores were falling into line, one by one, often painfully and slowly. The Miami efforts had been going on for a few weeks and we were on our way to help out.

When we arrived, around fifty people, black and white, crowded the ten-stool lunch counter. A young man with a bullhorn was telling us to line up neatly behind the people who sat at the counter on stools; we could relieve them when they needed to move around a little. Also, he reminded us, when the cops came we weren't to fight but to maintain a nonviolent attitude: "Just go limp and make them drag you out." The reminder about the inevitability of the police coming made the idea of being arrested real. Until that moment it had just been a fleeting notion, a worst-that-could-happen fantasy. After all, we were the good guys, the innocents. Who'd want to put us in jail?

Despite the threat of police and arrest, for the first hour or so the demonstration was, if anything, disappointing. It was like hanging out with friends. We all chatted and laughed and had a good time feeling proud of ourselves for taking a stand, playing and singing the familiar folk songs, and we could all feel the energy building as we belted out the old spirituals and union hymns that had been reworked to become movement songs. The fun lasted until the police showed up.

Even before the officers came through the doors, this whole thing was striking me as just a little silly. It was more like hanging out in the living room of a fraternity house than it was a serious protest. Everyone knew each other, so a lot of greeting of old friends went on, a lot of back slapping and joking and hitting on the movement girls. The truth was that standing up for justice and doing the right thing had many of the elements of a social situation, a party. There was much banging on Harmony acoustic guitars and singings songs like "We Shall Overcome," but the inescapable truth of the matter was that most of us were much more concerned with how cool we were than in getting minorities their fundamental rights.

The arrival of the cops changed the game. The possibility of doing jail

Introduction

time made what we doing real. The kid with the bullhorn reminded us that now was our opportunity to make a real statement by going to jail for our beliefs and to go limp when the officers tried to arrest us. Lawyers were standing by to arrange bail, he said. Since I didn't want to go to jail, the presence of lawyers was little comfort. I looked at Barry and Mason. They looked back at me and we all decided, without speaking, that this was a good time to make our way back up to Fort Lauderdale. We snuck out the door while the cops were ordering everybody to leave. I hoped no one saw me leave. I didn't want anyone, especially the movement girls, to doubt my commitment; I was doing enough of that myself. I wondered, *Could you be committed to the cause but not to jail?* The answer I came up with was a conditional yes, the condition being if you were as big a hypocrite as I was. Although it took some time to fully understand and internalize the insight, I learned that day the fact was that I was not an activist; my mind and body did not leap to direct action. No, I was a witness, an observer. As a budding poet and writer, my job was to examine what was going on, to put it in perspective and line it out in symbols, so that others could pick up on it.

I tell you the Woolworth's story to make a larger point. For most of us, participation in the movement was mere fashion, something we did every once in a while to enhance our self-esteem or to show we belonged to the group. No matter how much we opposed segregation or the war, our real commitment was not to direct action in the streets. For some, it was the music, for others it was the cool points, for yet others it was the sense of belonging, but only for a few was the action in the streets a calling. No, most of us much preferred to talk a good game and let others who were braver and perhaps holier than we were risk their lives and freedom.

Folk Music and the New Left in the Sixties is a book about those others, the ones for whom the movement went far beyond fashion. Sometimes they were right, sometimes they were wrong. Sometimes they were sharp and on the ball, sometimes they were incredibly obtuse. As we shall see, they were never competent at organization or detail; they were strongly influenced by, and were members of, the culture they were trying to change. Some worked for change by going into the streets, some did it through their songs, and some did both. But, given all of that, the important fact is that these were young people truly committed to a vision and willing to make incredible sacrifices to help bring that vision into being.

That afternoon in Miami gave me my first insight into the truth of protesters and protest and that was this: there were the serious ones who really wanted to make a difference and there were the faddists, who were on the line simply because it was the thing to do that season. The faddists were atmosphere, essential to the cause because they provided fertile ground to grow the numbers of the serious ones. Every movement in America has always suffered from this division. From the Greenwich Village Bohemians of the twenties and thirties to the Beats in the forties and fifties to the hippies and movement people of the sixties, those making a decision to act outside of the main culture have always suffered from the fact that a small portion of the people who identify themselves with any group are the artists, the movers and shakers, while the rest are the hangers-on, the ones who wear the clothes, speak the lingo, come in from the suburbs to play at being a member of the subculture and, like adolescents in public places, are more interested in the reactions they get than in the movement itself.

The Dominant 5 Percent

According to the British writer and philosopher Colin Wilson there is a dominant 5 percent of our population that is responsible for nearly all of the advances of its subculture. Wilson states that the most successful crimes are committed by 5 percent of criminals, 5 percent of actors become stars or work steadily, 5 percent of writers are able to make a living by their efforts, 5 percent of executives run most of the major corporations of America—these men and women are the dominant 5 percent.[2] The people we are examining here, rebels and musicians both, were members of the dominant 5 percent.

In the late sixties, during the days of rage, the concept would alter slightly, reaching its extreme and melding into what the writer A.E. Van Vogt called the "right man."[3] The right man is a person driven by an out-of-control need for enhanced self-esteem. He has to feel in control always and needs to be adored not just by his mate but by everyone. As Terry Malloy, Marlon Brando's character in the classic *On the Waterfront*, might have said, he needs to be a contender. Since he needs to always be correct, the right man will never admit he is wrong.

When protestors became armed revolutionaries it was because the dominant 5 percent of movement people either had been all along or became right men. In all movements it has to be this way because—though they are often negative members—Van Vogt's right men nonetheless belong to the dominant 5 percent. Because of this man's tendency to take what he wants in any way he chooses, Van Vogt came to call him the "violent man" as well as the "right man." He is a man driven by a manic need for self-esteem—to feel that he is a "somebody." He is obsessed by the question of "losing face," so he will never, under any circumstances, admit that he might be in the wrong.[4] Donald Trump is, of course, a prime example of the "right man."

Wilson connected the right man to the dominant 5 percent in this fashion: "The right man problem is a problem of highly dominant people. Dominance is a subject of enormous importance to biologists and zoologists because the percentage of dominant animals or—human beings—seems to be amazingly constant."[5] Like the other examples of the dominant 5 percent, the right man—who might be female (in Van Vogt's day the masculine pronoun was used exclusively)—is, for better or worse, an active leader. All leaders, for example, come from the dominant 5 percent and can only be replaced with another member of that group. The Irish writer George Bernard Shaw once asked the explorer H.M. Stanley how many of his followers were capable of assuming leadership if he himself got sick and had to relinquish his post. "One in twenty," Stanley said. "Is that approximate or exact?" Shaw asked. "Exact,"[6] was the reply.

The most dramatic evidence demonstrating the truth of the dominant 5 percent, though, comes from the Korean War, where the Communist Chinese discovered that it was not necessary to guard every American prisoner of war. All they had to do was locate the dominant 5 percent and put guards on them. They were the only ones who caused trouble or tried to lead escapes. The other 95 percent did what they were told and did not attempt to escape. They were content to be POWs.[7] It becomes clear, then, that the movement—whether it centered on civil rights, changing the colleges and universities, ending the Vietnam War, or simply trying to bring down America through a revolution—consisted of leaders and followers, heavies and juniors, the 5 percent and the 95 percent.

Just as I learned that I was an observer rather than an activist I learned that the heavies were the people I needed to observe. This book will try to tell the story of the dominant 5 percent. The juniors will have a voice in these pages, and certainly the heavies were not always the pure and selfless creatures we would have wanted. But they made things happen, and they will be the focus.

Introduction

The Plan for the Book

This book organically divides into three parts:

1. The Background: The New Left did not spring out of nowhere. The move to the suburbs, the Eisenhower years, the McCarthy era, the car culture, and the emerging teenage subculture all contributed to the rise of a fresh interest in the politics of personal and cultural freedom by the young that culminated in a rejection of their parents' world. Some simply rejected that world and huddled together, forming their own subculture. Their parents and the media referred to them as hippies. The term freak was used interchangeably with hippy. Known primarily by their uniforms—long hair, pink-lensed sunglasses, fringed leather jackets, bell-bottomed jeans, beads, and paisley shirts, most of the freaks were the juniors, often kids who still lived in their parents' homes while dressing the part and going to the Fillmore East on the weekends, where they would dream of living in the East Village. They were the sixties equivalent of the weekend Beatniks of the fifties, the ones who took the subway down to the village on the weekends and hit the bars and coffeehouses while trying to pass as a regular instead of a tourist. Yet from the ranks of the juniors emerged the heavies—the movers and shakers who created and sustained a movement. These were Wilson's dominant 5 percent, and this text will be mostly concerned with their work and its results.

2. The Politics: The heavies became the members of the emerging New Left. Generally they'd grown up in left-wing homes and become radicalized in college. After they graduated many became Freedom Riders in the South, taking their lives in their hands while striving to integrate the interstate busses. In 1962 the heavies, led by Students for a Democratic Society (SDS) spokesman Tom Hayden, wrote the Port Huron Statement, which Uberliberal sociologist Straughton Lynd pronounced as the founding document of a New Left.[8] The term struck a chord and became the name by which the movement would be known, both in the media and internally. We will discuss just how all of this happened, and our examination will be, as much as possible, nonjudgmental. The goal is to understand and learn rather than to approve or disapprove. As is the case with any movement, the New Left offered much to approve of and just as much to reject. However, to do either without understanding is a mistake.

3. The Music: The movement had its own soundtrack. Like the Old Left

Introduction

before it the New Left marched to the strains of folk music, and that musical cradle is the major focus of this work. It is important to understand the symbiotic relationship between the action and the songs that propelled it. Without the songs the movement probably would not have gotten where it went and achieved what it did, and without the movement an entire genre of song—the protest, or topical, song—would never have achieved the level of artistry and acceptance that it did. The goal is to take a close look at these interacting factors and, as a result, put together and analyze a significant moment in the growth of American culture so that we can know what it accomplished and whether or not it ultimately failed in its goals the way it did in its actions. The question is, why did a movement with so much potential and promise wind up destroying itself and, instead of uniting dividing this country?

One further note: scholars of folk music could conceivably quarrel with my definition of America's folk music. As I see the genre, rather than being locked in tradition—imitating the voices and styles of British, Scottish, and Irish musicians of centuries past—it is a living, growing, and changing form. It is the music of the people and the people are never still. We are a changing, evolving, technological people and our music will necessarily change, evolve, and take advantage of technology just as we do. As Regina Bendix has written, folklore scholarship has moved on from the old "authentic vs. phony" arguments. Because of technological advances the twentieth century, she says, has seen a redefinition of what constitutes folk expression. As a consequence, the very idea of authentic and spurious folk voices is disappearing. As society grows more complex, so does the music.[9] Woody Guthrie himself stated the following in a complaint about a magazine article he had read:

> The writer says that we haven't got any more folks songs, ballads, ditties because we can't make any more about machinery, atoms and electricity and that folk music can't be made up no more because the tractor is taking the place of the horse, the gas engine is pushing out the wagon, the western frontier is all settled, the gold is all dug up, the songs are all made up, and all are now only echoes of the good old past.[10]

Guthrie not only feels this view is wrong but he also sees it as "dangerous."[11] Writing to his wife, Marjorie, he said, "The very instant the classics stop being changed, or folk songs, the biggest part of them is dead on the spot. There are certain big principles that stay alive in all forms of art, but unless every single day's headline news and every day's happenings and historic trends are worked into all forms of show business, right then it's a dead bird."[12]

Introduction

Therefore, the position that this book takes is that folk music is a changing, growing, and very much alive art that both reflects and helps to change the culture that it grows out of. When Bob Dylan abandoned acoustic music for electric he did not leave folk music, he simply changed its presentation. Folk, folk-rock, and psychedelic music are all branches from the same folk tree. The dominant 5 percent create and lead the changes. These pages tell the story of how they created a movement and lost it when the very events they created transformed them into van Vogt's right men.

Part I
Mississippi Needs Folk Singers

Chapter 1

Background

The sixties as we know them could not have happened if it hadn't been for the huge and abrupt changes that occurred in the fifties. The common conception of the fifties is that they were a time of retreat, a time of longing for peace and quiet after the turbulent forties, a decade that saw the Second World War followed immediately by the Korean War. In the popular conception of the decade, it is as though the adults of the country said, "We've had enough. It's time to relax, forget about war, make a pitcher of martinis and just kick back, watching our brand new TV sets." Yet this was the decade that brought into being all of the elements that led to the creation of the idealistic political rebellion of the young. By examining, even in a generalized fashion, the main currents of the decade we can begin to see connections.

The picture we have of the decade of the fifties is, of course, oversimplified. As Todd Gitlin has written:

> "The Fifties" were multiple, of course, according to whether you were from California or North Carolina; different, too, depending on whether you were eight or eighteen or fifty-eight, female or male, black or white, Irish Catholic, protestant or Jewish, an electrical worker or a salesman of appliances, or a housewife with an all-electric kitchen or the president of General Electric; and this is not to speak of differences in family style or personality.[1]

Still, there was a dominant impulse in the decade and that was to retreat. It was a pattern that has happened throughout American history. Every war has been followed by a need to relax and escape. So the nation had been there before. At the end of the First World War we welcomed in the twenties, a decade of decadence and hard partying, of Bohemians and others flirting with the edges. The immediate post–Second World War years of the late forties played out this pattern. By the time the fifties hit, America decided to get off that particular highway and take a different route. In the fifties America retreated, played it cool, decided what the nation had been through entitled

1. Background

us to a life where the waters did not produce waves. The country entered an age of exhaustion.

Although it sounds contradictory, America in the fifties also entered an age of progress. Eisenhower built the federal highway system, which, by opening up the suburbs, led to a new way of living, one that perfectly suited the rising mega corporations. Even though we think of the fifties as the period of time that gave rise to the giant corporations, those companies were not a new factor in American life. Corporations have always been with us, so while the corporate life dominated the fifties it did not originate there. One hundred years earlier, Abraham Lincoln had said, "I see in the near future a crisis approaching that unnerves me and causes me to tremble for the safety of my country.... [C]orporations have been enthroned and an era of corruption in high places will follow, and the money power of the country will endeavor to prolong its reign by working upon the prejudices of the people until all wealth is aggregated in a few hands and the Republic is destroyed."[2]

In fact, the original thirteen colonies had been first explored and settled by employees of corporations, but in the postwar fifties the growth and influence of these companies became pervasive. These businesses sought conformity beyond all other values. They valued sameness, almost as if they believed that any sign of individuality would cause psychic landslides to crush the business. They sought to control all aspects of an employee's life, including approving of his wife—the corporate life was overwhelmingly male—and suggesting which suburban neighborhood he should live in and how he should dress. Among other big businesses of the day, GE and IBM insisted on uniforms for their white collar employees: gray suits with matching ties and white shirts. A retired IBM executive described for me the way the corporation dictated areas of his life that he might have preferred to keep private. To go to work for IBM, he said, was to be issued a pamphlet describing how to behave, how to dress, what type of car to drive, how your wife should dress and behave—everything the rising young executive should know in order to succeed through conformity.

If you were not a budding young executive, the culture encouraged you to still strive to live like one. You bought the house in the suburbs, had cocktail parties with your friends, and got your opinions from *Time* and *Life* magazines, which described and defended the status quo. The fifties brought this vision close to fruition. Sociologists of the day wrote treatises on the dangers of the mindless conformity that appeared to characterize the times. In 1950 David Reisman published *The Lonely Crowd*, in which he argued that society was moving from an inner-directed to an other-directed model. Where once, Reisman said, people searched for meaning inside themselves, now they sought meaning through the social, religious, and political institutions America had created. C. Wright Mills in his classic 1951 study *White Collar* lamented the rise of conformity and its corresponding loss of independence. By 1956 he was convinced that the battle for personal autonomy had been lost, and in *The Power Elite* he argued that we were being ruled by a military, political, and corporate oligarchy. Actor, writer, and student of culture Peter Ustinov said about the prevailing times, "In America, through pressure of conformity, there is freedom of choice but nothing to choose from."[3]

Conformity was the rule of the day, a rule that led to a profound emptiness. On a material basis, the lives of Americans were better but the psychic cost was high. At the time, the corporations made the economy cook and the cost of living was still low enough that a family could survive on one income, leading most suburban wives to stay at home. The men rode trains or drove cars to empty jobs that were segmented and specialized so that they rarely saw the fruits of their labors, while the women encountered emptiness in their homes. It was the age of the development of the tranquilizer, which found a welcome in those homes. An astonishing number of American housewives were prescribed the mood-stabilizing drugs to help them cope with the emptiness and boredom of their stay-at-home lives. Tranquilizers were seen as miracle drugs, the triumph of corporate pharmacology over conditions they had done so much to create.

The conformity and emptiness weren't just created and driven by the corporations. Politics, of course, played a vast part. Eisenhower, who had no political experience when he took office as president, was a product of the military. He became famous by planning and executing the D-day invasion and as a result of this fame both parties tried to recruit him as their candidate. After months of being courted, he chose the Republicans and won easily but was known as "a great general but a poor president."[4] Arguments have been made that he was actually a much more involved and better president than he appeared to be at the time. Whatever the truth of the matter is, one glaring error of his presidency stands out: he did nothing to stop senator Joseph McCarthy's three-year reign of terror, which did so much to give rise to the radical right that so terrorized our nation.

1. Background

The Rise and Fall of Tail-gunner Joe

McCarthy was elected to the U.S. Senate from Wisconsin in 1947. For three years he languished in obscurity while desperately seeking a higher profile. Then, in 1950, he found the issue that would propel him into the national limelight and proceeded to use it to become the most feared man in America, leaving in his wake a trail of broken lives. From the beginning of his career McCarthy showed none of the traits that make a good leader. He succeeded through a series of lies, innuendo, and personal attacks on his enemies. He was one of van Vogt's right men. During the war, for example, he served in the Marines, a branch he chose because he felt it would look better on a resume when he ran for office. McCarthy awarded himself the nickname "Tail-Gunner Joe," falsely claiming to have flown thirty-two missions so that he could qualify for a Distinguished Service Medal. He was very proud of a letter of commendation he received, signed by his commanding officer, Admiral Chester A. Nimitz. The only problem was that the letter was a fake; he wrote it himself.[5]

Once out of the service, McCarthy ran for the Senate, challenging the three-term incumbent, Robert La Follette, Jr., for the Republican nomination He made points among the voters by accusing La Follette of ducking active duty in the armed forces, even though La Follette had been forty-six when the war started. McCarthy nailed the nomination by accusing La Follette of war profiteering. Thus handily disposing of his Democratic opponent, McCarthy spent his first three years in the Senate earning himself first place in the Senate press corps' poll of the worst U.S. senators. Determined to become a man to be reckoned with instead of one to be laughed at, McCarthy used the opportunity of a speaking engagement at the Republican Women's Club in Wheeling, West Virginia, to make his strike: "In February 1950, appearing at the Ohio County Women's Republican Club in Wheeling, West Virginia, McCarthy gave a speech that propelled him into the national spotlight. Waving a piece of paper in the air, he declared that he had a list of 205 known members of the Communist Party who were 'working and shaping policy' in the State Department."[6]

In those Cold War years, when the Russians were seen as America's mortal enemies, charges like McCarthy's were taken seriously—even though they were ludicrous. Committees were set up in both houses of Congress to investigate his claims and McCarthy, despite the fact that he unearthed no Communists, known or cloaked, became a power, going from the worst senator to the most feared. His list, of course, was fraudulent, but McCarthy was not as interested in rooting out Communists as he was in acquiring power:

> These people on the list were in fact not all communists; some had proven merely to be alcoholics or sexual deviants. Regardless, McCarthy relentlessly pushed through and became the chairman of the Government Committee on Operations of the Senate, widening his scope to "investigate" dissenters. He continued to investigate for over two years, relentlessly questioning numerous government departments and the panic arising from the witch-hunts and fear of communism became known as McCarthyism.[7]

Not content to find Communists in every closet, he began ransacking those closets for homosexuals, determined to drive anyone gay out of government. His anti-communist and anti-gay stances led to almost constant fights with Democratic president Harry Truman, who McCarthy continually referred to as being soft on Communism. Later he upped the ante, claiming that Truman, if not a Communist himself, was certainly united with them.

By the time Eisenhower took office, McCarthy was the most powerful man in America, and the military genius who had defeated foreign armies was afraid to criticize McCarthy, even though he knew and said privately that the man was a dangerous demagogue. By 1953, though, like most right men, McCarthy had gone too far. He decided to use a subcommittee he chaired to investigate the United States Army: "This was the final straw for then president Dwight D. Eisenhower, who realized that McCarthy's movement needed to be stopped. The Army fired back at the accusations, sending information about McCarthy and advisors abusing congressional privileges to known critics of McCarthy. Reporters, Drew Pearson included, and other critics soon hopped on board, publishing unflattering articles about Joseph McCarthy and his methods of seeking out the supposed communists in America."[8]

When the army fought back, the hearings were televised. Every day for six weeks twenty million American citizens got to see McCarthy in action—bullying, harassing, threatening, coming across as reckless and lying. His popularity plummeted. Pioneering television journalist Edward R. Murrow put the symbolic bullet in the fallen McCarthy's head. On his news analysis show, *See It Now*, he ran an episode called "A Report on Senator Joseph R. McCarthy" in which he used film clips of the Senator speaking, using McCarthy's own words as rope to hang him with. Murrow concluded his show with these famous words:

1. Background

> This is no time for men who oppose Senator McCarthy's methods to keep silent, or for those who approve. We can deny our heritage and our history, but we cannot escape responsibility for the result. There is no way for a citizen of a republic to abdicate his responsibilities. As a nation we have come into our full inheritance at a tender age. We proclaim ourselves, as indeed we are, the defenders of freedom, wherever it continues to exist in the world, but we cannot defend freedom abroad by deserting it at home.[9]

He followed this up with a second show that focused on the story of Annie Lee Moss, an African-American soldier who had her life and career ruined by McCarthy. Furious, McCarthy came on Murrow's show to defend himself and accused the reporter of being linked to Russian espionage groups. This time, after hovering off the edge of the canyon like Wile E. Coyote for three years, McCarthy fell and crashed; to accuse army heroes and bureaucrats of being Communists and spies without producing a shred of evidence against them was one thing but to accuse America's favorite TV journalist? McCarthy was through. Discredited and reviled, within three years he drank himself to death.

McCarthy was gone but the damage he had done lingered, mostly in the actions of the House Un-American Activities Committee (HUAC), which was established in 1938 to investigate the infiltration of Communism into the lives of America's private citizens. From the very beginning the committee engaged in a kind of mindless overkill. One congressman asked a theater director who was testifying whether the playwright Christopher Marlowe, a contemporary of Shakespeare, was a Communist. Also, the committee considered investigating the KKK but passed on that one on the grounds that, as Mississippi senator John E. Rankin said, "after all, the KKK is an old American institution."[10] Although as a senator McCarthy had nothing to do with the HUAC, it really took off when witch-hunts made his name a household word. The committee widened its focus and began looking for anyone who was a perceived threat to the American way of life as guaranteed by the Constitution—at least as the anti-communist archconservatives on the committee read it. Their methods, as well as their goals, were questionable:

> The committee employed several controversial methods to accomplish its goal of ferreting out suspected Communists. Typically, an individual who raised the suspicions of HUAC received a subpoena to appear before the committee. During the hearing, the suspected Communist was grilled about his or her political beliefs and activities and then asked to provide the names of other people who had taken part in allegedly subversive activities. Any additional figures identified in this manner also received

subpoenas, widening the committee's probe. Individuals who refused to answer the committee's questions or to provide names could be indicted for contempt of Congress and sent to prison. Subjects of HUAC investigations had the option of invoking their right to avoid self-incrimination under the Fifth Amendment, but "pleading the Fifth" created the impression that they were guilty of a crime. In addition, those who refused to cooperate were often blacklisted by their employers. They lost their jobs and were effectively prevented from working in their chosen industry.[11]

HUAC investigated the film industry and when writers and performers refused to answer their questions or would not give the names of others, the committee saw that they were banned from working for the studios:

> It was the casting call no one in Hollywood wanted to receive. In October 1947, when the House Un-American Activities Committee (HUAC) convened a hearing in Washington, D.C., to investigate subversive activities in the entertainment industry, 41 screenwriters, directors and producers were subpoenaed. Most witnesses were "friendly"—that is, willing to respond to the committee's central question: "Are you now or have you ever been a member of the Communist Party?" And those who confessed to membership were offered the opportunity to name "fellow travelers," thereby regaining their good standing with the committee and, by extension, the American film industry. Ten witnesses—all current or former party members—banded together in protest, refusing to cooperate on First Amendment grounds (freedom of speech, right of assembly, freedom of association) and affirming that HUAC disagreed: It found the so-called Hollywood Ten in contempt of Congress, fined them each $1,000 and sentenced them to up to a year in federal prison. All 10 artists also were fired by a group of studio executives—and the era of the Hollywood blacklist began.[12]

The famous Hollywood Ten were blacklisted and their careers and lives ruined. Musicians faced the same fate. Just as the screenwriters had been, they were asked about left-wing affiliations and ordered to give the names of others they knew who might be "red." Before the blacklist was crushed in the sixties, more than 300 artists, including Pete Seeger and the Weavers, had been banned from working at their craft.

When McCarthy fell, HUAC slid down the long ladder to oblivion. It was no longer feared or taken all that seriously as a social and political force. Reading the signs, President Truman now felt comfortable regularly denouncing it. His words carried power and, though the committee tried to carry on and still managed to wreck a few more lives, its power gradually diminished. It hung on until 1975 and, as we shall see, the New Left had a lot to do with its decline.

Conformity, then, was the dominant idea that drove American lives, conformity brought about by the unquestioning acceptance of the status quo and a refusal to question the basic assumptions on which we were building a society, coupled with a fear of outsiders who advocated another way. People who had fought two wars in ten years to protect this way of life were not in any mood to see it questioned or challenged.

In 1957 the humorist and social critic S.J. Perelman summed up the state of our culture by titling one of his books *The Road to Miltown*. To intellectuals like him, our age was characterized by a need to escape from the crushing everydayness and emptiness through the use of chemicals like the newly developed tranquilizers. Most middle-class Americans, however, accustomed to a liquor-fueled suburban culture, simply saw the new tranquilizers as one more rung on the ladder to the good life.

The Birth of Teen Culture

If grownup middle-class America were happy and content, their children were not. Kids, especially those in their teens when the suburban diaspora took place, were most dramatically affected. The move to the suburbs radically altered the nature of teenage life. Once, these kids had been able to walk out their doors and find entertainment with their friends in the neighborhood. To move around, they used public transportation, which was widely available. Corner shops, neighborhood theaters, ice cream shops, empty lots and fields where baseball could be played—all of these were readily available. A teen had a sense of belonging to the larger life, a notion of an uncluttered meaning of life as a member of a community. As Paul Goodman wrote in 1960, at one time a young man could find a good job repairing cars in his neighborhood garage, where every day he would encounter his neighbors and friends. He could meet girls and make new friends. He could be a part of a community.[13] The suburbs and the new pervasiveness of the corporate culture killed all of that. How could he be a part of a community when the people he knew were scattered all over a series of developments, walled off from each other by income and status? How could the young man make his way in the world if he could no longer live in a community that contained people of all classes, races, and ethnicities? The kid who once mingled with the whole population found himself stratified, stuck as though trapped in amber in an inescapable grouping of people of his own race and class.

Now he had to rely on the schools to find companionship, schools which, with the rise of the suburbs and the conformity of postwar life, found their mission subtly altered from the teaching of individual thinking to a kind of group-think. Rather than striving to turn out people capable of changing the system, the schools aimed at getting people to fit into the existing system. In their halls and classrooms, kids learned that they were being guided into lives that were depersonalized, systemic, and habitual. From the first grade on they learned that they were not very important as individuals and were much more valued as future consumers. So they learned to fit in, to seek approval from the group by indulging only in socially approved activities, like sports, cheerleading, and school clubs. They also learned to dress like everyone else, to talk like everyone else, to look like everybody else, to read the same books, to listen to the same music. In short, they learned to *be* everybody else. They also learned that they were officially branded as teenagers and that fact carried with it a sense of secondary citizenship. Voting, drinking, having sex, possessing the ability to make yourself understood to adults—all of these actions and more were suddenly off the table.

As scattered as teens were and with the lack of public transportation, a car was essential to life; without one, you were not only stranded but also judged as somehow inadequate. With a car, you could obtain a little freedom. So a car culture emerged, with its attendant drive-in movies and restaurants and teen-centered dances and meeting places. Cars not only widened physical borders, they opened up new possibilities of an inner life also. They made dating possible and became a source of new music and entertainment; the car without a radio was not really a vehicle at all.

So, as far as adults and most teens went, life was good. For those young people who could *think*, however, American life in the suburban fifties was characterized by a soul-crushing emptiness. It was out of this cohort that a group of college students who sought a bigger meaning in their own lives tried to find that meaning in political activism. They would help themselves by helping those less fortunate than themselves. This group became known as the New Left and were almost immediately identified by their conformist elders as un–American and subversive.

Chapter 2

Senator Keating Discovers a Crack in the Nation's Foundation

As the radical politics of the New Left was being developed, it was already centered in folk music. From the union songs of the Wobblies to the anti-war songs of the Almanac Singers, folk music already characterized progressive politics. Now the young idealists who were creating a movement were also listening to folk music, using it for guidance and inspiration. In this chapter we begin to explore the connection between folk music and radical politics.

What was the connection? In order to examine the symbiotic relationship between the two forms, we go back to September 26, 1963, when Kenneth Keating, then the Republican Senator from New York, took to the floor of the senate and approached the well, clutching his notes close to his chest, an air of anticipation emanating from him. When he had been recognized, he spread his notes on the podium, took a deep breath and revealed that he had recently discovered a new source of creeping, festering communism turned loose on our shores, a new way for the Communists to slowly but ultimately consume our society.[1] That new scourge, he said, was folk music, which was subversive to its very roots. Through folk music, he said, the Communists would further their effort to turn workers against their bosses: "No one could possibly imagine the members of the board of directors of General Motors sitting around a conference table composing ditties in honor of defense contracts, while it is not surprising that coal miners should have come up with a protest song, "Sixteen Tons," crying to Saint Peter not to call them to heaven until they can pay their debt to the company store.[2]

Keating immediately lost whatever credibility he had with the young by getting his basic facts wrong. Coal miners did not write "Sixteen Tons." The song was composed by master finger-picking country guitarist Merle Travis, who originally recorded it for Capitol Records. His record failed to make much of a stir but a cover version by the countrypolitan singer and television star, Tennessee Ernie Ford, reached number one on the *Billboard* charts (and was entered into the Library of Congress's National Recording Registry in 2015). While the song has entered the domain of folk music, "Sixteen Tons" is not the traditional folk song Keating thought it to be. Regardless of its origins, the fact was that Keating saw danger in the song. "Sixteen Tons," he claimed, specifically and unfairly attacked mine owners and by extension all corporate executives. He also said that it portrays workers as little more than slaves and called the song very thinly disguised communist propaganda. And it is not the only subversive song Keating discovered.

He also objected to the folk chestnut, "Darling Corey," a traditional song long in the public domain about a female maker of illegal whiskey that had recently been made popular by the Kingston Trio and was a favorite of other groups. Originally recorded by Clarence Gil in 1927, it was also done by Buell Kazee the same year. In 1941 the Monroe Brothers issued a record of the song and it made its way into the early repertoires of Burl Ives and Pete Seeger.[3] Senator Keating, however, showed no evidence that he was familiar with the history of the song. He was, however, familiar with conservative political stances and saw "Darling Corey"[4] as violating them. Keating objected particularly to the verse in which Darling Corey is alerted that the revenue men are coming to destroy her still.

He claims that the song obviously approves of criminal activity on all levels but mainly it attacks the internal revenue system: rather than get her tax stamps and make whiskey legally, Corey will simply move her still and continue to avoid paying taxes on her product. "Darling Corey" says we have to be on guard against the revenuers, while "Copper Kettle," Keating says, is even more explicit. It tells the story of a family that has been in the business of making illegal whiskey for several generations without paying any sort of whiskey tax since the great Whiskey Rebellion of 1791. To the senator, the danger here is palpable and self-evident. As Keating says: "If enough people get around to singing this at hoot[e]nannies, Americans might get the idea that they don't have to pay their taxes. After all, the family in question got away without paying them for 171 years. And if the government loses the ability to collect taxes to pay for our defense effort, we would be wide open for a Communist takeover, would we not?"[5]

No matter how absurd the story sounds, it really happened. Senator Keating really read these words into the Congressional Record. Did he truly

2. Senator Keating Discovers a Crack in the Nation's Foundation

believe that all it would take for people to stop paying taxes was hearing a song a few times? Keating made the speech and appears to have believed as much of what he was saying as a politician ever does. Perhaps he overstated the danger deliberately; perhaps there was an element of fun in his statement; but the basic fact is he believed in the communist menace and believed in the power of folk music to spread radical ideas. His ultimate answer to the problem he alone had diagnosed was a full investigation of Communist infiltration of folk music by the House Un-American Activities Committee, an investigation that he called for but that never happened, perhaps because Keating's fellow senators appear to have been less concerned with this particular source of the red menace than he was. In fact, although it is hard to read tone in a printed typescript, the written text suggests that Minnesota senator and later presidential candidate Hubert Humphrey was openly mocking his fellow senator, encouraging Keating to sing, rather than simply quote, the lyrics. When Keating demurred because he didn't have a guitar handy, Humphrey enthusiastically volunteers to get him one.

While Keating was never able to get his investigation of folk music, the Republicans did manage to see the danger he spoke of and to investigate nearly every folk singer of note. As we've seen, most of the artists of the fifties—Pete Seeger, Lee Hayes, Woody Guthrie, Cisco Houston, Oscar Brand, and many others—all suffered at the hands of various congressional committees. (Joan Baez, Phil Ochs, Peter, Paul and Mary, and Bob Dylan, along with many of their musical contemporaries, all were, at one time or another during the sixties, harassed by federal and state authorities, and the FBI accumulated large files on all of them.)

Folk Music as a Danger to the Republic

While the songs Keating quotes are not technically protest songs, he perceives them that way. And that's what he sees as being so dangerous and communistic in folk music. What we have in this speech, then, is the first indication that the music of the Folk Revival is dangerous. When you consider that during the days of the folk revival, most of these songs were presented to the public by such safe acts as The Brothers Four, The Highwaymen, The Serendipity Singers, and the New Christy Minstrels, the only thing edgy about the versions Americans heard was the performers' flat-top haircuts.

During this time, however, the folk world was widening as two separate and distinct types of folk music were emerging: the more commercial trios and quartets, who made the music pretty and benign; and the individuals, like Bob Dylan and Phil Ochs, who wrote their own material and contributed many important protest songs to the mix. Keating was right: the music was dangerous. But to find the danger, you had to go beneath the surface, had to stop watching the performer and look at what was being performed. On top is the show business; below that is the politics.

Consider a song Joan Baez is noted for: "We Shall Not Be Moved." Originally conceived of during the labor movement of the early twentieth century,[6] "We Shall Not Be Moved" was a song of liberation and empowerment. Having outlived its original purpose, it became a sort of secular hymn and moved over into the entertainment side. When the civil rights movement erupted, however, the song became relevant again and regained all of its power.[7] It is now recognized as one of the great protest songs, as it shows the importance of standing up to illegitimate authority, of expressing and acting on your beliefs. The power of the song is beneath its surface, accessible to those who need it.

One person's protest song, though, is another's entertainment. A case can be made that some of our most famous protest songs don't belong in that category at all. Consider the Bob Dylan composition "Blowin' in the Wind." From the moment the song was introduced, it was seen as the very model of the protest song,[8] taking on war, social injustice, slavery and racism, and man's indifference to his own fate and to everyone else's. Released just as the crisis in Vietnam was cranking up, the song was made a massive top 40 hit by Peter, Paul and Mary and was quickly covered by nearly everyone who had access to a studio. Joan Baez, Peter, Paul and Mary and, of course, Dylan himself recorded it. Phil Ochs was known to have sung it at rallies. "Blowin' in the Wind" became the operational definition of the phrase protest song. From the moment he introduced the song, however, Bob Dylan has insisted that it was not a protest song.[9] The fact is the song did not attack anything or anyone—and Dylan wrote plenty of songs that did. What it did was ask some profound questions, pointing out that answers were out there and could be found. The song was the perfect example of why Phil Ochs insisted that what he and his cohort were writing were topical songs rather than protest songs. Did the appellation matter? Not really. The song quickly found its way into the culture, where it continues to work its magic.

What Exactly Is a Protest Song?

During the civil rights era, songs were loosely labeled protest songs if they argued against the "separate but equal" status quo—if they provided an alternative to the conventional. Actually, as far as the songs went, it wasn't always necessary to advocate for integration as long as you argued loudly enough against segregation. Speaking of the protest songs of the early sixties, Dr. Martin Luther King, Jr., said, "The freedom songs are playing a strong and vital role in our struggle. They give the people new courage and a sense of unity. I think they keep alive a faith, a radiant hope, in the future, particularly in our most trying hours."[10]

For our purposes, the protest songs that accompanied the struggle to end slavery mark a good starting point. "No More Auction Block for Me," "Sometimes I Feel Like a Motherless Child," and "Oh Freedom" (a favorite of both Joan Baez and Odetta) widened both the appeal and the reception of the form. Singers and songwriters, such as Phil Ochs, kept the songs coming, putting a more up-to-date and directly political spin on them, which carried them to new audiences. In addition to the Greenwich Village clubs and bars, Ochs and his contemporaries performed at many political events, including anti–Vietnam War and civil rights rallies, student events, and organized labor events.

Show Business and the Protest Song

Ochs was equally at home singing for anti-war protesters as he was performing for general audiences at Town Hall or Carnegie Hall, two venues he played often due to his huge popularity in New York City. Politically, Ochs described himself as a "left social democrat."[11] He also saw himself as a harmless journalist who worked in the song form. As we'll see when we dip into his life more, he also viewed himself as a star. His goal was to be big in show business—to be as rich and famous as the recordings he had not yet made could make him. He wanted to be as big as his idol, Elvis Presley, and was convinced that an album of protest songs written and performed by an adequate singer whose guitar playing, according to rock critic Robert Christgau, would not suffer had his hands been webbed[12] was going to sell millions of copies.[13] When that did not happen, Ochs' life changed and the powerful songs like "The Power and the Glory," "Draft Dodger Rag," "Changes," "Crucifixion," "Love Me, I'm a Liberal," and "I Ain't Marching Anymore" quit coming.[14]

As he was forced to watch other artists having major radio hits with topical songs, it hurt him. He felt overlooked, felt that no one would take him seriously. And for a short period of time in the early sixties, protest songs were all over the FM airwaves. Buffy Sainte-Marie's song "Universal Soldier" was a hit for both herself and later for Donovan. Tom Paxton became famous writing anti-war songs, like "Lyndon Johnson Told the Nation," about the escalation of the war in Vietnam; "Jimmy Newman," the story of a dying soldier; and "My Son John," about a soldier who returns from war unable to describe what he's been through, among others. P.F. Sloan's famous "Eve of Destruction," performed strongly and sincerely by Barry McGuire in 1965, became the first protest song to hit number one on the Billboard charts.[15]

The American civil rights movement went to the churches for inspiration, changing the lyrics of African-America spirituals so that they became political songs. The use of religious music emphasized the peaceful, nonviolent nature of the protests. These songs were also easy to adapt, since they generally followed a call and response format that did not require trained singing voices. They were as their originator, Martin Luther, intended them to be, songs of the people. As he wrote, "Next to the word of God, the noble art of music is the greatest treasure in the world. It controls our hearts, minds and spirits. A person who does not regard music as a marvelous creation of God does not deserve to be called a human being; he should be permitted to hear nothing but the braying of asses and the grunting of hogs."[16] Adaptations of Luther's hymns, their context changed to fit the needs of the civil rights movement, were carried across the country by the Freedom Riders and their folksinging accomplices.

When the anti-war movement gained its energy, the music turned electric, edgy—like the movement itself in these times. Country Joe and the Fish brought improvised rock to the arena, music that carried the danger of failure with it. The Jefferson Airplane, The Who, even Simon & Garfunkel brought a restless and insecure energy to the music. Peter, Paul and Mary talked about how they could travel with a candidate and possibly sway an election. They tested this theory by traveling with Senator Eugene McCarthy during his 1968 presidential campaign. He didn't win, of course, but can it be said that Peter, Paul and May weren't a benefit to his campaign? We had a decade where politics, social change, and music all intersected into one huge mass that forever changed our culture, our politics, and the way we listen to and play music. It was a time that changed us all forever. No wonder Senator Keating was afraid.

Chapter 3

The Schizophrenic World of the Protest Song

American popular music—whether rock, folk, or any other category—has always existed simultaneously in both the artistic and the commercial worlds. It is the job of the popular artist to create artifacts that will move people in some way, but people can only be moved by art that they have experienced. If it does not circulate among the public, a work of art cannot achieve its goal. If it is not distributed, it might as well not exist. Therefore, the music has to find a public of some size. It has to be art and show business at the same time. The music also must exist on many levels, simultaneously moving both artist and audience. The job of the protest artist has always been to walk that line, to use show business to reach beyond the already initiated and win new converts to the cause.

It can be a schizophrenic world; trying to maintain the right balance can be frustrating for an artist. Phil Ochs serves as an example. We have mentioned his singing for anti-war protestors and playing Town Hall and Carnegie Hall. Yet, while he was succeeding in the large halls, he also performed at small coffeehouses, political rallies, and protests large and small. He helped pioneer the college circuit, encouraging his manager to book him on campuses, often as part of a package with his friend and fellow folk singer Eric Andersen. As also noted earlier, Ochs described himself as a "left social democrat" and saw himself as a journalist whose medium was primarily the song form. As his goal was to be big in show business, to be rich and famous playing the music he wrote and loved, Ochs—even as the executives at his record company tried to scale back his ambitions—remained convinced that his was the album that would break the pattern, offer substance, and achieve huge sales simultaneously.[1] When that did not happen, Ochs' well of formidable songwriting apparently went dry.

Although it does not seem that this would be the case, for many writers and performers protest was a competitive field. Ochs was a case in point and struggled with feelings of rejection when he saw other performers—Buffy Sainte-Marie, P.F. Sloan, Tom Paxton—become famous and successful writing anti-war songs. Although, as we'll see in a later chapter, East Coast protest writers belittled Sloan's "Eve of Destruction," it climbed quickly up the charts. The list continues. Vince Martin and Fred Neil cowrote and recorded "Tear Down the Walls" in 1964, a song that asked us to "let peace and freedom in." It became a hit. Describing the song, Martin says, "It's not an anti-war song. It's not anti-anything. It's pro-peace. It argues for peace and freedom." Martin remembers growing up in Brooklyn singing Gregorian chants in church, then discovering country music and falling in love with it. By the mid-fifties he had begun his professional career by singing Hank Williams tunes in Brooklyn nightclubs. He was signed by Glory Records, which also had the folk group the Tarriers under contract. Putting Martin together with the Tarriers, Glory issued their single "Cindy, Oh Cindy," which became a big hit. After that one and a couple of follow-up singles that became minor hits, Martin moved to Greenwich Village: "When I went to the Village, I found and followed the political side of music. It was soothing and exciting. We thought it was necessary. I got into it and realized it was a way of reaching people and possibly changing things. Back in the sixties, we really thought we could change the world, felt we could change things with a song. It was a wonderful feeling."

Folk and Gospel Both Served the Movement

Many of the young people felt the same way Martin did, so protest songs captured the mood of the times and became very popular. Before the rise of topical songs, the American civil rights movement had gone to the churches for inspiration, changing the lyrics of African-American spirituals so that they became political songs. The use of religious music emphasized the peaceful, nonviolent, and cooperative nature of the protests. Texas-raised folk singer Carolyn Hester, whose first album was overseen by Buddy Holly's producer, Norman Petty, got to know Buddy Holly very well, singing and playing music informally with him. Both of them strongly opposed the segregation that dominated their West Texas homeland. She remembers her feelings about it:

> Segregation created a hurt I carried with me. Civil rights was very dear to my heart, it was very important to me. That's one reason I got into folk music. One of the most important things about folk music was that you could speak your mind about things

like that. I remember the first Columbia album, I sang "When Jesus Lived in Galilee" and one of the other early albums had "I Want Jesus to Walk with Me." They were religious songs and were black in origin. And they spoke to me, said important things that I wanted to say. I always felt I was one of the more rhythmic of the folk singers. I got that partly because I was friends with Buddy Holly, who was very rhythmic and was also influenced by black music.

These spirituals were also easy to adapt, since they generally followed a call and response format that did not require trained singing voices.

The Music Changes as the Movement Changes

When the anti-war movement began to gain its energy, the music itself caught that same vitality and sense of urgency. It had, as folk music always does, evolved to fit the new conditions. The Byrds brought hard-driving, passionate, and deeply felt folk-rock to the arena, music that carried a dark sense of danger with it. Ritchie Havens, the Beau Brummels, Jim Post, David Blue, Judy Collins, and Tim Hardin brought a restless and insecure energy to the music, an unsettled music to match unsettled times. Peter, Paul and Mary were early proponents of direct action and helped organize several major demonstrations and rallies. When Harry Belafonte asked them to perform at the 1963 March on Washington, the trio saw an opportunity. Peter Yarrow said, "It was our intention not to entertain, not to make people take a moment off, but to focus on why we were there. And when we did it was euphoric."[2] At the march they performed protest songs: "If I Had a Hammer" and "Blowin' in the Wind."[3]

Because of activities such as these, America experienced a decade where politics, social change, and music all intersected into one huge mass that forever changed our culture, our politics, and the way we listen to and play music. It was a time that changed us all forever. And it was a change that was met with increasing resistance by the social and political establishment, resistance that would itself be met by direct challenges from the New Left.

Chapter 4

Bob Moses Attacks Mississippi

If folk music was going to delve deeply into protest songs, it only made sense that the songwriters and singers take their talents into direct action, and this is what happened. The man who made it happen, the man who brought the folk singers to the civil rights movement, was a young folk singer and political activist named Robert Parris Moses. Born in Harlem in 1935, Moses was an early convert to the movement. A graduate of Stuyvesant High School in the Bronx, he went to Hamilton College and then picked up a master's degree in philosophy from Harvard. In 1958 he was teaching at Horace Mann High School in the Bronx when he had a vision that, in keeping with his personality and philosophy, he immediately acted upon.

Americans had always followed charismatic leaders, Moses reasoned, and the results were, more often than not, disastrous. Following leaders had created a segregated society, a culture of and for middle-aged white men. Continuing to give our collective fates over to some charismatic individual that we assumed would turn things around for us would only lead to more of the same. People in power did not relinquish or share their power. Instead they tried to acquire more. What was needed was a grassroots approach; instead of the charismatic leader, power had to be in the hands of the community. Ironically, he was able to pull off miracles in Mississippi because of his strong leadership.

Moses became the field secretary for the Student Nonviolent Coordinating Council (SNCC) and in that capacity took over the operating of the SNCC's Mississippi Project, which was, in essence, a voter registration project. His activities brought him into frequent contact with the police; he was arrested and beaten more than once and became the first black man to file assault charges against the Mississippi police.[1] When the people he filed charges against wound up in court the jury sided with them, and

Moses once more found his life in danger. The judge, claiming he could not protect him, gave Moses a police escort to the county line. Moses, however, refused to be intimidated. By 1964 he had become co-director of the Council of Federated Organizations (COFO), a central organizing group for all of the Civil Rights efforts in Mississippi. As the codirector, he began the Freedom Summer Project, which was essentially an extension of the voter registration drives he had been leading for several years.[2] It went beyond the previous efforts, however, by being more ambitious: COFO set up and operated Freedom Schools, Freedom Houses, and community centers all over the state.

Why Mississippi?

Of all the southern states, why did SNCC choose Mississippi as its target state? The reason why was that it had the largest black population and the lowest number of registered voters in the nation. Mississippi did not make it easy for African Americans to register to vote. In order to register, black citizens had to fill out a 21-question registration form and submit to a quiz by white registrars, a quiz that called on them to recognize and be able to interpret to the registrar's satisfaction any of the 285 sections of the state constitution. "To the registrar's satisfaction" is the key phrase. All Mississippi registrars were allowed full authority over questions of interpretation; any registrar could interpret any section any way he wanted to. When Moses started his work, only 6 percent of Mississippi's eligible black voters had managed to answer the questions to the satisfaction of the registrars, who had full and final authority to accept or reject registration applications.[3] Moses and his colleagues in SNCC decided this situation could not be allowed to stand and if it were going to be changed they'd have to be the ones to initiate and drive the changes.

They set out to do just that. When the project began rolling in earnest in 1964, more than 1,000 volunteers came from all over the country to work in Freedom Summer. Although Moses was the ringleader he worked hard to bring his vision of a decentralized community leadership into being, using his volunteers to recruit and train local leaders.[4] White locals did not welcome the volunteers. Over an eight-week period eighty volunteers were beaten by police, four were critically wounded, and four white workers and three African Americans were murdered.[5]

The Freedom Riders

Moses was a veteran of the southern civil rights struggles. He first came to Mississippi in 1960, having found an opportunity in the state to put his new theory about decentralized leadership into practice; he had been one of SNCC's earliest Mississippi civil rights workers. These first volunteers rode previously segregated busses across the south, trying to enforce the new federal laws that legalized the integration of interstate bus and train travel.[6] These activists called themselves Freedom Riders and sought to integrate not just the busses but also the stations and terminals, restrooms, and water fountains—all of which existed in two types: those marked "whites only" and the others for, as the phrase at the time put it, "colored."

Freedom riding was a dangerous undertaking. Most white southerners at the time were content with the way things were and saw the work of the Freedom Riders as communistic, a threat to, if not democracy itself, then certainly the southern way of life. As far as the majority of whites were concerned, the civil rights workers were outside agitators who were stirring up resentment and anger among their otherwise happy and contented "colored people." These enraged white people fought back.

At that time, not just public transportation was segregated in the south. Almost all aspects of southern life were split down the middle as cleanly as an English muffin. Blacks and whites might as well have been living in different nations occupying the same geography. Each race stayed to its own side and could no more mix than oil could mix with water. Towns and cities were divided into black sections and white sections. In the white neighborhoods, shops and stores were off limits to African Americans. All of the important government offices were held by whites, and whites actively excluded blacks from either holding office or determining who would participate in public service by holding office. Schools operated on the Supreme Court's separate but equal ruling handed down in the *Plessy v. Ferguson* decision of 1896, which stated that segregation was not a violation of the Fourteenth Amendment, in which "equal protection" under the law was guaranteed to everyone. As long as the facilities for each race were equal, then governments could maintain a segregated society.[7] Mississippi's facilities were separate but not at all equal. The police tended to enforce laws written by white men for white men and the courts backed them up to the extent of letting the murderers of black men and boys walk free.

Moses knew he could not change an entire culture, so he figured he

4. Bob Moses Attacks Mississippi

would begin by concentrating on a smaller aspect of it: public transportation, which at that time was segregated in the South. African Americans were forced by law to occupy only the rear seats of a bus or train. Freedom Rides were journeys by civil rights activists on interstate buses into the segregated South. While the Freedom Riders are generally credited with beginning the battle to integrate public transportation in the Deep South, the movement actually began much earlier. In 1946 a young Virginia resident named Irene Morgan took a bus from her home town to Baltimore, Maryland. The law at that time required her to ride in the back of the bus but she refused, claiming that since this was an interstate bus, Virginia laws were superseded by federal laws. Morgan was arrested, convicted, and fined ten dollars. Ordinarily, that would have been the end of the matter, but Morgan's case took a turn when Thurgood Marshall heard about the situation. Marshall and the NAACP took on the case, arguing that since an 1877 Supreme Court decision made it illegal for states to forbid segregation, it was also unconstitutional for a state to require it. Marshall's argument carried the day.[8] The Supreme Court declared that segregation was unconstitutional for passengers engaged in interstate travel. But there was a long line from declaring something illegal to actually changing the practice. Bob Moses set out to change the practice.

Moses, as president of the Congress of Racial Equality (CORE) as well as codirector of the Council of Federated Organizations (COFO), was in a position to organize the Freedom rides. His own experience showed him how dangerous this particular undertaking was. Everywhere the busses stopped they were met by violence. John Lewis, now a United States congressman, was among the Freedom Riders beaten unconscious, and several busses were firebombed, forcing their riders to run for their lives.[9] Birmingham Public Safety commissioner Bull Connor openly granted the local Ku Klux Klan members fifteen minutes to beat up the Freedom Riders before he moved his men in to stop the carnage.[10] White violence against the riders threatened to shut down the activities, but SNCC kept the pressure up by continually bringing in new activists. Since violence would not stop the movement, Mississippi officials turned to another tactic: mass arrests.

On May 24, 1961, the Freedom Riders arrived in Jackson, Mississippi, where they were summarily arrested and jailed for "breaching the peace" because they used "white only" bathrooms and water fountains. Not even jail stopped them. Using Martin Luther King, Jr.'s, Birmingham Jail tactic, they refused to be bailed out and released. They announced that they would not pay fines for unconstitutional arrests and illegal convictions.[11] At that time,

Mississippi law granted inmates thirty-nine days behind bars before they lost their right to appeal. The Freedom Riders declared they would stay in lockup the full thirty-nine days the law granted them before accepting bail. After the end of their legally granted safe time, they posted bond and file an appeal questioning the constitutionality of their arrests. The Freedom Riders also saw that, as Martin Luther King, Jr., had realized in Birmingham, they could get more publicity for the cause by staying in jail.[12]

Jackson authorities did not make their thirty-nine day stays pleasant. The prisoners were beaten, piled up like sardines in cells that were too small and cramped, and forced to work outside in Mississippi's 100+ degree summer heat. Some were moved to the notorious state prison at Parchman. All of these excesses wound up accomplishing what the riders figured they would: they won sympathy and support for the cause. The worse the Mississippi police and corrections officers treated them the more sympathy the riders won from the rest of the country. The public outcry led President John F. Kennedy to issue a stronger desegregation order. From that moment on, African Americans were no longer forced to sit at the back of the bus, and restrooms and water fountains were no longer segregated.[13]

The riders had won a major battle. But the war still raged on.

The Voter Registration Drives

Fresh from the Freedom Riders' victory, Mississippi's black leaders called on SNCC to help register voters and to build organizations that would help African American citizens get a bigger slice of the pie. So far, they could only smell the aroma of pie coming from white neighborhoods. Keeping all of the pie for themselves helped keep white supremacists in power. The SNCC could help the black leaders correct the balance. Again Bob Moses took the lead. After a series of beatings, arrests, and the occasional assassination of voting rights workers by the White Citizens Council and the Ku Klux Klan, Moses saw that no single civil rights group was powerful enough to triumph, so he urged a merger of groups. In February 1962 representatives of SNCC, CORE, and the NAACP got together to form the Council of Federated Organizations (COFO), which Moses was chosen to lead. Not long after that, Dr. King brought his Southern Christian Leadership Foundation (SCL) into the fold.[14] In every part of Mississippi that COFO tried to organize, white people fought back, reaching into their usual bag of tactics: beatings, shootings, arrests,

4. Bob Moses Attacks Mississippi

and the burning of schools and churches. The literacy tests that black voters had to pass were rewritten to make them so hard that it was impossible to pass one.

Moses was not used to losing and didn't intend to get used to it. He decided that in order to succeed he'd have to go beyond the simple act of registering voters; he needed schools, meeting halls, whole new approaches to community. Nothing could happen as long as the residents relied on outside leaders; in order to ultimately succeed they'd have to take their destinies into their own hands. What was needed in order to both register voters and build a self-sustaining community? The answer was simple: Folk singers.

Chapter 5

Here's to the State of Mississippi

Phil Ochs did not want to go to Mississippi. He had heard how, just a few days earlier, Robert Parris Moses, the man who was trying to talk him into going south and singing for the Freedom Riders, had been beaten senseless and arrested by white men in Amite County. He also knew that when Moses challenged the attackers in court before, he wound up being escorted by police to the county line after an all-white jury acquitted the men who beat him almost senseless.[1] And this was not the first time Moses had attracted violence in Mississippi.

Ochs wanted nothing to do with it. Sure, Moses came to the civil rights movement early. In 1961 he became the director of SNCC's Mississippi Project and, in that position, was asked to register African-American voters in the state.[2] According to Bruce Watson, Mississippi had made the least progress in the field of civil rights and was determined to maintain its record. In Georgia, 44 percent of the African-American population was registered to vote, in Texas 50 percent, and in Tennessee 69 percent. In Mississippi, however, a mere 6–7 percent of the African-American community was registered and eligible to vote.[3] Moses was determined to change those figures and he was asking Phil Ochs, among others, to help him do it.

There was little in Phil Ochs' background to indicate that he would become a mover and shaker in the movement. Born in El Paso, Texas, on December 19, 1940, Ochs grew up the son of an army doctor who had received a medical discharge. Ochs' father, Jacob "Jack" Ochs, returned home with a case of bipolar disorder and suffering from severe depression, two conditions from which his son would also suffer later in life. His conditions rendering it difficult for him to hold down a job, Jack Ochs spent his working life floating from hospital to hospital, so the family moved often, finally settling in Columbus, Ohio.[4]

In high school, Phil Ochs demonstrated an interest in the discipline, regimentation, and spectacle of the military, which led him to choose to

5. Here's to the State of Mississippi

attend military school instead of the public high school. He had earlier demonstrated a talent for music, playing the clarinet in the orchestra at the Capital University Conservatory of Music; at the age of sixteen, he became the orchestra's principal soloist. Classical music was only one of his interests, though. At this time, he developed what would become a lifelong fascination with the work of Buddy Holly and Elvis Presley as well as the country music of Hank Williams, Sr., and Johnny Cash.

Ochs spent three years at Staunton Military Academy in Virginia and after graduation attended Ohio State University. There he got his life turned around and found his direction by meeting a fellow student named Jim Glover:

> It was the wall of Elvis pictures which first caught the eye of the student from the floor below as he passed Philip's room one day on his way to study group. "Heartbreak Hotel" was on the phonograph. Jim Glover walked into Phil's room to get a closer look.
> "Where'd you get the pictures, man?"
> "I collect them," Philip said, without looking up from the magazine he was reading while he sat on his bed.
> "Do you have any pictures of Woody Guthrie?"
> "Never heard of him."
> Jim asked Philip if he'd ever heard of the Weavers. He said no.
> Or Pete Seeger? Not him either. Jim took him down to his room. He wanted to play some of his own records. A couple of 78s later, Philip told Jim he was looking for a new roommate. The next day he helped Jim move his stuff upstairs.[5]

While giving Ochs a basic education in folk music, Glover taught him to play guitar and introduced him to radical politics. Soon the two of them were playing out, billing themselves as the Sundowners, although Phil preferred to refer to themselves as the Singing Socialists. The act broke up when Jim Glover moved to New York City to become a professional folk singer. Phil stayed in Ohio, working small clubs and coffeehouses, and began fusing his interest in politics with his interest in folk music by writing and performing topical songs. Soon he followed Glover to New York and began the slow but steady process of becoming Phil Ochs, the second-most well-known composer of protest songs in America. Electra Records signed him to a contract and in 1964 his first album, *All the News That's Fit to Sing*, was released, followed a year later by *I Ain't Marchin' Anymore*. Both albums contained pro-civil rights and anti-war songs.

Now, however, Robert Moses was asking Ochs to live what he was singing; he wanted him to go into the territory he'd been writing about, taking his life in his own hands and become an activist rather than an artist. Writing topical songs was one thing, Ochs thought. Sticking your face inside the lion's mouth to sing them was something else altogether. Moses's request that Phil Ochs and his folk-singing compatriots go to Mississippi came about because the 1964 Newport Folk Festival had been the most successful one ever. A total of 77,000 people had attended, up from 30,000 in 1963.[6] That turnout gave Moses an idea. If the performers from the festival, which had been a harvest of protest songs, went south to sing those songs for the Freedom Riders, who were crisscrossing the state in a dual effort to integrate the state's mass transportation system and to register voters, they could open up the voter lists by adding thousands of new names.

As we have seen, even though the Supreme Court had affirmed integration in 1961, public transportation remained segregated in the Deep South and local Jim Crow laws declared that African Americans were to occupy only the back of busses.[7] As we also discussed, the actions of the original thirteen young people who went south as Freedom Riders inspired thousands of idealistic young white kids, primarily college students and recent college graduates, to go south to help integrate the transportation system.[8] As Moses, the president of CORE, had organized the Freedom Riders, he was fully aware of how dangerous this particular mission was. He knew of the violence perpetrated by Klansmen and other white supremacists, the firebombing of busses, and the fact that the Klan was given permission by Bull Connor to beat up the Freedom Riders for 15 minutes before he ordered his deputies to stop them.[9] He also knew that when violence didn't seem likely to stop the activists the authorities turned to mass arrests. By the time Ochs was offered his opportunity to go into the front lines and face the hatred, the Freedom Riders had become a familiar topic in civil rights circles.

On May 24, 1961, when they first arrived in Jackson, Mississippi, they were summarily arrested and jailed for "breaching the peace" because they used "white only" bathrooms and water fountains.[10] But as we have seen, not even jail stopped them. Following Dr. King's example, they refused to be bailed out and released, announcing that they would not pay fines for unconstitutional arrests and illegal conviction.[11] The state of Mississippi lost the public sympathy game and this time they lost big. President Kennedy issued his new desegregation orders pulling white and colored signs forever, ending separate drinking fountains and bathrooms. From then on, lunchrooms and terminals would be integrated, as would the busses. Bob Moses had his victory. He did not, however, feel like retiring from the ring. Being able to move freely and drink water where you wanted was a major victory, certainly, but why not go bigger? None of this progress made any real difference if people could not cast a vote, so acquiring voting rights was Moses's plan from the beginning. He would secure small victories that would lead to securing the big one: the vote.

The Mississippi constitution, drawn up in 1890, contains clauses on poll taxes, residency requirements, and literacy tests that were designed to prevent the black population from voting. When the Freedom Rides succeeded, local black leaders in Mississippi such as Medgar Evers asked SNCC to lead a voter registration drive. Moses, ready to build on his victory, said yes and Mississippi Summer resulted.[12] Moses had two goals for the summer's activities. The first, of course, was to register voters. The second was to show the rest of the world how absurd and dangerous this situation was. That's why he needed folk singers.

The Folk Singers Go South

Moses was making progress, but changing the dominant culture of Mississippi was a slow and dangerous process marked by arrests, beatings, shootings, arson, and murder, all committed by white supremacists. Now he wanted to bring the Freedom Riders' work to a higher level of public awareness. A group of thirty-five of the nation's finest and most popular folk singers could accomplish that. This was the situation facing Phil Ochs when Moses came to Newport.

As a member of the dominant 5 percent of the civil rights movement, Moses did not get turned down very often. In fact, all he had to do was bring up the idea and most of the singers were ready to go. Carolyn Hester, at that time one of the most popular folk performers in the United States (she had been recently been named by the *Saturday Evening Post* as "The Face of Folk Music"), declared, "You almost didn't want to stand up and say you were an American, if you didn't go." There was no getting around it: Phil Ochs *had* to put his body and his life on the line by going south.

Contemporary folk artists like Joan Baez, Peter, Paul and Mary, Eric Andersen, Jackie Washington, and Len Chandler were enthusiastically on board for the trip. Bob Dylan, never one either to be pressured into a decision or to follow someone else's directive, went back to New York after the festival. At the festival he had introduced a new song, one he had just written which was perhaps the best topical song of its time. "Only a Pawn in Their Game" was about the murder of Mississippi civil rights leader Medgar Evers. The veteran actor, folk singer, and writer Theodore Bikel, already in Mississippi, could not understand why Dylan had turned down the opportunity to come to Mississippi and sing that song for the people who had inspired it and needed to hear it. He called Dylan and told him he had to come down and sing that song for the people. "I can't," Dylan said. "I'm broke. I don't have the money." Bikel sent him a round-trip airplane ticket and Bob Dylan came down to join the company.[13]

No one provided a plane ticket for Phil Ochs. He drove down from New York with Eric Andersen, another folk singer with whom he'd performed at Newport and who, when they got back, was to be featured on Vanguard's *New Faces of 1964* album. Phil, who was drunk most of the way down, had to let Andersen drive. At this time he had no idea he was suffering from bipolar disorder, but knew he was getting more and more paranoid as they entered what Andersen called "Southerntown, Mississippi." In the sixties paranoia wasn't unusual among progressives but was a natural response to the fact that, in more cases than not, the FBI was monitoring the words and actions of the New Left. After his death, for example, the FBI released a file of more than 500 pages on Ochs.[14] Under those conditions, a touch of paranoia was not outside the norm and Phil Ochs began feeling it as soon as they entered the South.

When he and Andersen had been there for two days, the bodies of James Chaney, Andrew Goodman, and Michael Schwerner were found. On June 21, 1964, Goodman and Schwerner—two New York City members of Moses's Council of Federated Organizations who were in Mississippi for the voter registrations drive—were, along with Meridian, Mississippi, activist James Chaney, arrested while driving through Meridian. After questioning by the police, the three young men were released, but as they drove off they were followed by a group of white supremacists, a group that included members of the Meridian police department. They were pulled over and shot, then their bodies were dumped in an earthen dam.[15] When their corpses turned up, a shock went through the entire protesting community, both local and from out of town. All of the folk singers on the trip recognized that Mississippi was in a dangerous time and was a dangerous place, but their efforts had to be undertaken nonetheless. Carolyn Hester said, "We sang in churches, we sang in people's houses. It was hard, and it was scary, and we were staying in their homes, on their side of town, and making their lives more difficult and more dangerous. But it was all ... necessary. It was all necessary. I'm not sure we did anything except go there and say we see you, we love you, and we're with you. I don't know if we accomplished anything more than that. But we did do that."

5. Here's to the State of Mississippi

Phil Ochs agreed it was necessary, but, already paranoid, he became convinced that he was going to be murdered. Still, he went ahead and performed. However, each time he went onto the rickety homemade stage, he made Andersen stand watch, scanning the crowd for assassins. His paranoia grew by the day and he could not wait until the week he had pledged to the cause was up so he could go home. However, when he wasn't singing, he was out talking to the crowds, working them like the journalist he had trained in college to become, conducting interviews, and writing down in the reporter's pad he always carried what the local people had to say. When he got back to New York, all of those quotes would come in handy.

According to the Ochs biography *Death of a Rebel*, one night that fall he and Eric Andersen were playing the Gaslight. While Andersen did the opening set, Phil Ochs sat with Dave Van Ronk at the bar drinking as Ochs told Van Ronk how horrible Mississippi had been. Van Ronk was not impressed. Mississippi had no lock-hold on ugliness, he said, declaring that Ochs could have found just as much racial hatred down the block there in the Village. Even as Ochs took the stage, they continued arguing.

After a couple of songs, Phil Ochs asked the crowd to raise their glasses and join in a toast. As they did, he broke into "Here's to the State of Mississippi."[16] The song was built on his observations from his time in that southern state, as well as quotes from the citizens he had interviewed. He sang about the bodies beneath the state's muddy waters, about the still-segregated schools that did not teach black kids but instead taught white kids to hate, about the cops he accused in the lyrics of being murderers and more. The crowd in the Gaslight went berserk over the song, cheering, whistling, stomping, standing. That was more than the old-line Marxist Van Ronk could take. Storming his way to the stage, he screamed that Phil had it all wrong. Why shovel blame on Mississippi when it just as bad down the block as it was down South? Phil, he said, had reduced the problem to a "liberal's mentality, so very unimportant."[17] Phil didn't think the song was unimportant at all. What he had wanted to do was to express all of his rage and anger and confusion, to provide an emotional response to the horrors that he still felt about Mississippi Summer. He wanted an Aristotelian purgation, where, by expressing his choking emotions, he could rid himself of them. If he could not conquer racism by going into its heart, he could fight it the best way he knew—through a good topical song.

Chapter 6

Carolyn Hester Goes to Mississippi

Carolyn Hester's story is emblematic of the journey folk singers embarked on when they decided to build careers singing the old songs. Hers is an archetypal story. When she came to Greenwich Village to further her career, she had no idea that the Village was going to turn her into a world-traveling singing activist. As far as a career goes, she had come a long way already and was steadily becoming better known. She had released her first album, *Scarlet Ribbons*, on Coral Records. That record came about in an unusual way and served to show how open the folk music community was back in the early days before the folk revival. She had been playing guitar and singing around Texas, where she grew up, when her mother heard that a man named Norman Petty owned and operated a recording studio in nearby Clovis, New Mexico. Her mother cold-called Petty and informed him that her daughter sang folk music and he should hear her. Petty invited Hester to come up to Clovis to audition. Hester was excited by the invitation; one of the artists Petty recorded was Buddy Holly, whom she revered. "My mother didn't know who Buddy Holly was but I did. We went up there, I sang for Norman and he said, 'Why don't we make a record?' We recorded my first album and it came out on Coral Records. I was signed to Coral, Buddy was on Brunswick and both labels were owned by Decca."

Hester and Holly became good friends. He taught her some of his songs and played guitar on four of her recordings, the tapes of which are long lost. Both the studio copies and her personal copies have disappeared. It has long been rumored that Holly played guitar on *Scarlet Ribbons*, but Hester says that isn't true. He did, however, play on other sessions that were lost before they could be released.

6. Carolyn Hester Goes to Mississippi

Greenwich Village Days

Hester's New York move grew out of the restlessness that nearly every developing artist feels. It came about because she wanted, at the age of eighteen, to live "in my own mind." She had a classmate who aspired to be a dancer, so when they graduated from high school, the two of them and a third girl drove to New York City. "That first night we were in Greenwich Village, I saw it was going to be amazing but I didn't know a whole lot of my life was going to be in Greenwich Village."

At that time, Greenwich Village served as the center of alternative culture in New York City. It always had. In the twenties it had become a haven for the city's Bohemians, sheltering and nourishing such avant-garde artists as poet Maxwell Bodenheim, dancer Isadora Duncan, and playwright Eugene O'Neill. The off-off Broadway theater started there and by the forties experimental theater companies such as the Living Theater and the Theatre of the Absurd had their homes in the Village. The music scene was thriving: The Village Vanguard, The Village Gate, and the Bottom Line all operated simultaneously.

By the late fifties the Beats came to the Village in search of cheap rent and an escape from the conformity that the Eisenhower years had created. There they could be themselves. The folk singers followed the Beats, and by the early sixties clubs and coffeehouses like Gerde's Folk City, Cafe Au Go Go, Cafe Wha, and the Gaslight blanketed the area. Every Sunday afternoon, all of the folk singers gathered in Washington Square Park, playing and singing for the love of the music.[1] This then was the neighborhood that Carolyn Hester settled in. It was also the neighborhood that helped turn her into a civil rights and anti-war activist.

Hester had not been there long when her burgeoning career received a jump-start. One of her roommates was an actress who landed a job at Circle in the Square Theater in Washington, D.C. The company was going to be doing Ibsen's *The Purification*, and they had a musician on stage for the entire performance. That musician was jazz and classical guitarist Charlie Byrd. "He said he'd developed an interest in folk music and my friend said, 'I have a friend who is a folk singer.' Byrd said, '[H]ave her come on down, maybe we'll have a folk night or something.'" So Hester took a Greyhound bus down to D.C. and auditioned for Byrd with George Gershwin's "Summertime." Byrd was impressed. Hester remembers, "What happened was,

Charlie Byrd said 'I'm going to be going to Brazil with Stan Getz to do shows and record.'" Byrd owned a club in Annapolis, Maryland, where he performed nightly and needed to cover the time he was going to be gone with other performers. "Mose Allison did two weeks. Shirley Horn did two weeks and I did two weeks." Hester's career climbed from that appearance, and she began receiving offers to perform in better venues. "I played the Blue Dog Cellar in Baltimore and [folk music DJ] Dick Cerri came walking in. He said, 'I know you played for Charlie Byrd and I have your record and have already put it on the air. You'll have to come do my show.' So I became quite at home in the D.C. area."

After a second album was released on the Clancy Brothers' Tradition label, Hester had become important enough to be signed to Columbia Records by the legendary producer John Hammond. Preparing for her first album for that label she told Hammond, who was producing it, that she wanted the noted session musicians Bill Lee (bass) and Bruce Langhorne (lead guitar) to play. She also asked for a young harmonica player who had never recorded before named Bob Dylan, whom she had met at Gerde's Folk City. She had been headlining there, and one weekend night for her last song she announced she was going to do a song Buddy Holly taught her. After she sang, a kid in the audience crowded up front and asked her if she really had known Buddy Holly. She said she had, and she and the kid talked for a long time about Holly and his music, which the kid loved. That kid was Bob Dylan. The two stayed in touch, became friends, and when she signed with Columbia, Dylan approached her about participating in the recording session.

"Bob heard I was recording a new album and asked if he could play guitar on it. I told him I already had a guitar player and asked if he wanted to play harmonica. My father had played harmonica on my first album and I loved that sound. We got in the studio with John Hammond producing and he heard Bob and signed him to Columbia. That's how that happened."

Her association with Dylan has been a long one. They have remained friends since they met. She has joined him in concert many times and has played any number of tribute shows with him. In fact, she says that when Dylan got his Nobel Prize, "I was asked to do an op-ed for the *Los Angeles Times*, so I wrote about how we came from all over, gathered in the village and built ourselves a fortress of folk. Right now, Dylan's music is very much needed so I was glad to hear he won that award."

6. Carolyn Hester Goes to Mississippi

Freedom Summer

From the time she was a little girl Hester had the idea of equality on her mind. She was very young and living with her family in Washington, D.C., when the Second World War broke out. Remembering those days, she tells how she became aware of racism and how that knowledge changed her:

> My brother and I were displaced children, like in London when the bombing started. My folks worked for the government in Washington so when the air raids started to come, my parents decided we should go down to Texas. Until then I was living in the inner city and my schoolmates were from all kinds of countries. It was a nicely regarded school and I was just an ordinary kid.
> When I got down to Texas, living with my grandparents, I found out that the lady who came to my grandmother's house once a week to clean house wasn't able to sit down and have lunch with my grandparents. And my grandparents were lovely people. I was so in love with them. I was shocked when the maid told me. I said[,] "[L]isten, grandma and grandpa are going to have lunch too, so let's go in and join them" and she said, "[O]h, no, I can't do that."
> I said, "What?"
> She said, "Black people can't sit at the same table with white folks."
> That never left me. That really hurt. I sorted that out. My grandparents never said anything bad about black people. My parents were for sure almost like a different culture. When my father was a teacher in Texas, he coached black debate teams, never said anything bad about black people. I knew my parents were different from my grandparents. They never spoke badly about any minority. It was like there was this invisible law saying blacks and whites couldn't mix.
> I was like nine years old and inequity came through in my eyes and that never left me. Then there was Martin Luther King and I learned that it takes a village thing.

Mississippi Bound

In her first days in Greenwich Village, Hester met Gil Turner, who during the days of the folk revival was a legend there. Turner, a folk singer who served as the emcee at Gerde's Folk City, was nothing if not well rounded. He was an editor at *Broadside* magazine, where he selected protest songs for publication in its pages. He was also a Shakespearean actor and a Baptist minister. He founded the folk group the New World Singers, with fellow folk singers Happy Traum and the ubiquitous Bob Moses, which became the first group to record Dylan's "Blowin' in the Wind." In fact, Turner introduced "Blowin' in the Wind" to the public by being the first person to sing it on a stage. He was also the writer of one of the first protest classics, "Carry It On," which almost every folk singer of note—including Judy Collins, Buffy Sainte-Marie, Kate Wolf, Joan Baez, Peter, Paul and Mary, and Carolyn Hester herself—recorded.

Since Bob Moses played in the New World Singers with him, Turner was around when Moses was planning Freedom Summer and joined in enthusiastically. When he was getting ready for the trip south, he invited Hester to come along. She went and they "met up with a lot of other folk singers and that's how we all got down to Freedom summer." In Mississippi Hester experienced a culture shock bigger than the one she went through when she found out the maid could not eat lunch with her grandparents: "I remember that even in Mississippi, things seemed much more dire than in Austin or Dallas where I grew up. I'd be in the black community and just see hard working people, but when I was in Hattiesburg and Jackson and all the other small places we went, you would see children wandering listlessly, aimlessly. It was like a third world country. It broke my heart." For Hester, going to Freedom Summer was not really a choice to be made but an imperative. She felt she had no choice: "What was driving me in those days was that I had to go to Mississippi. I didn't tell my parents I was going but it was so vital to me that I felt I don't want to be an American anymore if this is what's going on. I had to get up and do something and I think generations were thinking that. I was in my mid-twenties and there were people older than me and people younger than me."

She went south at a particularly dangerous time. "Goodman, Chaney and Schwerner had just been murdered at the time we started driving down through New York and about a week or so later, their bodies were discovered and it was a truly frightening experience. Still, it was something I had to do." Hester and the other folk singers drove from town to town, singing wherever they could—from the back of pickup trucks, to open fields, on rickety homemade stages—wherever they could spread the news and the music. Although she and the others gave all they had to the experience, Hester to this day isn't entirely certain that their efforts accomplished everything they might have. Since the host families let the visiting performers stay in their homes it made the lives of Mississippi's citizens more difficult and perhaps even more dangerous. She can't be sure the musicians accomplished very much but one thing they definitely did was to stand up, to be present, to give support to the African Americans' struggle. They let them know that they were loved and respected. In truth, they helped to accomplish much more. Before Freedom Summer, fewer than 7 percent of African Americans were registered and able

6. Carolyn Hester Goes to Mississippi

to vote. The state had no black officeholders. Today most of the barriers to voting have been eliminated and Mississippi has over 1,000 black state and local officials—more than any other state in the union.[2] Carolyn Hester and the other veterans of Freedom Summer can take a lot of the credit for that.

As Hester's career flourished, the *Saturday Evening Post* put her on the cover and called her the "Face of Folk Music." She played concerts and appeared on television shows all over the world—often teaming up with other legendary folk figures—and she is proud that folk music has always been integrated:

> I used to do shows with Mississippi John Hurt. I'd go on first and he'd be sitting in the audience listening and then he'd nod off—he was already in his seventies then—but he'd wake up when I did "East Virginia" because he knew it was his turn to sing.
>
> And Odetta. She was a buddy. Thank God, it could have been a thing where they wouldn't let blacks and whites make music together. That would have been horrible for me. And Odetta, she was such a buddy. My life was so much nicer because of her. We laughed and screamed together.

Freedom Summer didn't end Hester's activism. She made topical and protest songs the centerpiece of the double album she cut live at Carnegie Hall and frequently marched against the Vietnam War:

> One march I remember happened when my mother had to fly from Texas to Baltimore, then she came up to New York where I was living. This was '62 or something, so I said, "Mom, there's going to be a peace march. I was going to go. Would you want to go and march?" And she said[,] "I'd love to do that."
>
> So we went out, my mom and I, and we did that and on the way a man stood next to me and before I knew it this man moved closer to me and I felt something was wrong with my hand and I saw that he had put out his cigarette on my hand. He evidently didn't approve of what we were doing so he was just going around putting out cigarettes on people.
>
> I recovered from that and when we got back to the apartment, my mom said, "Thank you for that. It's so important. Thanks for letting me do that with my generation."

Why do it? Why put your life on the line in the deepest South and why put up with the disrespect by, and hatred from, strangers? The answer is simple, according to Carolyn Hester: "There's that idea, you're not going to be surrounded by hate."

Chapter 7

Joan Baez Boards the Mississippi Train

Joan Baez knew Harry Belafonte and Harry Belafonte knew Mississippi. Having had some unpleasant early experiences there, the man best known at that time as the Calypso King refused to play the segregated South, so he did not tour the region from 1954 to 1961.[1] When he began touring there again, he was powerful enough to enforce some conditions. His shows had be open to everybody. Once he played to integrated audiences, he saw no reason why everybody shouldn't, so he joined Dr. Martin Luther King, Jr.'s, efforts to integrate the South, which Baez also signed onto. In fact, since King was trying to pay for his civil rights activities out of his $8,000 per year salary, Belafonte helped finance his civil disobedience.[2]

Harry Belafonte put his body on the line in Mississippi during the 1961 Freedom Rides, but primarily he made it possible for many others to do so as well.

He grabbed the check for the whole operation. Then when Bob Moses organized the Mississippi Freedom Summer, Belafonte picked up that tab too. He also talked Sidney Poitier into flying down to Greenwood, Mississippi, that August, carrying $60,000 in cash to donate to the movement. For Poitier, the thought of two black men being stopped by southern cops with that much cash on them was enough to frighten him half to death. But Belafonte said jokingly, "They might think twice about killing two big niggers." Poitier might be nervous about the prospects for survival but he was on board. The money was for SNCC, to pick up the tab for their operations that summer.[3] As it turns out, Poitier was right to be concerned. The two of them flew down to Mississippi in a Piper Cub:

> The Piper Cub arrived right on time. So did the Klan. Three SNCC cars waited on the tarmac in the muggy darkness. From the small plane stepped the two celebrities, Belafonte's wide smile instantly recognizable, Poitier's on screen serenity seeming on edge. James Forman greeted the pair, shook hands and steered them to the middle car. The

7. Joan Baez Boards the Mississippi Train

convoy pulled out and drove through the airport gate. Suddenly headlights flashed in the distance. Belafonte holding the satchel stuffed with cash, noted how comforting it was to see SNCC support all around them but Forman told him the headlights belonged to the Klan.

The Klan cars chased the convoy all the way to Greenwood, frequently ramming the rear car, which served as a block so that the Klansmen could not get ahead of the convoy and cut it off. Poitier remembered the event as "a ballet, though a nerve wracking one."[4]

Belafonte became the unofficial checkbook for the civil rights movement; he had also helped organize and pay for the 1963 March on Washington where Dr. King gave his "I Have a Dream" speech and Joan Baez sang. It is safe to assume that neither the Freedom Rides nor the Voting Rights Drive could have happened as they did and when they did without the efforts and cash infusions of Harry Belafonte.

In 1961, when Baez first started touring in Mississippi, she went through what Belafonte had experienced in 1954. She was surprised that in one of the states with the heaviest black population, her audiences were solid white.

> I did discover, however, that no blacks were at my concerts and would not have been allowed in if they had come. The following summer I wrote into the contract that I wouldn't sing unless blacks were admitted into the hall. The movement was beginning to swell in ranks and spirit and I returned to the south and discovered that no blacks came to my concerts anyway because they had never heard of me. We had to call up the local NAACP for volunteers to integrate an audience for someone they'd never heard of.[5]

Playing another card from the Belafonte deck, she had insisted that her audiences be integrated, that anyone who bought a ticket be admitted, and that tickets be sold to anyone who asked for them. Even though southern brokers and promoters complied with her demands, her audiences were still as white as a Klansman's dress uniform. In order to increase her recognition among minority audiences, she began booking shows in black schools and theaters. Baez determined that she should play black schools on the grounds that even if they didn't know who she was, students would turn out for the show because it was better than school.[6]

When she performed a concert at Miles College, a traditionally African-American school in Birmingham, a protest of segregation was being held in the downtown area and Baez went down to participate in it. Sheriff Bull Connor, the same man who had given the Klan permission and extra time to beat up protestors and the same man who was later seen on national TV turning attack dogs loose on protestors, "was giving orders to prepare for the fire hoses, tear gas, attack dogs, and arrests."[7] Baez was furious because she could not be arrested; she had a concert she had committed to and could not fail to show up and sing. She rushed to the venue and when she stood backstage, watching the hall fill up, "I was fearing for my life."[8] As they watched white people walking silently to their seats, one of the faculty members of the college said to Baez, "This is the first time whites have ever stepped foot onto this campus."[9] Baez writes about that show in her autobiography:

> Perhaps it was partly because of the electricity we could feel emanating from the center of town, miles away, where the kids were at that very moment being arrested and filling paddy wagons singing and praying, scared to their bones but bolstered by each other's presence and by the knowledge that they were doing right in the eyes of God. Images of the kids gave me courage and the concert was beautiful.[10]

So Joan Baez's Mississippi summer was different from that of Ochs and the others. Most of her civil rights work centered around her support for Martin Luther King, Jr., for whom she and Bob Dylan sang at the 1963 March on Washington:

> I was in Washington in 1963 when King gave his most famous speech: "I Have a Dream." It was a mighty day, which has been described many times. I will only say that one of the medals which hangs over my own heart I awarded to myself for having been asked to sing that day. In the blistering sun, facing the original rainbow coalition, I led 350,000 people in "We Shall Overcome" and I was near my beloved Dr. King when he put aside his prepared speech and let the breath of God thunder through him, and up over my head I saw freedom and all round me I heard it ring.[11]

Baez not only sang at the March on Washington but worked closely throughout the early 1960s with Dr. King (whom she had met in the 1950s when she was a high school student). She marched arm in arm with him in Selma and other cities, sang at rallies in churches throughout the South to support civil rights activists, and flew down to the Deep South to walk young black children into school buildings when they were integrating white schools—doing so because she knew these little kids would be subjected to far less brutal violence from the local sheriffs and the local racist hoodlums if she was there to attract the TV cameras. (She was a very big star at that time—a far bigger star than her then-boyfriend Bob Dylan was during the early 1960s, although his fame would soon eclipse hers.) Baez, who was raised by Quaker pacifists, continued to be a major figure in civil rights and human rights struggles for decades afterward.

7. Joan Baez Boards the Mississippi Train

Where Did This Woman Come From?

In 1958 Joan Baez, a seventeen-year-old kid at the time, entered Boston College as a drama major. In Boston, which was a major folk music town, she fell in with the lefty folk crowd and began performing at the Boston area clubs and coffeehouses, including the legendary Club 47 (still operating today under the name Club Passim). There she met the city's progressives, a group of young people whose humanist politics matched hers. She was able to spend her time ignoring college and concentrating on her two favorite things: progressive politics and folk music.

Hers was a fully developed and extraordinary talent almost from the beginning and her musical reputation grew quickly. In 1959 folk singer Bob Gibson took her to the Newport Folk Festival, where she was an immediate hit. Credited with discovering her, Gibson told a reporter that discovering Baez was like discovering the wind: she was out there, bound to be noticed, and no one could take credit for a natural force like that.[12] At Newport she sang duets with Gibson on the festival's main stage and their songs were selected to appear on the sound track album. By the time the festival ended, Baez had been offered recording contracts by both Columbia and Vanguard Records, which had issued the soundtrack album. She says the difference between them was that "one [Columbia] was commercial and had mostly to do with money and the other was not so commercial and had mostly to do with music."[13] Albert Grossman, the manager of Bob Dylan, Peter, Paul and Mary, Bob Gibson, and other top acts, was courting Baez at the time and wanted her to sign with Columbia. She chose Vanguard and Grossman lost interest in her except to tell her every time he ran into her that no matter how well she was doing, she could have done a lot better if she had gone with Columbia and signed with him.[14]

From the beginning, Baez was socially and politically committed. Because her father was Mexican, Baez had been bullied during her childhood. This treatment was at least partially responsible for her commitment to civil rights and the resolution she made early on to divide her career in halves: 50 percent show business and 50 percent activism. In 1965 she founded the Institute for the Study of Nonviolence and refused to pay the portion of her income tax that she believed would go to pay for military spending, citing the fact that she was opposed to war as a justification and writing an open letter to the Internal Revenue Service, which read in part as follows:

Part I. Mississippi Needs Folk Singers

I am not going to volunteer the 60% of my year's income tax that goes to armaments. There are two reasons for my action. One is enough. It is enough to say that no man has the right to take another man's life. Now we plan and build weapons that can take thousands of lives in a second, millions of lives in a day, billions in a week.
No one has the right to do that.
It is madness.
It is wrong.[15]
Her second reason was more personal and judgmental. War, Baez said, was "stupid."[16]

Her commitment to civil rights deepened even more in 1961 when Baez was introduced to Bob Dylan by her brother-in-law, writer and folk-singer Richard Farina. The pair hit it off and soon became personal and musical partners. At that point, Baez's popularity far exceeded Dylan's, so she carried him on tour with her, greatly expanding his audience as well as expanding her own repertoire. Her covers of such Dylan songs as "Don't Think Twice" brought him attention from a larger public. Even after they broke up, the pair remained close. In 1969 Baez recorded *Any Day Now*, a two-record set that consisted totally of Bob Dylan's songs. During the 1975–1976 season she toured as a part of Dylan's Rolling Thunder Review.

Politics, however, were never far beneath the surface of Baez's interests. Even her marriage had the overtones of a political act. In 1968 she married David Harris, an anti–Vietnam War activist who was sent to prison for his activities in the protest movement. They divorced in 1973 after having one child, Gabriel.

Why Joan Baez and the Others Used Folk Music as a Weapon

Joan Baez and the other folk singers recognized early that the civil rights movement was about more than just speeches and proclamations. For example, when Dr. Martin Luther King, Jr., gave his "I Have a Dream" speech to the biggest crowd ever gathered in Washington, D.C., he was preceded at the podium by Harry Belafonte, Paul Robeson, and Peter, Paul and Mary, as well as Joan Baez, who sang "Oh Freedom," a song from slavery times that had been resurrected by the people at Tennessee's Highlander Folk School, which trained future civil rights leaders. Baez sang the old refrain "Before I'll be a slave, I'll be buried in my grave and go home to my Lord and be free" and got a massive positive response.[17]

7. Joan Baez Boards the Mississippi Train

From the beginning, the civil rights movement relied on folk music. Today when historians and journalists look back on the days of voting rights activism they don't choose to remember and write about the organizing, the deadly dull days of running mimeograph machines and spreading fliers all over the neighborhood. They don't recall the endless meetings where the type of participatory democracy advocated by the Port Huron Statement insisted that everyone be allowed to speak and that all decisions be group-approved, so that meetings ran on for hours after a decision could have been made, leading to frustration and animosity and the rise of factionalism. No, they don't recall any of the daily and decidedly unglamorous work of keeping a movement on track, focused, and moving forward.

What is remembered is the music of artists like Joan Baez, Phil Ochs, Bob Dylan, Pete Seeger, the Freedom Singers, Peter, Paul and Mary, Harry Belafonte, Carolyn Hester, Guy Carawan, Eric Andersen, Paul Robeson, Odetta, and the others, performing on makeshift stages, standing on truck beds and in churches and homes across the South, getting the message out in song, reminding people that no matter how divided the nation was, joining together as one was the only thing that was going to make it work, encouraging people to take their own destinies into their own hands. Historians and social critics also remember all the anonymous or formerly forgotten performers who spread the word from the rickety stages of coffeehouses throughout America.

The speeches inspired but the songs created togetherness, gave the victims of segregation comfort and tools to make changes. The music showed people they were not alone, that others had been there, too—or if they hadn't been there, they were still able to empathize with those who were there because we are all human, so we know what suffering is. The speeches were designed to move people to action, but people can't act without hope. The music provided the hope.

The artists who turned out for Freedom Summer were encouraging people to put their bodies and lives on the line. The men and women trying to register to vote were facing jail, loss of jobs, beatings, and death. That sort of sacrifice was not an easy thing to make; even if the activists won everything on the table, they were still going to suffer in the process of winning. The folk singers reminded people to "keep their eyes on the prize," to stand up for what was right instead of settling for what was safe. Because of those efforts and the efforts of the armies of people demanding their rights, our world is different and better.

Part I. Mississippi Needs Folk Singers

Joan Baez is one of the people who used her art to alter our world. Although she worked as much outside of the movement as within it, choosing her own way of serving, she served, responding positively to requests for her appearance at rallies, marches and protests, using her voice for what she saw as the greater good.

Chapter 8

Peter, Paul and Mary

Ian Tyson of Ian and Sylvia once said that folk music has always been there—sometimes hard to find but always there. When Peter, Paul and Mary emerged, folk was in one of its hard-to-find phases. As we saw from Senator Kenneth Keating's comments, the McCarthy era had postulated a connection between communism and folk music, which resulted in a blacklist of the generation that included Pete Seeger, the Weavers, Cisco Houston, and Woody Guthrie.[1] These were the artists who immediately preceded the musicians of the folk revival of the early sixties, which gave us the rise to popularity of the protest song. Before that, protest songs were used to build community among activists; after that they made the top forty. Peter, Paul and Mary were one of the groups that made that happen.

With the nation still reeling from the witch hunts of Joe McCarthy and his followers, the delight that the House Un-American Activities Committee took in throwing American citizens over the cliff, and the Cold War paranoia, an aura of Red-baiting was constructed around folk music, like a moat around a castle, even as the genre became incredibly popular. In fact, its very popularity made the music suspect because it was popular among the young. The nascent left-wing political stirrings of college students were creating a generation gap at the same time that the recent election of John F. Kennedy promised an end to the right-wing oppression and militarism that had characterized the culture during the Eisenhower years. It was that generation gap leading to the election of John F. Kennedy that led to folk music's coming out of hiding and into the sunlight once more.

Carolyn Hester credits the election of John F. Kennedy with the rise of folk music. "It's been said that if Kennedy had not become president, there could not have been a Bob Dylan," she declares. Whether or not the connection is that direct, it is accurate to say that the Kennedy election created a climate in the country of hope. Even if its actions did not always lean to the left, his administration lightened the mood.

Part I. Mississippi Needs Folk Singers

The Village folk revival or, as Dave Van Ronk called it, the Great Folk Scare, was kicking off during the rise of Kennedy's Camelot, and the artists who would later become Peter, Paul and Mary all chased it to Greenwich Village, arriving there separately. Peter Yarrow, recently graduated from Cornell with a degree in psychology, showed up to build a career as a folk singer, while Noel Paul Stookey, just out of Michigan State, came there to become a standup comic. Mary Travers was already on the premises; she'd grown up in the Village and had been singing around for a few years already, primarily as a member of the Song Swappers, who backed up Pete Seeger on two of his albums, and as a member of the cast of comedian Mort Sahl's Broadway show *The Next President*.[2]

In those days, as noted earlier, the members of the Village community would gather in Washington Square Park on Sunday afternoons to play and sing informally, not necessarily to build their careers but to have fun. The three singers who would become Peter, Paul and Mary met in the park and first sang together there, although the idea of uniting as a trio did not occur to them. Each one still continued to pursue a solo career.

If the idea of forming a trio did not cross their minds, it did cross Albert Grossman's. Grossman, one of the most powerful managers in folk music, was continually on the search for an act that would make both good music and good money in the marketplace. He looked at the huge success of the Kingston Trio and decided he wanted a piece of that. There was room for another folk trio, especially if it had something the others did not. Grossman studied the field and saw that what the other groups lacked were three essential elements: a woman singer, which hadn't been seen since the Weavers disbanded due to the blacklist, a sense of humor, and an overall sense of fun. He made a decision: he would put a group together. It wasn't as easy a task as he'd figured it was going to be. His first attempt to flesh out his vision consisted of his clients Bob Gibson, Hamilton Camp, and Carolyn Hester, but they didn't quite have the intangible qualities he was looking for. So he kept on trying until he came up with the combination of Peter Yarrow, Noel Paul Stookey and, again, Carolyn Hester, who decided the fit wasn't quite right and left. Mary Travers came in to replace her and this time everything clicked. Albert Grossman was the most appropriate manager for a group like Peter, Paul and Mary. As Peter Yarrow said,

> [Albert] was concerned first and foremost with *authenticity*. Did the music have real substance, value and honesty? But he was also concerned with having an impact and influence in the larger world, the heartland. It was a very rare combination. Everybody

8. Peter, Paul and Mary

was ready for the change, but how could you reach them? How could you tap the public's ability to take in and incorporate our taste? Albert realized it wasn't enough to just write and perform songs, that there was a multitude of ways to be successful and to *happen*, to become important, to be wanted by that public. It was necessary to couple artistic success with enormous economic success in order for that to take place.[3]

The newly formed trio named themselves Peter, Paul and Mary for two reasons: first, the name had a Biblical ring to it, recalling the phrase Peter, Paul, and Moses and, second, it recalled a song Odetta sang, "I Was Born About 10,000 Years Ago," which refers to Peter, Paul, and Moses joining in a game of ring around the roses. A name touching on Odetta and the Bible? How could it miss?

After about six months of rehearsing, the trio made its debut at Gerde's Folk City. The circumstances were less than auspicious. Peter Yarrow was playing the club as a single when Grossman went to Mike Porco, who operated Gerde's, and offered him the trio. Porco said he would not pay the extra twenty dollars for all three singers, so Grossman put it up himself, allowing Peter, Paul and Mary to make a subsidized debut as a trio.[4] They had not yet polished their trio act, so for this, their debut performance, Yarrow did a solo set, then Stookey did his comedy routine, followed by a solo set by Mary. Only after all three had performed separately did they do a trio set, because they had only twelve songs, the twelve that made up their first album, which was not enough to make up a night at a club. After that appearance, Grossman brought in vocal arranger Milt Okum, who had previously coached the Chad Mitchell Trio and the Harry Belafonte Singers. Okum helped them find the three-part vocal harmonies that made their sound unique. After his coaching, the trio made a more proper debut at the Bitter End and signed a contract with Warner Brothers Records.

Their first album contained "If I Had a Hammer," which had been written by Pete Seeger and Lee Hayes for the Weavers. A strong anti-war song with a hook that could not be escaped and a chorus that almost demanded that you sing along with it as well as a strong political statement, it was the perfect song for the emerging civil rights movement. Seeger, who came up with the melody for the song, later said he could never get the tune quite right, but Peter, Paul and Mary got hold of it, tweaked it a little, and solved the problems he could not. "If I Had a Hammer" became a standard of the civil rights movement. Just how big a part Peter, Paul and Mary played in the movement has been questioned. They walked a tight line between entertainment and activism from the start, mixing humor and light-hearted songs with their protest material so that they came across as tough but soft simultaneously. As Peter Yarrow said, on the occasion of the group's receiving the Songwriters Hall of Fame Lifetime Achievement Award, "The songs we sing invite the participation of the listener, who is central to finding a way of creating the life of the song. It's the difference between poetry and didactic writing. One tells you, '[T]his is it,' and the other says, 'Let's find this together.'" Noel Paul Stookey amplified Yarrow's comments: "Whether it's your own material or somebody else's material, it's essential that you identify with it thoroughly. It's like you want to archive it; you want to freeze it in terms of your perspective on it, then move on, because folk music is that volatile and comments not only on overall human concerns but also on the specifics."[5]

This philosophy of music and its purpose allowed the trio to walk straight down that center line between entertainment and activism. Although progressive politics was a part of their makeup from the beginning, they picked and chose the battles they would enter carefully, choosing to skip Mississippi's Freedom Summer. They did, however, go in 1963 to the Million Man March on Washington, where they sang "If I Had a Hammer" and "Blowin' in the Wind" before Dr. King spoke. They also showed up for nearly every march for civil rights: Washington, Selma, Alabama. Paul Stookey said, "You have to put your body on the line from time to time in order to make a statement or change a law."[6] Coretta King, Martin's widow, praised their efforts, saying, "Peter, Paul and Mary are not only three of the greatest folk artists ever, but also three of the performing arts' most outstanding champions of social justice and peace. They have lent their time and talents to the civil rights movement. labor struggles, and countless campaigns for human rights for decades, and their compassion and commitment remain as strong as their extraordinary artistry."[7]

As important as their activism was, however, the trio's most significant contribution to the civil rights movement was probably their championing of the topical songwriters. They recorded Bob Dylan's material very early, having a hit with "Blowin' in the Wind" before his own recording of it was released. Their hit version of "Don't Think Twice, It's All Right" lifted Dylan's own album containing the song, *The Freewheelin' Bob Dylan*, into the top thirty. At that time, Dylan was being managed by Roy Silver, who also had among his clients Bill Cosby, Joan Rivers, Cass Elliot, and Hamilton Camp. Al Grossman saw there was money to be made from Bob Dylan and tried to buy his contract from Silver, who wanted ten thousand dollars. Grossman thought this was an excessive amount to pay for an unknown folkie with a

8. Peter, Paul and Mary

voice like a frog's and whose first album had topped out at 2,500 copies. Peter, Paul and Mary, great fans of Dylan's, put up $5,000 and Grossman made the deal. Even though their investment entitled them to a share of Dylan's profits, they did not take an ownership stake. They put up the money simply because they liked Dylan's work and wanted him to have the best management possible.[8] They were also great supporters of the new breed of protest writers like Phil Ochs, Tom Paxton, Peter La Farge, Janis Ian, and the others, recording their songs and working to bring the topical song artists to a larger audience by using them as opening acts on their tours.

But as we shall see, it was as anti-war activists that Peter, Paul and Mary had their biggest impact. We'll discuss that aspect of their professional and personal lives in the second section of this book. In the meantime, we'll take a look at Bob Dylan's contributions to the civil rights movement.

Chapter 9

Bob Dylan
The Reluctant Spokesman

When we speak about Bob Dylan, we have to be aware of the swirling, escalating presence of contradictions. He is a show business performer but a very private man. He is a Jewish folk singer but expressed surprise to his friend Richard Farina when they saw a Jewish folk singer perform. He is a songwriter, but his tunes are often lifted directly from other songs. And his name is Robert Allen Zimmerman, but he became Bob Dylan because, as he said, "You're born, you know, with the wrong name, the wrong parents. I mean, that happens. You call yourself what you want to call yourself."[1] He takes great delight in inventing himself, presenting a complicated, ever-changing persona to the public and press but—despite the fact that he's spent his entire adult life in show business—hates to be treated like a celebrity. He loves to lie to the media, and many people feel he hides behind his lies. His autobiography is said to contain over 200 incidents of plagiarism.[2]

Indeed, well-founded accusations of plagiarism surfaced in 2001 with the release of the appropriately titled *Love and Theft*. Both the *New York Times* and the *San Francisco Chronicle* noticed wholesale theft of both lyrics and tunes, even though the album credited all words and music to Dylan. In the songs on the album, Dylan had taken words and sentences verbatim from the English language translation of Dr. Junichi Saga's 1991 Japanese gangster memoir, *Confessions of a Yakuza*. Additionally, almost every tune on the album was lifted from an older song. "Rollin' and Tumblin'" was simply new lyrics to Muddy Waters' song of the same name. "Beyond the Horizon" was "Red Sails in the Sunset." "When the Deal Goes Down" was "Where the Blue of the Night (Meets the Gold of the Day)" and so on.[3] Dylan's biggest venture into plagiarism, though, appears to be his memoir, *Chronicles*. In it, he lifts material from *Time* magazine as well as novels by Jack London, Sax

Rohmer, R.L. Stevenson, Mezz Mezzrow, Mark Twain, and Marcel Proust, among others.[4]

The plagiarism accusations aren't meant to show that Dylan is not the major artist he is thought to be. Indeed, his writings over the years have proven conclusively that he is one of the best songwriters of his times. Additionally, the fact is that, since they are part of the ongoing folk process, many of the great folk songs of all times use borrowed tunes. Dylan has done this from the very beginning of his career. "With God on Our Side," for example, uses the Irish tune "The Patriot Game." These accusations simply show that Bob Dylan is, and always has been, a complex riddle of contradictions who has carefully and completely built a wall between himself and his public. Lifting from other people's work is most likely designed to create and maintain a distance.

Very early in his career Dylan was saddled by the media with the designation "the voice of his generation," a role he was never comfortable with and which he tried to reject. But it was hard to escape. So many people thought he was speaking for them that they made it impossible for him to be the normal person he wanted to be. He had to put up with climbing out apartment windows and going down fire escapes to avoid the army of obsessed fans that lurked outside his building.[5] He also had to tolerate over-the-top fans who called themselves Dylanologists and went through his garbage cans, looking for evidence of who he really was and what he really stood for.[6] Faced with that sort of unwanted attention and a demanding media, he has responded by lying, evading, and withdrawing. He created and embodies a fictional, almost mythological, character.

Also early in his career, Dylan was very much a part of the civil rights and protest song movement. Among his songs that had a direct bearing on race relations were "Blowin' in the Wind," "When the Ship Comes In," "Oxford Town," "The Lonesome Death of Hattie Carroll," "Only a Pawn in Their Game," "The Times They Are A-Changin'," and "The Death of Emmett Till." Obviously, then, at that time, Bob Dylan's greatest contribution was the inspiration that these songs created. Many civil rights workers went South as a result of listening to Dylan's topical material. His songs were not his only contribution. His then-girlfriend, a long-time activist named Suze Rotolo, had introduced him to political action, and after he met Joan Baez at Newport and began touring with her his direct action increased greatly. Both of them appeared at the 1963 March on Washington.

Part I. Mississippi Needs Folk Singers

Music at the March on Washington

Baez and Dylan are the performers most mentioned regarding the march but actually the music was pervasive and wide-ranging. Gospel singer Mahalia Jackson opened the morning's music with two powerful songs, "How I Got Over" and "I've Been 'Buked and I've Been Scorned." Marian Anderson sang "He's Got the Whole World in His Hands," and Joan Baez did "Oh Freedom" and "We Shall Overcome," which she turned into a sing-along. Then Dylan took the stage for three songs, "The Times They Are A-Changin'," "Only a Pawn in Their Game," and, as a duet with Baez, "When the Ship Comes In." Peter, Paul and Mary did two songs that were already becoming movement standards—Dylan's "Blowin' in the Wind" and Pete Seeger and Lee Hayes' "If I Had a Hammer." Odetta sang "I'm on My Way," and the Freedom Singers reprised "We Shall Overcome" with Baez, Dylan, Peter, Paul and Mary, and Theodore Bikel.[7]

From the beginning, then, folk music drove the civil rights movement and Bob Dylan created a lot of it. By creating the music, he helped create a movement. "Without the songs of the movement, personally I believe that there wouldn't have been a movement," Rutha Mae Harris, one of the original Freedom Singers, told NPR. "We needed those songs to help us not to be fearful when we were doing marches, or doing picket lines. And you needed a calming agent, and that's what those songs were for us."[8]

Who Is Bob Dylan Really?

Who was this person who, despite his wish for privacy, became a living symbol of everything his fans wanted, this man who continually built walls between himself and his public but still had to live with fans who imprinted themselves upon him like baby ducks, the man who constantly said he was just a song and dance man but could never escape the people who tried to find themselves in him, this man who did so much for the civil rights movement while claiming not to have any interest in politics?

Born on May 24, 1941, in Duluth, Minnesota, Dylan spent the first seven years of his life there. In 1948 his family moved to the city of Hibbing, Minnesota, where he spent a fairly normal childhood, going to school, forming local bands, and performing Little Richard songs in high school talent shows. In 1959 he appeared at a Hibbing High School talent show as Elston Gunn and the Rock Boppers; even at the age of seventeen, he preferred to protect his sense of his identity.[9] Within a couple of years, still as Elston Gunn (spelled with three *n*s now), he played piano in pop singer Bobby Vee's band. Meeting Vee in a record store after hearing the established singer was looking for a piano player, Dylan introduced himself as Gunn and told Vee he'd just come in off the road with Conway Twitty. Vee hired him but later discovered Dylan could play piano only in the key of C, so he didn't last long in that band.[10] Bobby Vee later said, "It was ill-fated. I mean, it wasn't gonna work. He didn't have any money, and we didn't have any money. The story is that I fired him, but that certainly wasn't the case. If we could have put it together somehow, we sure would have. We wished we could have put it together. He left and went on to Minneapolis and enrolled at the University of Minnesota."[11]

Later, even after the Elston Gunn role-playing, after he'd found fame, he continued to try on identities like suits. However, he denied that he was creating himself, telling an interviewer that he did not create Bob Dylan, instead Dylan had always been there. As Donald Brown said, "If Bob Dylan has 'always been here,' then the name is more than a name; it's a role or spirit, something Robert Zimmerman could inhabit, enact, become."[12] Yet, other statements Dylan has made over the years would appear to contradict this one. He told Mikal Gilmore in 2001 "the folk song created an identity for people like himself, 'an identity which the three-buttoned-suit postwar generation wasn't offering to kids [his] age.'"[13] It would appear, then, that from his teen years on Dylan was inventing personas that allowed him a safe wall to hide behind.

His heroes at this time were not folkies. He worshiped Hank Williams and Buddy Holly, whom he saw perform in Hibbing, Little Richard, Johnny Cash, Elvis Presley, and James Dean, who was already dead but well on the way to becoming a legend. Dylan played rock, not folk music—his piano style was said to owe a lot to Little Richard—until he went to the University of Minnesota, where, like so many college students of the day, he was introduced to the music of Woody Guthrie, which led him into the world of folk music. He discovered folk music in Dinkytown, a bohemian neighborhood near the university that had just overcome its Beat-inspired reputation as a cradle of jazz and was transforming into a center for folk music clubs and coffeehouses. He hung out there, soaking up the folk world and learning to play guitar and harmonica so that he could follow up on his new goal in life: "to be Guthrie's greatest disciple."[14]

During the depression era, Woody Guthrie had carried the folk songs of America all over the country, singing in union halls and bars, at hootenannies, on the radio, and on records. Like John Steinbeck's Tom Joad—a fictional character who was the protagonist of *The Grapes of Wrath*, a book both Guthrie and Dylan admired greatly—wherever there was a need Guthrie was there. Guthrie wrote an autobiography, *Bound for Glory*, which made such a strong impression on Dylan that Dylan began dressing, speaking, and performing like Guthrie. Dylan later wrote that "folk songs transcended the immediate culture" and Guthrie's songs, in particular, were "totally in the moment, current and even forecasted things to come."[15] After that discovery, nothing made sense for Dylan but to drop out of school, go to New York, and visit Guthrie, who was at that time dying of Huntington's disease in the Greystone Park Psychiatric Hospital in New Jersey. When Dylan arrived in Greenwich Village, he amused the folkies there, who thought of him as nothing more than a Woody Guthrie clone.

From Zimmerman to Dylan

In 1961 there was a knock at the door of teenaged Arlo Guthrie's house on Mermaid Avenue, in the Coney Island section of Brooklyn. The sitter answered it and on the porch stood a scruffy kid covered with road grime who introduced himself as Bob Dylan and said he'd come to see Arlo's father, Woody Guthrie:

> The babysitter, according to Arlo's recollection, was "really frightened" of the uninvited guest. There was something about him that was a little odd, from the mumbling way he talked to the way his eyes moved about the room. The baby sitter, Joady and Nora were all uncomfortable; they wanted the stranger to leave, but Arlo, enamored of Dylan's "high, laceup engineer boots," invited the teenager into the house. They chatted a little about Woody and the hospital and music.... After an uncomfortable hour-long visit, the babysitter finally convinced Dylan to leave.... Nora and Joady were relieved to see the stranger go, but Arlo wasn't. The guy was pretty interesting.[16]

After being told Guthrie's location in the hospital, Dylan visited him frequently and sang his idol the song he'd written for him, "Song for Woody," which used the melody of one of Woody's songs, "The 1913 Massacre." That initial meeting led to more, and becoming acquainted with his hero had a huge effect on the fledgling folk singer. When Dylan performed, he told audiences that he'd been roaming around the country, retracing Woody's steps.

9. Bob Dylan

His identification with his hero was so complete that he almost became Guthrie.

Robert Zimmerman had invented a persona named Bob Dylan, who was more a myth in the making than an actual person. As we have seen, from the very beginning of his public life he concentrated on creating his alter ego. His early interviews were laced with lies and legends—even the place of his birth was obscured. He was from Denver, Wyoming, or any other place that entered his myth-making mind. He would, with a straight face, say he was raised in a carnival, had made music with Leadbelly, had been a cowboy, ridden the rails, and whatever other outrageous, distorted, and exaggerated clams he could think of. Robert Zimmerman was building a myth that he called Bob Dylan and appeared to be intent on making the legend larger than life. In this way, he protected his own privacy, which was very important to him. The mythical Bob Dylan became the wall that stood between the public and Robert Zimmerman.

Starting in the winter of 1961 Dylan worked clubs and coffeehouses around the Village, where he got to know and become friends with other performers. He was especially taken by the Clancy Brothers and Tommy Makem and was closest to the youngest brother, Liam, to whom he said that his goal was to become as big as the Clancy Brothers.[17] He also met Phil Ochs during this time, and Ochs picked up Dylan's trick of leaving his apartment by going down the fire escape to avoid the flocks of fans waiting outside—even though at that time, since Ochs was just beginning, there were no fans lurking outside his door.

Dylan worked in obscurity until September of 1961, when Robert Shelton, music critic for the *New York Times,* reviewed his show at Gerde's Folk City. That write-up brought him to the attention of record companies. But nothing came of it until Carolyn Hester hired him to play harmonica on the first album she made for Columbia Records. During those sessions, as stated earlier, he met and impressed John Hammond, who signed him to a record deal.[18] His first album, *Bob Dylan,* was released in August of 2002 and could not under any circumstances be considered commercially successful. In its first year of availability, the album sold around 2,500 copies and Columbia executives wanted to drop Dylan from the label. Johnny Cash, at that time a major Columbia artist who sold millions of records, spoke up for Dylan, as did John Hammond. Dylan kept his deal.[19]

Dylan Breaks Through

That August he legally changed his name to Bob Dylan. It was at about this time that Roy Silver sold Dylan's contract to Albert Grossman, as discussed in the section on Peter, Paul and Mary. Grossman figured the best way to break Dylan as an artist would be to develop him a reputation as a major songwriter. To this end, he had his newly signed client record nearly every song he'd written and distributed the resulting reel-to-reel tapes to other performers in an effort to get them to record his songs. The tactic worked. Soon, artists on both sides of the Atlantic were placing Dylan songs on their albums and the original tape was widely bootlegged as *The Witmark Demos* (which finally got a legitimate release as volume 9 of the *Bootleg Series*). That effort got Dylan started. Also helping was the fact that he teamed up with Joan Baez for two crucial years. In *Chronicles*, Dylan describes seeing Baez on TV before he'd even left Minnesota. He wrote, "I couldn't stop looking at her, didn't want to blink.... The sight of her made me sigh. All that and then there was the voice. A voice that drove out bad spirits ... [and] she sang in a voice straight to God."[20]

Maybe the sight and sound of Baez reached Dylan, but the converse was not true. Baez first saw Dylan in 1961 at Folk City and was not impressed. It wasn't until she saw him again at Club 47 that she was able to appreciate what she was hearing.[21] He had become a different man, grown and matured as a singer-songwriter. They met that night and first sang together at the Monterey Folk Festival shortly afterward, which began a two-year professional and personal partnership.

The release of his second album, *The Freewheelin' Bob Dylan,* put him on the map. That record, begun in April of 1962 and finished in April of 1963, was much more carefully done than his first one. According to Donald Brown, it took a solid year to make it, because Dylan was aware that he needed better material than he'd recorded on *Bob Dylan*. He also recognized that to get the sort of material he needed, he'd have to write it.[22] He wound up with thirteen fine originals and two covers, pretty much a direct reversal of what he'd put on his first album.

Among the originals are some of the songs that remain in his repertoire to this day: "Masters of War," "Blowin' in the Wind," "Girl from the North Country," "A Hard Rain's a-Gonna Fall," "Don't Think Twice, It's All Right," "Oxford Town," and "Bob Dylan's Dream." The weight of these songs was balanced by lighthearted and funny, if quirky, numbers like "I Shall be Free" and

9. Bob Dylan

"Talkin' World War III Blues." *Freewheelin'* was successful on every level. In its first month of release, it bettered the first year's sales of *Bob Dylan* and continued to move 10,000 units a month, bringing Dylan an income of $2,500 per month.[23] It also created a demand for personal appearances across the country, and Dylan found himself playing the bigger theaters and festivals.

He was also moving away from active involvement in the civil rights movement. He had become an activist at the continued urging of Suze Rotolo, whose parents were union organizers. As a result of her prodding, he began singing at CORE rallies. In 1962 he was doing benefits for SNCC. At the Newport Folk Festival in 1963, he was joined onstage by Peter, Paul and Mary, Joan Baez, and the Freedom Singers, who all did "Blowin' in the Wind" together and then encored with a sing-along version of "We Shall Overcome." During his set, he introduced "Only a Pawn in Their Game," the song that inspired Theodore Bikel to fly him down to Mississippi.

Dylan's time in Mississippi was both the high point and the beginning of the end of his activism. The "voice of a generation" tag drove him away again. The website *about entertainment* explained: "Feeling co-opted by white movement leaders and despising their expectations of him to become its star champion, Dylan began his retreat. Although he never stopped supporting the black struggle, becoming a Pied Piper for liberal guilt-afflicted whites was a hypocritical role he was unwilling to play."[24] As he always had, Bob Dylan went his own way, though as we shall see, he never really escaped being the voice of his generation.

Chapter 10

After the Summer Comes the Fall

So what happened as a result of Mississippi's Freedom Summer? Did the invasion of the visiting folk singers turn the situation around? Were the African-American citizens of Mississippi finally able to vote? Did the ten weeks of activism make a positive difference? The last three answers are no and no and yes. Freedom Summer did not result in thousands of new voters being registered. The numbers of registered voters remained about the same at the end of the summer as it had been when the invasion began.[1] However, the summer did call international attention to the conditions in the American South and had a great deal to do with the eventual breakdown of the system. Before the summer of 1964 the national media had paid little attention to the suffering of African Americans in the Deep South. After that, it could not be ignored.

What grew out of the summer's actions? Many of the benefits were educational. A system of some thirty to forty Freedom Schools was established to teach such forbidden subjects as basic literacy, math, black history, and constitutional rights. Held in private homes, churches, and outdoors, the schools enrolled both children and adults and operated on progressive principles that vastly influenced the educational reform movement of the sixties. Fifty Freedom Libraries were established across the state, providing books and lessons in literacy to citizens who'd never had libraries in their communities before. As was the case with the schools, the libraries were set up wherever they could be put: in private homes, churches, and abandoned houses.[2]

Other benefits were more political. One of the major goals of Freedom Summer had been to establish a Democratic Party that actually represented the people—all of them. The summer had been planned to culminate at the time of the Democratic convention, where the activists planned to attempt to get an alternative delegation recognized and seated. In this effort to give people control over their own lives and destinies, Bob Moses led in the creation of the Mississippi Freedom Democratic Party (MFDP). He saw the alternative party as necessary because the regular Mississippi Democratic Party was segregated and had a history of violent racism. The goal was to get the MFDP recognized as the legitimate Democratic party in the state. That goal was never reached because Lyndon Johnson, afraid of losing the support of southerners during his reelection campaign, refused to seat the delegation at the 1964 Democratic convention.[3] The COFO continued to build the party, though, and finally the Democratic Party was integrated and African Americans began winning elections in the state.

Ironically, racial tensions had caused the creation of an integrated force to bring racial justice to Mississippi. Those same tensions destroyed that force. The popular view among some African-American activists was that only media attention had caused positive changes and the media paid attention only because white people had become involved. Not until the bodies of Goodman, Chaney, and Schwerner were found did the FBI take an interest in the rampant crime against African Americans in the state. When they searched the waters for the white activists' bodies, the Feds found the corpses of eight murdered black men.[4] The question raised by the black community was simple and important: Why hadn't the FBI come to investigate any of those deaths before young white men were being killed? Why had the government ignored those murders? Did they value white supremacists votes more than black peoples' lives?

These questions led to others that divided the civil rights movement like barbecued ribs. Ignoring the leadership of Bob Moses, the young black activists demanded to know why white people were leading a movement to help change the lives of black people. Why weren't African Americans leading it? And why were these white people advocating Ghandian nonviolence when blacks were being brutally murdered by the white power structure? No, there was no need for white leadership, a segment of the African-American population said. What was needed was for blacks to lead their own causes, to be responsible for their own destinies, to develop their own personal and political power, instead of borrowing it from white leaders. No, Ghandian nonviolence was not for them; it was a nice theory, but it did not work against people so committed to a way of life that had never existed anywhere but in their diseased minds that they were willing to kill to protect it. What was needed was access to guns to fight back against white killers. From now on, they declared, the work would continue but it would be led and carried out by black people.

Part I. Mississippi Needs Folk Singers

Bob Moses Quits

The white activists, forced out of the civil rights movement by this first flourishing of black power, moved on to other causes. So did many of the African Americans. Bob Moses, who had done so much to build this movement, left it, declaring that he had become too strong, too central to the movement, so that people who were capable of standing up by themselves continued to lean on him, to use him as a crutch. If the movement was to flourish, he believed, he would have to leave it. Gitlin reports that Moses then began a long and strange journey that eventually took him out of direct political activism altogether. Going by his middle name, Parris, instead of his last, Moses turned his attention to the war in Vietnam. He temporarily dropped his surname, using only his middle name and began participating in the campaign against the Vietnam War. Getting more deeply into anti-war activities, he left SNCC and journeyed to Africa. There he decided that African Americans must win their full freedom without the help and leadership of whites. He cut ties with the white activists he had recruited and the ones who had followed them into the fray. Upon his return to the United States, he went back to graduate school at Harvard, earning a master's in the philosophy of math. When his daughter told him that her high school in Cambridge did not have an algebra teacher, he filled the gap, beginning a teaching career that occupied the rest of his working life.[5]

Part II
"Hey, Hey, LBJ, How Many Kids Did You Kill Today?"

Chapter 11

The Radicalizing of Tom Hayden

In the first chapter, we spoke of the alienated kids of the fifties, how they grew up in peaceful, joyless, and dead suburbs where they learned that they were being trained to become corporate drones and mindless consumers. Tom Hayden was one of those kids. As he wrote later, "Our generation was troubled by contradiction between the ideals we'd been taught and realities we experienced. We felt these contradictions, or paradoxes, in the form of *insults*—status rankings, bullying, belittling, snubbing, threats, punishments, sheer unfairness—that we either accepted and internalized or questioned, resisted, and, ultimately, defied."[1]

Nothing in his world made sense. Hayden and his generation knew that hiding under their desks, a strategy taught as duck and cover, would not protect them from nuclear blasts, although their government and their teachers said it would. They knew that the eternal war machine built by Eisenhower, who later warned us about the military-industrial complex he had helped to create, could not lead to peace. They sensed that the policy of mutually assured destruction would lead only to mutual destruction. They also sensed that, even if they survived, a life in the corporate world was going to deaden their souls and lead only to the empty lives their parents led.

No, something else was needed and the Beat generation, with their emphasis on choosing to be outsiders, on rejecting the dictates of our society, arrived just in time to show Hayden and his generation a possible alternative, a paradigm into which they could fit.. After reading Jack Kerouac's *On the Road*, Hayden accepted the author as a role model and did his own hitchhiking journeys around the country.[2] But then he discovered radical politics. Studying journalism at the University of Michigan, he became a member of the National Student Association, which he quickly found out was far too moderate for him. It was like being a mercenary soldier and joining the Boy Scouts. Maybe the organization had something to do with his goals, but it couldn't come close to where he needed to be. Using the idea that if what you needed wasn't there you create it, Hayden helped form the more radical Students for a Democratic Society (SDS), becoming president of the organization in 1962.[3] The year before, he had married Sandra Carson, who worked for SNCC, and as soon as he graduated from college Hayden joined the Freedom Riders.

But serving wasn't enough. Hayden needed to lead. He got his opportunity in 1962, when the United Auto Workers held a retreat at Port Huron, Michigan. As one of the top guns of SDS, Hayden was called upon to be the writer of record of the Port Huron Statement, a mission statement for SDS that was to be unveiled at that meeting.

The Port Huron Statement

The 27,000-word document called for participatory democracy, a type of bottom-up leadership where all major decisions were made by all members of the organization. Instead of a few people in power passing down a policy decision to the masses, power was given to the masses; no decision could be made without their input. While some on the left hailed this idea as a widening of freedom, others complained that it led to endless arguments and long, dull meetings in which nothing was accomplished because too many people served their own egos and agendas and could never reach a decision. Still, the left welcomed the notion of participatory democracy, which still serves as the operating model in groups such as the Occupy movement. The text of the Port Huron Statement called for three main thrusts of action: disarmament, changing the Democratic Party, and reforming colleges and universities.

Disarmament

Hayden's was the first generation to grow up with the threat of nuclear annihilation. At any moment, a button could be pushed by either of the world's two atomic powers and the world would end. This was, of course, an unacceptable development and the young radicals had been fighting it for some time. Ad hoc groups had been demonstrating outside defense plants for several years, but now, with the Port Huron Statement, disarmament

Part II. "Hey, Hey, LBJ, How Many Kids Did You Kill Today?"

became an official policy of the emerging New Left. The text read, "Universal controlled disarmament must replace deterrence and arms control as the national defense goal."[4]

Folk music contributed to the creation of this policy position. Songs about the threat of nuclear holocaust dominated the early sixties the way songs about dying teenagers dominated pop music. In 1962 Bonnie Dobson wrote "Morning Dew," a mournful song in which the planet is destroyed by nuclear weapons. The song was first recorded by Vince Martin and Fred Neil before going on to become a classic covered by dozens of musicians, including Dobson herself, Tim Rose, Melanie Safka, and such artists as the Grateful Dead, Nazareth, the Pozo Seco Singers, Long John Baldry, Jeff Beck, Robert Plant, and Lulu. "Morning Dew" was a song that captured the angst and fears of the time, a song that spoke what was on young people's minds and was quite powerful. It was one of those rare songs that changes things. Vince Martin remembers: "I learned the song from—actually I don't remember from who. It might have been Len Chandler or maybe Ritchie Havens. I taught it to Freddie [Neil] and we sang it around and then recorded it. That's it. I had no idea it was going to become a classic. You sing a song, turn it loose and it goes where it goes. 'Morning Dew' is the kind of song I really love."

The years 1962 and 1963 brought on songs about the nuclear holocaust. Malvina Reynolds contributed "What Have They Done to the Rain," which dramatized the issue of death from nuclear fallout. It also became a hit, recorded by Reynolds herself, Melanie Safka, Joan Baez, the Searchers, the Seekers, and Marianne Faithful. Bob Dylan contributed "A Hard Rain's a-Gonna Fall," "Masters of War," and one of the first songs to treat nuclear annihilation with humor, "Talkin' World War III Blues."

By the mid-sixties, after the Port Huron Statement restored the issue to popular consciousness, the songs took on a slightly different and sometimes more complex form. Instead of preaching a standard message, they looked at the issue from other angles. The Byrds did "I Come and Stand at Every Door," Crosby, Stills and Nash added "Wooden Ships" to the collection, and Lowell Blanchard and the Valley Trio began a short-lived trend to using nuclear weapons as a symbol of God's power by recording "Jesus Hits Like the Atomic Bomb," which was covered by dozens of gospel groups, including the Pilgrim Travelers. The Louvin Brothers urged people to get right with God so they could escape the coming nuclear holocaust in "Great Atomic Power." Rockabilly artists also mined the possibility of a nuclear holocaust for material. Warren Smith did "Uranium Rock," while Mary Robbins contributed "This Cold War with You," and Sonny Russell joined the throng with "50 Megatons." Wanda Jackson, who was billed as the female Elvis, had a minor hit in the States but a massive hit in Japan with "Fujiama Mama."

All of these songs created a mood in the young people who made up SDS and while they cannot be given all of the credit they certainly helped shape a mood that led the young to oppose war and the nuclear arms race. While the establishment politicians pursued a policy of mutually assured destruction, claiming that only the threat of the destruction of our entire planet would lead to peace and that beating back a perceived communist threat was the most important thing, the young were being conditioned by the music and by the New Left to reject those ideas and to try to create a world that loved and respected life. Universal disarmament was seen as the first step.

Changing the Democratic Party

At the time of the writing of the statement, efforts of the Democrats in Congress to make positive changes in civil rights and foreign policy were for the most part blocked by the Dixiecrats, a powerful group of reactionary southern members of the party who had broken off from the mainstream Democratic party and organized as a separate entity in 1948.[5] The specific goal of the Dixiecrats was to advance state's rights, thereby limiting the power of the federal government in order to make sure segregation remained the law of the land. In that way they could keep the federal government from advancing the civil rights of minorities. The Dixiecrats were also strongly anti-union.[6] In short, the group was committed to protecting what they saw as the southern way of life, which to them meant protecting Jim Crow laws and white supremacy. Adopting these positions, of course, meant that they opposed the granting or extension of voting rights.

The group formally broke away from the Democratic Party in 1948 when President Harry Truman ordered an end to segregation and discrimination in the military. This action caused South Carolina senator Strom Thurmond and Mississippi's Fielding L. Wright to pledge to leave the party and hold an alternate convention in Birmingham if Truman got the presidential nomination at the Democratic convention. When Truman won at the convention—who, in the eyes of the Dixiecrats added insult to injury by adopting a plank calling for civil rights—Thurmond and Wright made good on their threat and at their separate convention removed Truman's name from the ballot and offered up a ticket consisting of Thurmond for president and Wright as the vice presidential candidate. They called the new party the States' Rights Democratic Party and their platform read in part as follows:

> We stand for the segregation of the races and the racial integrity of each race; the constitutional right to choose one's associates; to accept private employment without governmental interference, and to earn one's living in any lawful way. We oppose the elimination of segregation, the repeal of miscegenation statutes, the control of private employment by Federal bureaucrats called for by the misnamed civil rights program. We favor home-rule, local self-government and a minimum interference with individual rights.[7]

The American people did not flock to the Dixiecrat Party in big numbers; the election was a disaster for the new organization as voters ignored them the way they would a sudden bad smell in church. After the shellacking the Dixiecrats endured in the 1948 elections the party officially folded, but the term lingered in the political lexicon and is still used to refer to conservative southern democrats. The former members of the party continued to hold power in the Democratic Party when the Port Huron Statement was written. About changing the Democratic Party, the manifesto read as follows:

> An imperative task for these publicly disinherited groups, then, is to demand a Democratic party responsible to their interests. They must support Southern voter registration and Negro political candidates and demand that Democratic Party liberals do the same (in the last Congress, Dixiecrats split with Northern Democrats on 119 of 300 roll-calls, mostly on civil rights, area redevelopment and foreign aid bills; and breach was much larger than in the previous several sessions). Labor should begin a major drive in the South. In the North, reform clubs (either independent or Democratic) should be formed to run against big city regimes on such issues as peace, civil rights, and urban needs. Demonstrations should be held at every Congressional or convention seating of Dixiecrats. A massive research and publicity campaign should be initiated, showing to every housewife, doctor, professor, and worker the damage done to their interests every day a racist occupies a place in the Democratic Party. Where possible, the peace movement should challenge the "peace credentials" of the otherwise-liberals by threatening or actually running candidates against them.[8]

We have previously discussed the music that came out of the civil rights movement, which was partially a result of the Dixiecrat Revolution and the Port Huron Statement. We will simply reiterate here that songs like "Oh Freedom," "We Shall Overcome," "When Will We Be Paid for the Work We've Done," and "We Shall Not Be Moved," inspired young people, black and white, and helped create the rebellion that broke the Dixiecrat's hold on the American South.

11. The Radicalizing of Tom Hayden

Reforming Colleges and Universities

In the fifties, colleges and universities, despite the rantings of conservative intellectuals such as William F. Buckley, were far from the hotbeds of radicalism that conservative intellectuals accused them of being. Conservative and cautious, given to maintaining society as it was, the colleges saw their mission as protecting the status quo. Built on a model that the Crusaders brought back from the Middle East in the 1400s, the schools looked to the past for inspiration and direction. In the humanities, the emphasis was on what was known as the "Established Dead" and the canon consisted of work by dead white men. The most widely used undergraduate literature text of the time, the 1962 edition of the *Norton American Literature* anthology, contained only one poem by a woman, the Puritan Anne Bradstreet, who advocated surrender to men.[9] Business programs were designed to lead their graduates into the corporate life, and in the social sciences humanist psychologists like Carl Rogers fought for acceptance of their theories and a place in the academic world at a time when B.F. Skinner's behaviorism ruled psychology departments.

Young women were shuttled into education programs, destined for teaching jobs, as teaching was considered at the time to be a secondary and female occupation. The four-year colleges that offered nursing programs were filled with females also, as the schools reflected society at large by continuing to look at nursing as a woman's occupation. Most nursing education was considered beneath the dignity of universities, though, and took place in specialized schools.

College politics were generally conservative. Student clubs and organizations like the Young Republicans and Young Democrats again reflected the larger culture; even in college, the young were being channeled into the existing system by both custom and by fiat. The University of California system, as we have seen, forbade students from creating more radical groups on campus. As the members of the newly formed SDS saw it, young people were idealistic and their schools were not. Overall, Hayden and his coauthors saw the universities as a conspiracy to keep the young in an ongoing state of apathy. The situation outside college was no better. The Port Huron Statement declared that all of the movements available to students—civil rights, peace, student, and labor—lacked the power to make positive changes, and people should look to the "only mainstream institution ... open to participation by individuals of nearly every viewpoint," the universities.[10]

How would the universities help the various movements? People of good will would reform the colleges by forming an alliance of students and faculty who would beat back the educational institutes' bureaucracies and make a place for public issues inside the curriculum, thus introducing debate and controversy into the picture and reforming the curriculum so that the schools would be relevant to the lives of the people who attended or worked in them. The statement was adopted, but by 1964, with the assassination of John F. Kennedy and the ascendency to the presidency by Lyndon Johnson, things changed in the political world and a new edition of the manifesto was issued, with a preface that stated that most of the original writers of the decree would not agree with all of its conclusions and that the first edition of the statement should be seen almost as a historical document.[11]

Still, it was the statement of the guiding principles of SDS, which carried its principles into Freedom Summer and then, when the mostly white activists found themselves pushed aside there, into the anti-war movement.

Chapter 12

Lyndon Johnson Fights a War on Two Fronts
In Vietnam and in the Streets

Groups like SDS were, at first, reluctantly content to work within the existing system. That attitude ended when a tipping point was reached in 1964. In September of that year a group of Freedom Summer veterans set up tables outside Sproul Hall at the University of California, Berkeley, in order to pass out information on their activities. Their purpose was to raise money to continue civil rights activities, an action that was prohibited by the current rules in effect at the university, whose trustees on the governing board had initiated a policy that said only the Democratic and Republican student groups could fundraise on campus.[1] As a reaction to the more radical students' actions, the university passed a whole new set of regulations forbidding anyone from advocating for a particular candidate or cause, outside speakers, recruitment, or fundraising.

Groups like SDS and CORE, fresh from having their heads beaten in by white supremacists, were not going to meekly fold their tents and slip away in the night like a defeated army. A graduate student named Jack Weinberg decided to test the rules and set up shop at a CORE table. When the university brought in the police, Weinberg refused to cooperate; he would not shut down his operations. As a result, he was arrested. That's when the situation exploded. A group of students spontaneously surrounded the squad car Weinberg was to be transported in. When the crowd swelled to nearly 3,000 people it became impossible to take Weinberg to jail. The police were forced to sit in one place, enveloped by protestors for thirty-two hours while the activists made speeches from the top of the car. After a day and a half of stalemate, the police surrendered, and the charges against Weinberg were dropped.[2] Thus the Free Speech Movement was born. It lost little time in making itself a power. On December 2, four thousand students gathered in Sproul Hall to

Part II. "Hey, Hey, LBJ, How Many Kids Did You Kill Today?"

try once more to get the administration to lift the new restrictions. Joan Baez showed up to lead them in song, proving that "We Shall Overcome" was not simply a voting rights song but applied to all people who saw themselves as oppressed. Free Speech leader Mario Savio made a famous speech in which he said, "There comes a time when the operation of the machine becomes so odious, makes you so sick at heart, that you can't take part, you can't even passively take part. And you've got to put your body on the gears, and upon the wheels, upon the levers, upon all the apparatus. And you've got to make it stop."[3] The state police arrested 800 students, leading to a student strike that shut down the campus. It reopened after the faculty senate voted to support the Free Speech Movement, a move that caused the administration to change its mind and lift the restrictions.[4]

The Free Speech Movement is still remembered as the beginning of the campus turmoil in the sixties, which we'll discuss later in this book. What is less well known, however, is the fact that the movement evolved into the Vietnam Day Committee. In May of 1965 an anti–Vietnam War demonstration took place at the Berkeley campus. It lasted 35 hours and drew more than 35,000 people. During that protest, New Left activists Jerry Rubin, Paul Montauk, Abbie Hoffman, and a few others formed the Vietnam Day Committee, which was designed to accomplish three major objectives: to coordinate antiwar action nationwide; to engage in militancy, including civil disobedience; and to take the movement beyond the campus. From the beginning the group explored the symbolism, sense of absurdity, and heavy use of symbolism Rubin and Hoffman would later become known for. One of their first actions was to lead a march of Berkeley students to the local draft board, where they presented the workers with a black coffin and then burned their draft cards.[5] After that they organized the National Day of Protest, a series of coordinated protests taking place simultaneously in Boston, New York, New Haven, Philadelphia, and about a dozen other cities. In San Francisco the original group held a sit-in at San Francisco State College, with the folk rock group Country Joe and the Fish playing.[6]

Country Joe and the Fish were probably the perfect band for the National Day of Protest, as an association with activism was built into the band's core. In 1965 two folk singers who had been working the California clubs and coffeehouses, Country Joe MacDonald and Barry Melton, teamed up to work as a duo. Both had leftist political backgrounds. Country Joe, in fact, published a radical underground magazine and was a veteran of the Free Speech Movement. To help the movement, he decided to put out a talking issue of his magazine and together with Melton rounded up a rhythm section to flesh out the band they called Country Joe and the Fish. That issue contained a recording of two of the band's anti-war songs, songs that later became classics of the movement: "I Feel Like I'm Fixin' to Die Rag" and "Superbird."[7] The issue was passed out to the crowd at an anti-war demonstration at Berkeley.

McDonald and Melton toured the Northwest playing SDS-sponsored events, which led to their National Day of Protest appearance. So for most of their career, and certainly for the most prominent and successful part, they were associated with the various protest movements. Country Joe and the Fish were to the Vietnam Day Committee what the laugh track is to a sitcom. As one would expect from a group formed by Abbie Hoffman and Jerry Rubin, the Vietnam Day Committee thrived on publicity, absurdity, cheap symbolism, humor, and shock value—all elements that the band exhibited as well. In that sense, the band was a perfect fit for the committee's actions. Their biggest song, "I Feel Like I'm Fixin' to Die Rag," for example, is black humor at its best, exhorting mothers to send their boys off to Vietnam so they can be the first people on the block to have their boys come home in a box. It urges Wall Street to support the war because it's war au-go-go with plenty of money to be made producing weapons for the armed forces. The last line of the chorus celebrates the fact that the war is going to kill all of us. The song drips irony like blood from a cut.

"Superbird" is a satirical look at Lyndon Baines Johnson, characterizing the president as a comic book super villain and pledging to use the comic book superheroes the Fantastic Four and Doctor Strange to bring him down. The opening verse asks what's that up in the sky and establishes that instead of Superman what we're seeing is an insane man: President Lyndon Baines Johnson. The singer claims he's going to bring Johnson down to earth, send him back to Texas, and make him work on his ranch. The song matches the operating philosophy of the Vietnam Day Committee by using heavily laden dollops of irony, twisted humor, unique symbolism, and a purpose that appears to be designed more to call attention to itself than to end the war.

The Anti–Vietnam War Tradition in America

Most people believe that the act of protesting the American presence in Vietnam was a product of the sixties. In truth, the first protest against our involvement in that land happened in 1945. Merchant Marine sailors rallied against the use of American merchant ships to transport French troops to that land.⁸ That demonstration, though, was an outlier, led by and participated in by people directly involved in the conflict. Opposition to the war by the general public was launched in 1963 by the War Resisters' League, a pacifist organization that had originally been formed to try to end World War I. They organized a demonstration in New York City outside the United Nations headquarters, which was quickly followed by the picketing of Madame Ngô Nhu, the sister-in-law of South Vietnam's president, Ngô Đình Diệm. Since Đình Diệm never married, Nhu was known as the first lady of South Vietnam. She was staying at the Waldorf Astoria hotel and the War Resister's League picketed her there. In December of 1964 the group teamed up with other antiwar groups to organize a national protest against the Vietnam War.⁹

Although ending the war in Vietnam or at least preventing it from escalating were the goals, the major fear was greater than that. In an atomic age any war could lead to nuclear war. Already the Americans had engaged in actions that revealed a dubious set of ethics—the use of napalm to burn down entire villages, for example—and it was not inconceivable that they would continue to move into previously off-limits circles.

War Creates Fear

Since the possibility of nuclear war hung like a cloud over the nation—presidential candidate Barry Goldwater advocated the limited use of nuclear weapons in Vietnam as early as 1963[10]—the folk music of the day reflected this fear. In England in 1963 the Ian Campbell folk group recorded "The Sun Is Burning," an anti-nuclear war song quickly covered by Simon & Garfunkel. Satirical songwriter Tom Lehrer contributed "Who's Next" and "So Long, Mom (a Song for World War III)," which, like most of his material, used black humor to make serious points.

Pete Seeger, the only man able to move freely back and forth between the Old Left and the New Left, had no use for humor when it came to nuclear war. Among the strongest of his anti-war songs is one that is generally not associated with him at all. In 1962 he adapted a poem by Zazim Hikmet, "I Come and Stand at Every Door," into a song that he recorded in 1962. The Byrds released their much better known version in 1965. Like the poem before it, the song tells the story of a seven-year-old victim of the bombing of Hiroshima who knocks at the doors of the living but remains unseen because,

12. Lyndon Johnson Fights a War on Two Fronts

when she died, as a result of the bombing the wind scattered the dust that had been her bones. The child's silent prayer is that we fight for peace today so that no other children of the world suffer her fate.

The music had become political once more. Pete Seeger, who had long served as the lightning rod, was once again, even as he was still blacklisted from the better clubs, tours, and television, faced with complaints that his music was too political. Seeger would refer to something his old friend Woody Guthrie had said. In 1940 Guthrie explained to Alan Lomax that *all* of folk music was political. He wrote the following in a letter:

> I think real folk stuff scares most of the boys around Washington. A folk song is what's wrong and how to fix it, or it could be who's hungry and where their mouth is, or who's out of work and where the job is or who's broke and where the money is or who's carrying a gun and where the peace is—that's folk lore and folks made it up because they seen that the politicians could find nothing to fix or nobody to feed or give a job of work. We don't aim to hurt you or scare you when we get to feeling sorta folksy and make up some folk lore, we're doing all we can to make it easy on you. I can sing all day and all night sixty days and sixty nights but of course I ain't got enough wind to be in office.[11]

Certainly in his days as a Woody Guthrie clone Bob Dylan believed what his role model had written. As we have seen, he wrote dozens of protest songs, many of them attacking the war. In a period from 1962 to1964, at the height of the nuclear fears, he wrote, among others, "Blowin' in the Wind," "Masters of War," "The Times They Are A-Changin'," "With God on Our Side," and "Talkin' World War III Blues." Yet even as he contributed to the anti-war mood that was growing, he was already having doubts. As stated earlier, the moment Dylan started to be defined as a spokesman, the voice of his generation, he backed off, rebelling against that identification. Comments he made at the time indicate he doubted that the writing and singing of songs would have any effect. At the 1963 March on Washington—where he sang "Only a Pawn in Their Game" and "When the Ship Comes In"—he wondered aloud, according to his biographer Anthony Scaduto, if anyone in the capital was listening and concluded they were not.[12] By 1964 he had ended his association with protesters and overt protest materials and concentrated on internal ideas. At the time, he said, "All I can say is politics is not my thing at all. I can't see myself on a platform talking about how to help people. Because I would get myself *killed* if I *really* tried to help anybody. I mean if somebody *really* had something to say to help somebody out, just bluntly say the truth, well obviously they're gonna be done away with. They're gonna be *killed*."[13]

Part II. "Hey, Hey, LBJ, How Many Kids Did You Kill Today?"

Since most of the Greenwich Village folkies at the time followed Dylan's lead, his withdrawal from protest caused a major case of disassociation. Some people saw it as the end of a direction, while a few forward-looking thinkers saw it as an opportunity to be heard. Phil Ochs was among the latter. Even though he had always been a hard-core Dylan follower, defending him when he was attacked for going electric, for example, Ochs was nevertheless his own man, determined to walk his own path to his own destination, which he saw as massive artistic and commercial success. After having been introduced to folk music in college by Jim Glover, Ochs got his head turned around by the music and, abandoning the journalistic career he had aimed for, began writing and performing songs.

If folk music changed Ochs, the Cuban revolution of 1959 turned him into a radical; as a journalism major he had begun writing political pieces, many for his own underground paper, *The Word*, in which he published exclusively radically tinged political stories.[14] When his only college friend, Jim Glover, dropped out of school to go to New York to become a folk singer, Ochs stayed behind for the time being, working in folk clubs where he met his idol and mentor, Bob Gibson, who became his strongest influence as a songwriter.

In 1962 Ochs arrived in Greenwich Village, where he described himself politically as a Social Democrat and artistically as a singing journalist. After briefly being managed by Albert Grossman, who also handled Dylan, Bob Gibson, and Peter, Paul and Mary, Ochs became a client of Arthur Gorson, who was close to SNCC, SDS, and the Americans for Democratic Action. By 1963 Ochs had become important enough to warrant an invitation to the Valhalla of folk music, the Newport Folk Festival, where he performed songs that would become civil rights anthems: "Too Many Martyrs," "Talkin' Birmingham Jail," and "The Power and the Glory."

In the year that followed Freedom Summer, things fell apart. As we have seen, the civil rights movement imploded, and the anti-war movement was at that time still firmly in the hands of the old, traditional left, which implicitly endorsed the Cold War by opposing communism and was committed to working within the system. At first Phil Ochs and the rest of the New Left went along with that posture. They supported Lyndon Johnson in his campaign for a full elected term in office. But their optimism and faith in the government was quickly shattered. The promise of change that the Kennedy administration had brought to Washington died along with John F. Kennedy, which led to Lyndon Johnson, who was viewed as a hawk, trying to extricate the nation from Vietnam by escalating the war.

12. Lyndon Johnson Fights a War on Two Fronts

The attempts to work within the system failed when Lyndon Johnson reversed Kennedy's policy of trying to withdraw our troops from Vietnam. The new president's act of sending more troops to that country led to new actions against the war. As Allen Guttman reports, the spring of 1964 ushered in an increasing number of protests against the war. In May the Progressive Labor Party and the Young Socialist Alliance organized a nationwide series of marches and demonstrations. In New York City several hundred students began a demonstration in Times Square that led to a march on the United Nations. Other marches were held simultaneously in San Francisco, Boston, Seattle, and Madison, Wisconsin. On May 12 a public burning of draft cards took place in Manhattan. Smaller, local demonstrations took place almost daily in almost every city in America. Slowly but unequivocably the nation's academics, intellectuals, and artists turned against the war.[15] Within a few years it would appear that the only member of the recognizable celebrity class who still supported U.S. efforts in Southeast Asia was Bob Hope.

Those events and attitudes informed the 1964 Newport Folk Festival. That year, Phil Ochs built on the reception he'd received the year before, introducing his famous songs "Draft Dodger Rag" and "I Ain't Marchin' Anymore." At the same festival Joan Baez teamed up with Mary Travers for a couple of songs, including "Lonesome Valley," and performed a traditional ballad that had gained new relevance, "The Unquiet Grave." An anti-war aura hung over the entire festival. The year before, Bob Dylan had been an uninvited guest of Joan Baez, performing with her. In 1964 he received his own invitation and performed, among other songs, "Mr. Tambourine Man," "With God on Our Side" with Joan Baez, and "Chimes of Freedom," all songs that nailed down his reputation as the spokesman for his generation, the very perception he spent so much of his energy trying to escape.

If Phil Ochs, Bob Dylan, and Joan Baez were able to light the fuses of their careers at Newport, a large part of the credit has to go to Peter Yarrow of Peter, Paul and Mary. When jazz impresario George Wein began the festival, he put together a board that consisted of Theodore Bikel, Bill Clifton, Clarence Cooper, Eric Darling, Jean Ritchie, Pete Seeger, and Peter Yarrow, who insisted from the first meeting that the gathering not be limited just to the traditional singers of Child ballads (ballads of Scotland and England and American versions) and other public domain historical pieces. No, Yarrow, said, the young singer-songwriters were doing important work that had to be recognized and brought to a larger audience. He won out and younger artists who were doing protest material got a chance to be heard by 30,000 people at once, instead of the forty or fifty who could fit into a coffeehouse.[16] Yarrow's very notion of inclusion, however, in many people's eyes weakened the impact of the festival. The unnamed author of a post on Wikileaks.com expresses the opinion that "the 1964 Festival 'overreached' itself: too many performers, too many different genres: in Theodore Bikel's words, 'giving both the individual performer and listener too little chance for expression or absorption.'"[17] In addition, critic Paul Nelson wrote snarkily that it had left him "unmoved to the point of paralysis":

> Under the misguided conception that a couple of regiments of folk singers were preferable to a Hand-picked two or three squads, the Newport Committee enlisted what looked to be every folk singer, or reasonable facsimile, on the North American continent, and proceeded to attempt to have them all perform in the space of a single weekend. Even God himself needed six days. Further, Newport proved to be less of a folk festival than a spectacular three-ring morality play of cult worship. The scores of traditional artists remained virtually unnoticed in the back pew, while the hungry throng of worshippers craved a blood sacrifice to mount on a pedestal, another golden saint to add to their socio-religious trilogy of Pete Seeger, Bob Dylan and Joan Baez.[18]

If this complaint is an accurate reflection on the 1964 Newport Folk Festival, it is also a reflection of two qualities that were prevalent in our culture at the time. The first was the SDS's idea of participatory democracy, which created a climate where everyone's ideas of who should appear at the festival were equally valid. The second was the chaos loose in our society at the time. Both ideas prevented a single vision from emerging and being acted upon. As we will see, both of those factors indicated that trouble blocked the road ahead like a fallen tree.

Chapter 13

The Music of the People

Folk music is often described as the music of the people. It is also most often thought of as acoustic music, so much so that when the Paul Butterfield Blues Band played an amplified set at the Newport Folk Festival of 1965, veteran folk song collector Alan Lomax, a traditionalist who on field trips discovered Leadbelly, Woody Guthrie, and Muddy Waters (whom he turned against when Muddy went electric), insisted on introducing the band himself. He gave them a patronizing introduction that included a five-minute capsule history of the blues, emphasizing that it was an acoustic music. It was an intimate personal expression, he said, made by a musician and his instrument, generally a guitar or banjo. With all the condescension a member of royalty shows to a footman he claimed that the next group needed a "lot of hardware" to play the blues and that he would leave it up to the audience to decide whether they could really play the music or not.

When Lomax left the stage, the manager Albert Grossman, who was about to sign Butterfield as a client, called out Lomax for his comments. Lomax shoved him out of his way. Grossman shoved back and the audience was treated to an on-stage fistfight between the spokesman for the old folk music and the spokesman for the new.[1] An hour or so later, Bob Dylan, inspired by what he'd seen in the Butterfield set, assembled an electric band to accompany him on stage for his own performance.

If folk music is the music of the people, by 1965 the people had changed and the music changed with them. Attitudes toward folk music were changing also. Eric Weisberg, the multi-instrumentalist and songwriter, claimed that more authentic folk music was being created everyday by groups like the Drifters than by all of the folk revival musicians. The music Weisberg admired was, like that of Butterfield and Muddy Waters, electric. Soon most folk music was amplified. The music went electric for several reasons, all of which came about as a result of a natural evolution, a change in Americans as a people.

First, one must consider the fact that folk music was originally played on acoustic instruments because electric instruments simply did not exist. New technology always changes the landscape it enters. As the futurist Marshall McLuhan famously pointed out, it was not the content of the medium that changed things, it was the existence of the medium itself.[2] Television programs did not change the leisure habits of Americans; the existence of TV sets did. McLuhan coined the famous phrase "the medium is the message" to explain this fact.[3] Consider the effects recording had on the early singers and players. When the first Appalachian musicians heard themselves on primitive recording machines, they immediately became self-conscious and began paying more attention to their performance, making changes that never would have occurred to them had they not been able to hear themselves play. The same changes occurred when amplification became common. When musicians began using electric instruments it was because the whole society had become electrified.

It was only natural that musicians would take advantage of this development. Folk music is authentic and to do as Alan Lomax demanded meant to pretend to be living in a world where electricity does not exist. Such an attitude is inauthentic. If you have spent your entire life surrounded by electricity, you don't know a world where there is none. Electricity is to our world what water is to a fish. As the music of the people, folk reflects the world in which we live—and we live in an electric environment.

Second, audiences had changed. Clubs, theaters and festival grounds got bigger and noisier. For any kind of performance, there is the problem of reaching people who are distant from the stage; to handle this, there has always been some sort of amplification. The Greek theater masks served as amplifiers, projecting the actors' voices to the last rows of 15,000-seat amphitheaters. For most of its history theater depended on the actors' ability to project, which resulted in an unnatural, exaggerated sound. The development of small condenser microphones that could be hidden in the costume allowed the actor to speak normally and still be heard. Acting styles changed as a result. What is true in drama is true in music. Muddy Waters switched to electric guitar so that he could be heard over the noise of crowded South Side Chicago clubs and bars. In so doing, he changed the nature of the blues forever, paving the way for Paul Butterfield and the others. Insisting that the music remain what it was in more primitive times is like insisting that we make only silent movies because that's how motion pictures started out. In fact, folk music was amplified long before Bob Dylan went electric. Before electric pickups were built into acoustic guitars, musicians in coffeehouses

13. The Music of the People

played through a sound system that used two microphones: one at waist level to pick up the guitar and one at face level for the voice. So no performers were taken by surprise when Dylan and the Butterfield Blues Band went electric.

Third, and for our purposes, most important, it is obvious that folk music changed because the culture that produced folk music and folk musicians changed. It became chaotic. Electric music is much more capable of capturing chaos than acoustic music is. As the war grew more and more out of control and the draft became more of a death sentence for our young men (women were exempt from the draft) the music reflected the horror and confusion the youth of the nation were experiencing. The stated reason the government had always used to justify the peacetime draft was that all American men were required to serve their country for two years. The implication was that the men would be alive at the end of those two years. With the war in Vietnam the assumption that draftees would be alive at the end of their required service disappeared like fog when the sun comes out.

Veterans of the Freedom Riders and Freedom Summer had already discovered to their own satisfaction that the American federal government was either not capable or not interested in keeping its promises. After their work—after they had put their lives on the line, been beaten, jailed, and murdered, had their churches and schools burned down only to find the same conditions in place after their efforts—they felt they had little reason to trust their government. The nation had been at war for most of their lives: World War II, followed by Korea and, just as the nation was beginning to think of Korea as a memory, Vietnam.

No one could say why America was in Vietnam anyway. Our involvement began when Eisenhower, supporting our French allies, sent advisers and began quietly upping the ante, presenting in a 1954 speech what he called, and what the nation came to call, the Domino Theory:

> He spent much of the speech explaining the significance of Vietnam to the United States. First was its economic importance, "the specific value of a locality in its production of materials that the world needs" (materials such as rubber, jute, and sulphur). There was also the "possibility that many human beings pass under a dictatorship that is inimical to the free world." Finally, the president noted, "You have broader considerations that might follow what you would call the 'falling domino' principle." Eisenhower expanded on this thought, explaining, "You have a row of dominoes set up, you knock over the first one, and what will happen to the last one is a certainty that it will go over very quickly." This would lead to disintegration in Southeast Asia, with the "loss of Indochina, of Burma, of Thailand, of the Peninsula, and Indonesia following."

Eisenhower suggested that even Japan, which needed Southeast Asia for trade, would be in danger.[4]

When Kennedy replaced Eisenhower, a moment of optimism sprang up. The new president at least tried to contain the war, to keep American presence in Southeast Asia under control. His assassination threw everything into turmoil. Lyndon Johnson went for a win instead of a withdrawal and American entered into a period of insanity.

The Role of Chaos and Nothingness

At first opposition to the war in Vietnam was led by Old Left intellectuals like Dr. Benjamin Spock and the Committee for a Sane Nuclear Policy (SANE), but these older activists were quickly joined by the student population, who had watched helplessly while the certainty of their lives was replaced by the chaos that springs from a sense of nihilism, of nothingness. The prime factor in their lives, the thing they had tried to escape by leaving their suburban upbringing behind, was that bewildering sense of nothingness. And that's what caused the chaos—nothingness.

To understand nothingness, we have to go back to the work of Friedrich Nietzsche, whose theory of nihilism paved the way. He thought of nihilism as the inescapable destiny of humankind, an inevitable condition that we will each arrive at independently, but which, whatever the timing, we will all come to. Sooner or later we will be forced to recognize that nihilism is our natural condition.

What exactly is nihilism? Nietzsche claims that it is an exhaustion of the spirit that comes from "seeking meaning too long and too ardently. It seems like a kind of death, an inertness, a paralysis … a desert-like emptiness. a malaise, an illness of the spirit and the stomach. One sees all too starkly the fraudulence of human arrangements. Every engagement seems so involved in half-truths, lies and unimportance that cause the will to believe and the will to act to collapse like ash."[5] We arrive at nihilism by waking up, which according to Nietzsche is a three-stage process: "Nihilism will be reached, first, when we have sought in all events a 'meaning' that is not there. We will recognize the waste of strength, the sense of shame that comes from the feeling of shame because we have deceived ourselves for so long. We wanted to achieve something but are forced to realize that '"Becoming aims at nothing and achieves nothing."'[6] Secondly, we will be forced to recognize that the uni-

13. The Music of the People

versal we have sought does not exist. There is no single force that organizes and unifies—no totality, no organization, no unity—in or beneath all events. If this is true, then obviously there is no whole that is superior to human beings. Hence, in Nietzsche's famous phrase, "God is dead." To put your faith in a God is to continue to maintain a self-deception. Finally, nihilism will be achieved when, as a result of the first two qualities, we are trapped in a place where we can neither accept nor reject our world. This leads to periods of frantic action in an effort to change the reality in which we live, the reality that is actually a collective fantasy. These efforts are of course futile and we are forced to discover that we are alone in an indifferent universe.

Nihilism became the most prominent philosophy of the twentieth century, characterizing the lives of people who had never even heard the word. As political and social conditions worsened, as wars failed to bring peace, succeeding only in generating more wars, as we became suspicious and hostile toward anyone different from ourselves, as we postulated that other governing philosophies were hostile and out to destroy us, as we maintained a posture as good guys even as we participated in practices just as shady as the ones we publicly deplored, nihilism grew, but under its more current names of existentialism and nothingness.

In his *The Experience of Nothingness,* a 1970 book written about the plight of the young in the sixties, theologian and philosopher Michael Novak identifies five conditions that lead to nothingness. Boredom, he says, is the first stage. The word boredom in this sense goes far beyond its usual definition. When applied to nothingness, the word means that everything is the same, that no one activity, action, or decision is worth any more than any other. It is the result of the discovery that everything is the same, that nothing one does makes any difference, so that all decisions are equal. The mystery and suspense writer Lawrence Block once grew tired of the feeling that his books had become "the same, only different," so he bought a Cadillac and spent five years driving almost randomly around the United States, visiting every town he could find that had the word Buffalo in its name. When asked why he was doing that, he shrugged and said that it was as good as anything else. That is a prime example of boredom.

In addition to boredom, there is the collapse of a strongly inculcated sense of values. The sensation of having been betrayed by their society was one of the biggest driving factors of the New Left. Their homes, where they had expected to discover meaning, contained none; their schools taught them that they were unimportant and did not count; their churches advocated for the status quo, maintaining a don't-rock-the-boat attitude when the young sensed that the boat was already sinking; and the government, which they had counted on to free them, sent them overseas to be killed, ignored them if they survived and returned, and did nothing about the hatred and racism that permeated the culture.

These factors, of course, led to the third factor, a sense of helplessness, which Novak describes as the feeling that the young have no control over their own lives. They have no personal or political power and, worse, the people in power have no power either. They have no idea how to use the power their status has granted them; they don't know what to do with it, except to protect it. The young were confident that if they did somehow attain power they would not know what to do with it, either.

Fourth, Novak says, we have the sense of betrayal by permissiveness, pragmatism and value-neutral discourse. The young rebels grew up in a society where no one said no to anything, where everything was relative and nothing was absolute. No one would say anything was right or wrong: do your own thing was the rule, even if your own thing was self-destructive or futile. Among the civil rights workers and the anti-war protestors, the prime rule was that whatever your trip is is fine, just don't lay your trip on anyone else. Novak claims that as a result of this, the young are being robbed of a fundamental right: "To learn a way of discriminating right from wrong, the posed from the authentic, the excellent from the mediocre, the brilliant from the philistine, the shoddy from the workmanlike. When no one with experience bothers to insist—to insist—on such discrimination, they rightly get the idea that discernment is not important, that no one cares, that no one either about such things—or about them."[7]

One of the main factors in bringing about the conditions that lead to nothingness arises from the fact that America built a society—a rational, efficient society—without contemplating the effect it would have on the people who had to live in it. The young, having no place in society to call their own, had to seek their own place, gave themselves over to drug experiences and unwanted intimacy, which manifests itself in mechanical relationships. As an example, consider the sexual revolution, brought on in the 1960s by changing social mores and the development of the birth control pill.

The sexual revolution led to more open and frank attitudes toward sex but also brought with it a series of mechanical relationships. Frequency and ease of sex did not necessarily lead to meaning and intimacy.

A person who suffers from the condition of nothingness is likely to come to prefer mechanical relationships. They are easier and closer to the surface, and one can escape troublesome emotions. There develops a tendency to substitute sex for love because sex is easier and less messy emotionally than love, even though it is actually empty. If, however, your entire life has been empty, then you expect nothing else. You also will probably not realize how empty and mechanical these relationships are. Nothingness is a chaotic state. We indulge in frantic activities to fill the void, to maintain the illusions that our lives are going somewhere; we spend energy trying to get energy, expend our power trying to get power, waste our time trying to make our time count. We bang our heads against the wall trying to tear down the wall.

The Music Changes as the Culture Changes

The lives of young Americans by the time of the anti-war protests had become totally frenetic. Is it any wonder that folk music did too? When Dylan went electric, the old guard at Newport got it all wrong. He didn't abandon folk music; he simply changed its presentation to suit the times. Much of the music he was writing no longer lent itself to the accompaniment of a single acoustic guitar. "Mr. Tambourine Man," for instance, played acoustically loses much of its power and fails to capture the sense of disassociation and despair that the young saw as reality. When Roger McGuinn and the Byrds electrified it, they also electrified the young progressive audience, who, even if they remained unable to find a meaning in the lyrics, could feel the authenticity of the song, authenticity that was missing from their lives. They were not bothered by the fact that they could not make literal sense of the lyrics, because little in their world made sense anyway. The very ambiguity of the words Dylan wrote and McGuinn sang simply made them applicable to many situations. Listeners were invited to fill them in, to flesh them out in their minds.

The fact remains, though, that even if it was electric music, it was still folk music. Everything about it reeked of folk, including the backgrounds of Dylan and the Byrds, all of whom had been acoustic players and still included folk instruments, themes, chord structures, and patterns in their music.

Electric folk music became the norm. Eric Andersen released his second album, *'Bout Changes and Things*, acoustically. For his third album, he re-recorded the second one, this time with electric instruments. Did that make the second recording rock or not folk music? No, it simply made it what he called it, *'Bout Changes and Things, Take Two.* Lomax, Seeger, and the others at Newport who objected to electricity were against it for all the wrong reasons. They had forgotten that folk music, like the society that created it, is a growing, changing, living art form and that the ballads they sang as symbols of musical purity bore little relation to what they had originally sounded like. They also either ignored or forgot that they had changed and altered the presentation of the songs they discovered and sang. They lost sight of the fact that folk music is a process, not an object.

Folk music, as music of the people, reflects the people. When the people's lives are on the brink, so will folk music be on the brink—and brinksmanship became the rule of the sixties.

Chapter 14

Music and the Prefigurative Culture

If nothingness characterized the music and the behavior of the young of the sixties, it is worth exploring where it came from. How did this sense of powerlessness sweep through the people of the most powerful nation on earth? The answer lies, at least partially, in a theory set forth by anthropologist Margaret Mead, a theory that hypothesizes that three different and separate types of cultures exist: *postfigurative*, in which children learn primarily from their forebears; *cofigurative*, in which both children and adults learn from their peers; and *prefigurative*, in which adults learn also from their children.

A postfigurative culture is one in which change is so slow and imperceptible that grandparents holding newborn grandchildren in their arms cannot conceive of any other future for them than their own past lives.[1] The children of the fifties who became the radicals of the sixties grew up in a postfigurative culture. Eisenhower was everyone's grandfather who held the young and predicted their future; Congress was the group of wise old men who guided the actions of the young, serving as modern-day shamans who read the signs and prescribed actions for the younger generations based on their visions. When Eisenhower sent advisers to Vietnam, he did it without the advice and consent of the young, who did not count. Most of the young people at the time could not even legally cast a vote. Only adults, defined as those over twenty-one, were viewed as mature enough to be qualified to vote. The young were disenfranchised and disempowered.

Their education was no better. One man remembered that when his son entered the first grade, he was overjoyed at the prospect. He'd been to a very good preschool and thought that now he'd get down to some first-rate learning, an idea that was reinforced by his tour of the school's facilities before he registered. When the boy saw all of the science equipment and the technological miracles available in the building, he made the mistake of assuming he would be allowed to use it. At the end of the first day, he came home furious, unable to contain his anger.

Part II. "Hey, Hey, LBJ, How Many Kids Did You Kill Today?"

"I'm not going back," he said.

"Come on," his father replied, "Whatever happened, it couldn't be that bad, could it?"

"I'm not going back."

"What happened?"

The boy fought for control and finally said, "They made us all go to the bathroom at the same time. Whether we needed to or not. They made us line up and go to the bathroom."

On his first day of school, the boy had been taught that he was not important; he and his needs did not count. Administrative convenience was more important. In the sixties educational reformers such as John Holt, George Dennison, Paul Goodman, Neil Postman, and James Herndon all attacked the deadening of the spirit that occurred far too often in America's public schools.[2] These attitudes continue and characterize far too much of American education. One young woman related the story of the day when she, then a high school student, walked into the restroom and interrupted a drug deal between three other students. One of them stabbed her in the arm. She went to the nurse and, after her wound was tended to, was sent to see the principal, where she expected to be asked who had stabbed her. Instead he asked where it happened.

"In the girl's bathroom."

"Are you sure?" the principal asked.

"Of course, I'm sure."

"Stop and think a minute and then tell me: are you sure it didn't happen off campus?"

"No, it was in the bathroom."

The girl reports that at this point she was getting confused. The principal continued to question her, implying that the stabbing must have taken place somewhere else. Although his attitude confused her, the young lady continued to insist it happened in the rest room.

Finally the principal said, "I don't think so. If it happened in the restroom, it would mean we had a drug problem on campus and we don't have a drug problem here."

To this man, maintaining a false image for his school was more important than the safety of his students. It isn't just administrative hypocrisy that creates problems for the young in schools. It is what is taught and how it is taught. Public schools originally existed to help integrate immigrant kids into American culture. To give these kids a boost, the schools passed on the collected knowledge of our past. Today the initiation of foreign-born kids into the soci-

14. Music and the Prefigurative Culture

ety is a much smaller part of the task of the schools, but they still cling to that outdated mission. The result? As Paul Simon wrote, "When I think back on all the crap I learned in high school, it's a wonder I can think at all."[3]

The kids of the New Left generation went to high schools and colleges that taught from a top-down model. An expert lectured and the neophytes took notes. More than one hundred years of educational research have conclusively demonstrated that the lecture system is the single worst way to learn anything, but it still dominates our classrooms. The operating assumption of the lecture system is that the listeners don't know anything. Again, the learners don't count; what matters is that with a lecture system schools can process many more students. If a school does not deal with students as individuals, as *people*, it can pack hundreds of them at a time in a hall and pontificate in front of them and then evaluate them based on how well they can fill in little ovals on paper with a number two pencil.

Even though, as we noted earlier, Marshall McCluhan pointed out that it was the medium itself rather than the content that created change, we should not overlook what the schools and colleges were teaching. Civics courses taught an idealized version of how our government works, ignoring the deal-making, the role of lobbyists, and the crazed, politically motivated investigations. Philosophy courses could be taken in which no one ever read a philosopher's work, instead studying commentaries on the philosophers. As Thoreau said, there were no philosophers left, only teachers of philosophy. English classes taught grammar rules that contradicted themselves and each other and tried to reduce the act of writing to a set of rules. Conformity beat creativity. History was presented to students as a big bag of omissions and lies and the things that were important, like truth, eternal verities, and the spiritual impulse were ignored. Schools created a top-down authoritative world in which the adult held all the power and instead of sharing it doled out the illusion of power as a reward in the form of student governments and administratively approved and absolutely safe political clubs.

For the majority of American youth the situation was just fine. Raised in homes where their parents ruled, attending schools where the administration ruled, they were used to being told what to do and under what conditions to do it by their elders. Having grown up in a postfigurative culture, they were accustomed to it and saw it as natural. It was their whole environment, water to the school of fish. In fact, when the generation gap created tensions, most young adults sided with the adult authority figures. In his essay "On Work," Bertrand Russell made the claim that the vast majority of workers would rather be told what to do than exercise their own judgment. Like a group of old cons waiting out their time until parole, most of the young in the Eisenhower fifties surrendered their autonomy, trading it for conformity and security. Instead of fighting nothingness, they accepted it as the normal state.

As a result, young America was depressed, feeling disaffiliated and powerless. Many had been through Freedom Summer and found the results of having put their lives on the line disappointing. After the summer they discovered that thirty-five of the churches they'd worked with had been burned to the ground, sixty of the Freedom Houses and homes they'd stayed in were firebombed, and the Freedom delegation to the Democratic National Convention had been turned away. The regular party refused to seat them, preferring instead to give official recognition and voting power to the racists, white supremacists, arsonists, and murderers who made up Mississippi's Democratic Party.[4] Small wonder they felt disillusioned, ready to reject the world of their elders.

The music these young people listened to reflected the world they saw around them. The Monkees, a fabricated group for a fabricated age, sang "Pleasant Valley Sunday," a Carole King-Jerry Goffin song about the emptiness of suburban life. Dylan contributed "Subterranean Homesick Blues," a song that attacked the futility of contemporary American life, and "Maggie's Farm," about the singer's refusal to play the game anymore. The Rolling Stones, after their American tour in 1964, wrote and recorded "Nineteenth Nervous Breakdown," which captured the chaos and intensity of life in this country, and "Mother's Little Helper," a song about American housewives' dependence on tranquilizers to fight off the aloneness and alienation of their condition.

As the civil rights movement was shifting away from its white allies and the war was beginning to escalate, a series of songs protesting all aspects of American life appeared. Bob Dylan sang that he had been "older then" but was "younger now," signaling a rejection of society's stated values, while Phil Ochs gave us, "I'm Going to Say It Now," a declaration of independence from the old ways. Eric Andersen contributed a number of songs about restless young people in search of a direction and a destination, such as "Thirsty Boots." These songs captured the mood of the young men and women who were in the act of creating the New Left as an alternative way of governing and being.

Even country music—that most conservative music genre—briefly entered the field of social protest. Jeannie C. Riley, who took on hypocrisy in "Harper Valley PTA," recorded "Generation Gap," a song that blamed the gap squarely on parents, with lyrics claiming that from the very beginning when a baby was sitting in his mother's lap there was the start of a generation gap. Her song also complained of bad parenting, the lyrics speaking of the parents' partying and drug use and their demands for a standard for their children's behavior while exhibiting none themselves.[5] In the hypocrisy of adults, Riley concludes, you'll find the origin of the generation gap.

Why a Generation Gap?

One reason would lie in sheer numbers. According to Todd Gitlin, the first generation of baby boomers turned eighteen in 1964. Between 1964 and 1970, 20,000,000 more reached the age of eighteen. These numbers are important because, as Gitlin says, "America's young were not only multiplying, not only relatively rich, not only concentrated on campuses and, thanks to the mass media—visible as never before. Suppose they were, en masse, in motion, breaking out of the postwar consensus, out of complacency, out of good behavior and middle-class mores, out of bureaucratic order and the cold war mood. Then the unthinkable might be actual, the unprecedented possible. You could safely kick out the jams, dissolve the old hesitations, break with adults, be done with compromises, *be done with it.*"[6]

Because these young radicals had grown up in a postfigurative culture, where all power and authority were top-down, their parents had held the role of old wise men; what they said was the operational truth, even if it turned out to be, as was frequently the case, wrong. The problem was that the parents of these new eighteen-year-olds were as riddled with nothingness and nihilism as their children were, but they could not admit they were empty and were trying to cover their emptiness with the correct suburban lives, whiskey and tranquilizers, cocktail parties and television, career climbing for the men and homemaking for the women. It was a life in which conspicuous consumption tried to cover a lack of meaning, where suburban churches sold the good life and rural churches maintained the racism and sexism that characterized the age. When the civil rights movement began to take hold, most churches railed against the granting of rights to minorities.

When the young grew up in situations like these, could they do anything else but revolt? Could there be anything other than a generation gap? Parents had preached to their children to be idealistic, and when their children tried to live up to what they'd been taught, the parents were horrified.

Chapter 15

Rise of the Prefigurative Culture

Postfigurative parents had raised prefigurative children. As Mead wrote, in a prefigurative culture adults learn from the young. When the motto of an organization is, as it was with the Youth International Party (Yippies), "Never trust anyone over thirty," then a prefigurative culture has come into existence. Phil Ochs once again caught the zeitgeist with his song "Love Me, I'm a Liberal," which attacked the hypocrisy of the old-left liberals and announced that the youth were moving in another direction. This song did not take on the southern, conservative, white supremacists and others that Ochs usually attacked. Instead he drew a deadly bead on hypocritical liberals who were properly moved when black civil rights leaders such as Medgar Evers or white liberal icons like Robert Kennedy were shot but felt radical leaders such as Malcolm X did not deserve the same compassion.

Ochs' song celebrates civil rights as long as that fight for justice remains on a safe level and avoids revolutionary change. The speaker in the song, Ochs' portrait of a typical postfigurative liberal, is all in favor of minorities as long as they don't live next door to him. In the concluding verse, the singer talks of his younger times when he attended leftist meetings and flirted with ideologies but now has become a turncoat, giving the names of his friends to congressional investigating committees.

The elders Ochs wrote about—in this case the Old Left—were not pleased. They had felt like Ochs had been one of them, a disciple, and now they discovered he had broken with the party line and looked upon them with contempt. Ochs had seen through their poses down to the hypocritical behaviors that rested, like nougat beneath the chocolate in a candy bar, beneath the artifice. To the old-left liberals Ochs had become a traitor. How could the young man who had written and sung songs that inspired them, songs that reflected what they believed they had taught him, turn against

15. Rise of the Prefigurative Culture

them like that? Ochs, though, had in reality done nothing more than satirize what he saw around him every day.

Bob Dylan also reflected on what he saw around him. "Chimes of Freedom," the aforementioned "My Back Pages," "The Times They Are A-Changin'," and "Paths of Victory" all give us a world in which the young and the parental generation might as well not live on the same planet so big is the breach between them. The young, no longer feeling they could learn anything from their elders, became determined to switch roles. They would become the teachers of the older generations. The New Left brought us what sociologist Carl Boggs called a prefigurative politics, which is characterized by different approaches to social and political relationships that, instead of reflecting the culture as it stands, reflects the culture the radical wants to bring into being. A prefigurative model turns the status quo upside down. Decision making, ways of viewing the culture, and human relationships all move from the powerful to the powerless. Practicing prefigurative politics means that the last shall be first.[1]

For these young white activists, who had been, in their eyes, unceremoniously kicked out of the civil rights movement, direct political action was still their mode of being. They simply turned from one cause to another, directing their attention to trying to stop a war. Until this time their movements had been led postfiguratively, by their elders. In fact, they had been led into the anti-war movement by the already-established American Society for a Sane Nuclear Policy (SANE) an organization formed in 1957 by elder statesmen like magazine editor and writer Norman Cousins and the Quaker leader Clarence Pickett. One of SANE's foremost members was Dr. Benjamin Spock, whose writings had taught mothers how to raise the members of the New Left. By 1965, however, the young had rejected SANE the way SNCC had rejected them. Now they would go it alone. They would create a prefigurative world in which they showed the previous generations how it should be done.

Escalating the War and the Protests

The catalyst for their action was Lyndon Johnson's decision to begin bombing North Vietnam, a move seen as another betrayal, since SDS had supported Johnson in the election campaign against Barry Goldwater. In February of 1965, almost as soon as the bombing began, SDS organized protests, marching on the Oakland [California] Army Terminal, from which troops departed for Vietnam. They led another march on the terminal in March and then began a series of teach-ins on campuses around the country—designed to educate students who had not yet gotten involved—about American policies in Southeast Asia.

By this time, Joan Baez, who would say without irony that "somebody had to save the world. And obviously, I felt I was the one for the job,"[2] had organized her Institute for the Study of Nonviolence, where she served as a teacher's aide to her own teacher and partner in the undertaking, Ira Sandperl. She and Sandperl showed up at demonstrations and teach-ins, where she sang and they both advocated and taught a civil disobedience guided by love and acceptance. The institute, headquartered in Carmel, California, was not greeted with shouts of joy from the local politicians, business leaders, and citizenry in general, who viewed it as a hotbed of subversion and did their best to close it down. Every time they succeeded in shutting its doors, though, Baez and Sandperl defiantly but lovingly managed to get them open again. The institute still exists as the Resource Center for Nonviolence.

Baez, Phil Ochs, and Peter, Paul and Mary became familiar faces at antiwar demonstrations and rallies. In March of 1965 SDS held its first anti-war rally in Washington, D.C., drawing an attendance of 25,000. Joan Baez, Phil Ochs, and Judy Collins sang there. That May the action shifted back to the West Coast, where the Vietnam Day Committee organized the largest teach-in to date. Some 35,000 came out for a thirty-six–hour event. Speakers included Dr. Benjamin Spock, socialist leader Norman Thomas, political journalist I.F. Stone, Alan Watts, Dick Gregory, Freedom Summer organizer Bob Moses, and Mario Savio. Phil Ochs also showed up. Among the songs he sang was his recent composition "I Ain't Marchin' Anymore."

Peter, Paul and Mary began to follow Joan Baez's regimen of mixing benefits with concerts, spending 50 percent of their time playing rallies and protests, a move that did not please all the members of their audience. Once, as people crowded into a lecture room to attend a teach-in at Hunter College in New York City, the group was standing in the hall, singing for the entering crowd. A young man going in muttered to his friend, "I paid twelve dollars to see them last night. I could have just waited a day and seen them for free." He was right; they had become ubiquitous, showing up wherever a crowd had gathered to either fight segregation or to end the war. The defection of a small number of their fans did not bother the trio; the cause, they figured, was important enough to place above their careers.

15. Rise of the Prefigurative Culture

By this time, Bob Dylan's withdrawal from public life had become more than a personal choice. A motorcycle wreck put him out of action for eighteen months, although in rejecting his role as spokesman for a generation and in his need to protect his privacy he probably would not have been involved in direct action anyway. Again, his feelings and sympathies were kept private. He intended to keep them that way. Still, just as they had for the civil rights movement, his songs helped propel the anti-war movement. As always, Dylan had his own take on the issue: "Masters of War" took on war profiteering, while "With God on Our Side" attacked the use of Christianity to justify mass slaughter throughout the centuries. His early foray into protest, the song he insisted was not a protest song, "Blowin' in the Wind," had posed questions without giving answers. Some were ambiguous, such as the number of roads that have to be traveled before a man is a man, while others—the number of cannonballs that will be fired before being "forever banned"—could not be more direct. Because the song gave no answers it remained relevant and easily transferred from the civil rights campaign to the anti-war movement. "A Hard Rain's a-Gonna Fall" describes a vision the speaker has had in which he has seen our world crumbling to pieces from war and destruction, and tells of guns and swords being used by children and a young woman whose body is burning, It is an apocalyptic song and only a part of it deals directly with war. The rest of the lyrics ring with Dylan's characteristic ambiguity. In the liner notes to *The Freewheelin' Bob Dylan*, Dylan himself said of the song, "Every line in it is actually the start of a whole song, but when I wrote it, I thought I wouldn't have enough time alive to write all those songs, so I put all I could into this one."[3]

Like good poetry, Dylan's major protest songs suggest, rather than declare. Most topical songs were designed to get the audience to act, to do something. Phil Ochs' songs were mainly designed to get his listeners out into the streets, actively protesting the war. Dylan wanted them to think, to try to figure out the conditions that brought these horrors into being; his songs suggest that these issues are much more complicated than people assume and that a simple song cannot adequately capture the essence. That song, though, can lead us to understand and, more important, to empathize. Then, like Dylan at "Maggie's Farm," we can quit being a part of it.

While Dylan retreated from direct activism, content to point out the problems, Phil Ochs continued to try to win converts to the peace movement. He wrote "I Ain't Marchin' Anymore," which urged people to march in the streets instead of in uniform to war, and collaborated with Bob Gibson on

Part II. "Hey, Hey, LBJ, How Many Kids Did You Kill Today?"

"One More Parade," which called on people to resist the temptation to march in the big parade. And, of course, there is the famous "Draft Dodger Rag," which was about exactly what the title implied and was the single happiest song about dodging the draft ever written. In it, Ochs used satire to encourage people to resist the draft. That title, his 1963 song, "What Are You Fighting For?," and "Love Me, I'm a Liberal" infuriated the Old Left. The two were, Ochs believed, the songs most responsible for his being investigated by the FBI. Even though he had written the patriotic hymn to everything that was great about America, "The Power and the Glory," Ochs was looked upon as un-American and was spied on by the government the rest of his life.

Joan Baez also suffered from accusations that she was not a "good American." A strong and confident woman always ready to act on her beliefs, she didn't just form her institute, she toured the country leading workshops and teach-ins in its name, marched in the streets, got herself arrested and sent to jail, and even refused to pay that portion of her income tax that went to support the war, forcing the government to sue for the money. Not a prolific songwriter, she relied mostly on traditional songs and covers of other protest material, such as the songs of Dylan and Ochs. Her set lists almost always included a crowd sing-along on "We Shall Overcome" and the song Pete Seeger had made from an old Russian poem, "Where Have All the Flowers Gone." To her, "Joe Hill," a song about the legendary Wobbly organizer, was an all-purpose protest song. She also covered other artists' songs. Her biggest hit single was a cover of Phil Ochs' "There But for Fortune," another all-purpose protest song that speaks against prisons, against our attitudes towards the poor and homeless, and against the war and discusses how fortunate the majority of us are to walk on this side of the thin line that separates us from those victims. Ochs recorded the song before Baez did; but his version is angry, an attack, while hers is sympathetic, refusing to cast emotional blame.

Peter, Paul and Mary also relied primarily on traditional songs and covers. With one foot in the commercial world, they could use their three-part harmonies and simple but imaginative arrangements to put these songs on the charts, as they did with Dylan's "Blowin' in the Wind " and "Don't Think Twice" and Ochs' "There But for Fortune," as well as the Weavers' anti-war classic, "Wasn't That a Time." Their versions of "If I Had a Hammer," "If I Were Free," "All My Trials," "This Land Is Your Land," and "We Shall Overcome" were familiar parts of the anti-war soundtrack, as was their own composition "The Great Mandala." Other Dylan songs they were associated with were "The Times They Are A-Changin'" and "When the Ship Comes In."

15. Rise of the Prefigurative Culture

The trio not only performed at anti-war rallies, they also organized them, a practice they'd begun with the 1963 Million Man March on Washington, which they helped arrange, and the march on Selma, Alabama, also one they helped put together. Their most dramatic contribution to the movement, though, came in 1968, when they decided to put to the test a comment Peter Yarrow had made offhandedly to a reporter that it was possible that they had enough clout to sway a presidential election by traveling with a candidate. When Democratic senator Eugene McCarthy had decided to challenge Lyndon Johnson for the nomination as a peace candidate, Peter, Paul and Mary signed onto his campaign and traveled the country with him, appearing at his rallies, singing and speaking to the crowds. McCarthy, for all his attractiveness to the young, was far too diffident to win the nomination. Whenever he was asked if he wanted to be president, he replied that he was willing to serve, an answer that indicated a certain lack of passion for his role in the political scheme of things. The major accomplishment of his candidacy was that he drove Lyndon Johnson into retirement, an action that threw the race for the nomination into a chaotic mess. The man who managed to climb out of the political tar pits to victory was Hubert Humphrey, and we will see the results of his presidential race in a later chapter.

In 1965, though, the year we were discussing, the most important topical song did not come from any members of our subtitle quartet. It was a protest song so different that the East Coast protest writers hated it, saying it was not truly folk music at all. Ironically, the very people who had changed the definition of folk music forever, who had widened it so that it included the work they were composing, were complaining that another composed song did not qualify, even though it was written by a man with solid folk credentials and sung by another.

In Los Angeles, 17-year-old P.F. Sloan wrote "Eve of Destruction." Barry McGuire sang it, and the single, released in the summer of 1965, was by fall number one in the nation. The song begins with military drumming, then the guitars come in softly, and McGuire's vocal, strong and convincing, his raspy voice sounding troubled and desperate, begins to sing a description of a litany of horrors that the speaker in the song sees all around. A Dylanesque harmonica gives the response to McGuire's verses, as his gruff and strong vocal tone plays against the fear and uncertainty the narrator feels. The fact that the tone of the voice fit the song the way a glove fits a hand was a lucky accident. McGuire's singing on the record was meant to be a reference vocal, designed to show roughly what the song sounded like. The plan was to do a smoother voice track later on. However, an employee of the record company leaked the single to radio disc jockeys, who got a great response from their listeners when they played it. So Dunhill Records, which released it, decided not to redo the vocal. It was evidently a wise decision. "Eve of Destruction" turned out to be the biggest hit of 1965.

Also in 1965, on the West Coast, Buffalo Springfield released a haunting song that captured the spirit of the times: "For What It's Worth." Specifically written about the riots on Sunset Strip that occurred when the police tried to stop teenagers from hanging out on the strip and attending the music clubs there, "For What It's Worth" turned out to be an all-purpose protest song whose lyrics were ambiguous enough to apply to the anti-war movement as well as to kids on the Strip. Together, "Eve of Destruction" and "For What It's Worth" created more of the same action they described, serving as anthems for activists.

Chapter 16

"Lyndon Johnson Told the Nation"

As the war grew more unpopular, President Johnson tried to end it by winning it. Just as generals described having to destroy villages in order to pacify them, Johnson would bring the end of the war by escalating it. In some way that only his administration understood, more would bring less. In July of 1965 he raised the number of men to be drafted each month to 35,000, more than doubling the already high previous number of 17,000.[1] In a move designed to hamper criticism of his method of conducting war he pushed Congress into passing a law criminalizing the burning of draft cards.[2] Rather than calming the movement, these moves drove more young people into the streets. The National Coordinating Committee to End the War in Vietnam immediately broke the law by holding a mass public draft card burning, at which Phil Ochs played.

The rise in the draft numbers created a dramatic rise in the number of songs about avoiding the draft. Phil Ochs wrote and recorded his classic, "Draft Dodger Rag," while the Flying Burrito Brothers wrote in "My Uncle" about heading for the nearest foreign border after receiving a draft notice. The Byrds released "Draft Morning," which used martial drumming, distorted guitars, and overdubbed sounds of war as a motif to describe the terror in a young man's heart when faced with conscription. Tom Paxton contributed "Lyndon Johnson Told the Nation," a song about the difference between Johnson's words and his actions. In it, a young draftee sits in a rice paddy in Vietnam remembering the time just a few months before when he'd been in the States and feeling secure in Johnson's declaration that he wouldn't have to go to Vietnam.

The most masterful and powerful of the anti-draft songs, though, proved that humor is one of the strongest weapons that can be brought to bear. Arlo Guthrie's eighteen minute "Alice's Restaurant Massacree" describes the day Arlo and a friend went to Thanksgiving dinner at the home of their mutual friends, Ray and Alice. Arlo and his friend decide to take the family's accumulated trash to the dump but when they discover the dump is closed, they drop the trash into a gully and return to Alice's, where they are promptly arrested by Officer Obie for littering and taken to court, where a blind judge fines the pair and orders them to clean up the trash. The scene then changes to the draft board at Whitehall Street in New York City after Arlo receives his draft notice. He is able to beat the draft because of his police record for littering and disturbing the peace. The song has become a classic and, although it was originally recorded in 1966, it still reaches a nationwide audience by being played on the radio, especially on NPR and the alternative stations of Pacifica Radio, every Thanksgiving.[3] In 2016 Guthrie did a year-long national tour celebrating its fiftieth anniversary. It is a song that has lasted far longer then the war it describes. "Alice's Restaurant Massacree" serves as evidence that art outlasts destruction.

But Was It Folk Music?

At this point, the transition from acoustic to electric music accelerated. Disillusionment, a sense of nothingness, and helplessness had all led to attempts to create a prefigurative society. And, as folk music is a force that continues to reflect the lives of the people, it became what those lives had become: loud, forceful, direct and chaotic, young, wild, sometimes stupid, sometimes raucous. It became what was played on the radio as rock & roll. Still, it was folk music. Almost everyone who played what was becoming known as folk-rock came from folk backgrounds. They had all been coffeehouse acoustic veterans who, just as Muddy Waters had back in the forties, went electric in order to be heard by their audiences.

Even if the delivery of the music was more technologically sophisticated than it had been just a few years earlier, its purpose was the same. As Mary Travers said, "Folk music has always contained a concern for the human condition. And since it brings people into it from different points of view, that can help illuminate what a consensus might be to important issues."[4] If that music was electric, as Peter, Paul and Mary's later music quietly was, then it could work on several additional levels that were important to the young radicals. Still, electric or acoustic, it was folk music. It became folk rock when the media decided a new term was needed to describe the amplified folk music of the Byrds.

What Was Folk-Rock, Exactly?

When the Byrds hit the top of the charts with their amplified cover of Dylan's "Mr. Tambourine Man" and Dylan himself began releasing albums recorded with electric instruments, folk-rock exploded commercially and artistically. What common denominators existed in songs that qualified them as folk-rock instead of just rock? Folk rock was, of course, drawn from folk sources. The Byrds covered Dylan's material and wrote their own, but they also recorded electric versions of traditional songs. In the terminology of musicians, guitars were played "clean," which meant musicians played without much distortion or the use of effects pedals and the vocals generally used three- and four-part harmonies. Often acoustic guitars were strummed in the mix, providing the rhythm while electric guitars took the lead. The music was clean, clear, often idealistic, and designed to get people to move politically as well as socially. It combined the best qualities of both worlds: the messages of folk music and the energy of rock. Today, because it draws from many influences and many genres, this music is called Americana.[5] It was the music of rebellion, just as rock was, but of *unified* rebellion, a prefigurative music that claimed its listeners had something to say that the guardians of the old postfigurative culture should listen to.

As the War in Vietnam Deepens, So Does the War in the Street

Yet even as the music and the movement advocated peace, the demonstrations often turned violent. The turning point was June 23, 1967, when Lyndon Johnson went to Los Angeles for a fundraiser and was greeted by a protest led by the Progressive Labor Party and SDS. Fifty-one protesters were arrested, but that did not end things. Without warning and without provocation, the Los Angeles Police Department waded into the crowd and began beating the protestors for no discernible reason. The American Civil Liberties Union reported, "Unresisting demonstrators were beaten—some in front of literally thousands of witnesses—without even the pretext of and attempt to make an arrest."[6]

By 1967 some 40,000 men a month were being called for the draft. A national Stop the Draft week was called by an ad hoc group called The Resistance. It took place in thirty American cities, with simultaneous demonstrations happening in which demonstrators blocked the entrances to induction centers, urging young draftees to refuse to go inside and to join them on the line. In Oakland, California, Joan Baez sang for the protestors and the draftees and then joined the protestors who sat blocking the doors, forcing the inductees to climb over them to enter the building. When the police arrived to break it up, Baez was, along with the other demonstrators, arrested. She spent ten days in jail.[7]

By this time, the majority of Americans had turned against the war. Polling revealed that most of them thought the nation's involvement in Vietnam was a mistake. This was bad news for the government, which reacted by increasing their efforts to win both the war and the hearts and minds of those who opposed it. Neither of those goals was ever attained. At first a movement consisting of a few Old Left intellectuals and then by New Left students, the Vietnam opposition grew quickly to include the clergy, educators from preschool teachers to university professors, young mothers, artists and performers, and journalists. Indeed, a prefigurative culture bloomed; the young leaders of the anti-war movements taught the adults that the war was morally, politically and practically wrong.

The unfair draft system was probably the major reason young men opposed the war. College and university students were entitled to deferments and could escape the draft as long as they remained in school, which meant a period of incredible growth for colleges and graduate schools. (This situation also led to the college reform movement, as we shall see later.) Given the ease with which privileged people could escape the draft through deferments, it is easy to see that someone had to take their places—and those people turned out to be the poor and the minorities. Individual local draft boards had the authority to pick and choose their draftees from the general population of registered young men. This fact, in practice, meant that a larger percentage of African-American men would be called.

In 1967 there were 29 percent of black men eligible for the draft as opposed to 63 percent of white men, but 69 percent of black men were called and only 31 percent of the eligible white men.[8] As the perception of the draft became more and more unfair, more people turned against it and acted in opposition to it. In October of 1967 resisters turned in their draft cards across the country; more than one thousand cards were returned to the Justice Department. Attorney General Ramsey Clark chose to prosecute only the ringleaders, Dr. Spock and William Sloane Coffin, the chaplain of Yale Uni-

16. "Lyndon Johnson Told the Nation"

---

versity. The strategy of taking only the organizers to court, though, did not last. Within just a couple of years, one-fourth of all court cases in federal courts were draft related. Over 200,000 young men were accused of draft dodging and 25,000 of them were prosecuted.[9] Among the ones sent to prison was Joan Baez's husband, David Harris.

Chapter 17

Impatience Leads to Escalation

As the war escalated, an all-too-familiar American attitude surfaced on the parts of nearly everyone involved: activists, government, and citizens at large. That attitude was impatience. In a sense, impatience had been bred into this generation from birth. The activists of the New Left were the first American children to have been raised with TV sets in their homes. Every drama and comedy they had watched growing up—and those shows numbered in the thousands—introduced a problem, explored it, and solved it in half an hour. Some problems were complex, and it took an hour to restore harmony to the universe presented by the program. That pattern, familiar from childhood, could not help but have an effect on them.

Consider what these young people had gone through. Raised to believe they would inherit the nation, they found every effort they put forth to create a nation they would want to inherit resisted and thwarted by the very postfigurative elders who had promised them that world. Prefigurative young people were ready to teach the old but the old refused their offerings. The nation remained postfigurative. Many of the youth had spent years trying to bring voting rights to Mississippi only to be driven out by the southern approach to justice and abandoned by the African-American groups that had recruited them. Certainly a voting rights act had been passed but had anything really changed? Then they had taken on the war. It had been a few years now and, while universally unpopular, the war still continued to gain steam. Like an erupting volcano's lava stream, they could see it approaching but could do nothing to stop it.

In 1968 they tried once more to work within the organized system by cutting their hair and shaving their beards so they could be "neat and clean for Gene" and campaigned for peace candidate Senator Eugene McCarthy, while Peter, Paul and Mary traveled with him.[1] McCarthy lost. Others supported Robert Kennedy, who also challenged Lyndon Johnson. Folk singer

John Stewart traveled with Kennedy, singing for his crowds. He had met John F. Kennedy when, as a member of the Kingston Trio, he was, along with the other members, invited to the White House. There he met and bonded with Robert. F. Kennedy. The two men became friends and when Kennedy tried for the Democratic nomination, Stewart campaigned for him, traveling with him and singing for his crowds. Kennedy was assassinated in 1968 in Los Angeles after winning the California primary.

We Want the World and We Want It Now!

The leaders of the New Left were young and privileged, used to having most areas of their lives the way they wanted them. Most of them had until now measured out their time in semesters. Every four months or so their situations and mental environments changed. One part of their lives ended and another began. Now they found themselves up against conditions that, rather than ending, just got more dangerous. Their work, to them, did not bring fast enough results. Abbie Hoffman captured that sense of lost patience: "Above all, what you have as young people that's vitally needed to make social change, is impatience. You want it to happen now. There have to be enough people that say, 'We want it now, in our lifetime. We want to see apartheid in South Africa come down right now. We want to see the war in Central America stop right now. We want the CIA off our campus right now. We want an end to sexual harassment in our communities right now.'"[2]

Impatience Leads to New Problems

The 1968 Democratic convention in Chicago changed everything. By the time of the convention, Jerry Rubin and Abbie Hoffman, who had emerged as the clown princes of the New Left, along with satirist Paul Krassner and Phil Ochs, had begun the Youth International Party, popularly known as the Yippies. The relationship between Phil Ochs and Jerry Rubin was a complicated one: "Everyone assumed that Rubin and Phil were the best of friends. Actually, Phil's association with Rubin was almost exclusively in the realm of political protest. His alliance with Rubin was symbolic—Phil Ochs the Che Guevera to Rubin's Fidel Castro.... Rubin made Phil politically acceptable with the radical fringe; Phil shared the literary stage with Rubin."[3]

Together they created a political party that was pretty much exactly as serious as the name sounded. Rubin, Hoffman, and Krassner quickly became known as the Three Stooges of the movement. Hoffman was given to pronouncements such as "Avoid all needle drugs, the only dope worth shooting is Richard Nixon," and "Sacred cows make the best hamburgers."[4] Jerry Rubin famously uttered pronouncements like "Don't trust anyone over thirty."[5]

Looking back on their behavior, we could easily be led to conclude that they cared more about fame and media attention than the revolution. They did things like going to the New York Stock Exchange and, from the viewing area, throwing money down into the crowd of traders on the floor. At one point, Rubin said, "I'm famous. That's my job."[6] Hoffman maintained, however, that there was a deadly serious purpose to the clowning. He explained their antics by saying that only by reaching the media could they reach the kids, and the best way to attract the cameras was by being outrageous.[7]

The Yippies called for a mass protest when the Democrats met in Chicago. They intended to disrupt the convention and nominate a real pig for president. The political establishment of Chicago did not want them there. The well-publicized conflict between the city and the Yippies guaranteed, as Hoffman and his cohorts wanted, that TV cameras would cover the events widely and thoroughly. Mayor Richard Daley was also aware that TV cameras would be focused on the city and wanted to have a peaceful and quiet convention in his town. He was, in fact, determined to have it. He warned the Yippies to stay away or he would order his cops to shoot to kill.[8] The two teams on the field were playing different games.

Rubin and Hoffman decided to warm up for Chicago by holding a War Is Over Rally down in Greenwich Village, which they billed as a "spring mating service celebrating the equinox, a back-scratching party, a roller-skating rink, a theatre, with you, performer and audience." It would be the start of the Yippies' "Festival of Life," a gathering and celebration that would conclude in Chicago.[9] Shortly before that, Phil Ochs had displayed his own impatience with the ongoing war by declaring it over, ending it in a song called "The War Is Over." He debuted the song at a War Is Over Rally he'd put together in Los Angeles. He had announced the rally in the alternative *Los Angeles Free Press*, saying, "Now some of you may not believe the war is over—and that, essentially, is the problem. The mysterious East has taught us about the occult powers of the mind, and yet we go on accepting our paranoid president's notion that we are actively involved in a war in Asia. Nonsense. It's only a figment of our propagandized imagination, a psychodrama out of *1984*.[10]

17. Impatience Leads to Escalation

The Folk singer Judy Henske, an old friend of Ochs' from the Village days, accompanied him to the rally. With his usual lack of organizational skills, Ochs had not bothered to get a permit for the demonstration, so, in the eyes of the police, his was an unlawful gathering, a mob scene. When Ochs and Henske arrived at the scene, the police were everywhere. A huge crowd of protesters were waiting and Ochs, with the eight months pregnant Henske by his side, led a parade along the Avenue of the Stars. All of the marchers were chanting, "The war is over!" When they reached the rallying ground, an empty lot across from the Century Plaza Hotel, Ochs leaped on the back of a flatbed truck and someone passed him up a guitar. The crowd went crazy and Henske, from the ground, told him "Ochs, you made it ... you're in the big time."

Ochs began to play and sing, getting out the first line of his new song when the cops attacked, charging into the crowd with clubs and bullhorns, demanding that they disperse immediately. Phil Ochs leaped down from the truck's bed, gathered up the pregnant Henske, and together they made it safely out, leaving thousands of demonstrators behind to be clubbed and beaten. Safely back at Henske's house, Ochs was insane with joy. The event had been a huge success, he said, working out exactly the way he'd wanted it to. They watched on the TV news as footage of kids being clubbed by riot police unfolded. Ochs was so happy watching the slaughter you would have thought he had forgotten to get a permit deliberately, just to provoke this reaction.[11]

Now, fresh from his self-perceived triumph, Ochs was back in New York City, where he helped organize and appeared at the Greenwich Village rally, singing his anti-war repertoire and inciting the crowd to come to Chicago, where he promised a free music festival. Rubin and Hoffman then called on the crowd to march on Grand Central Station, which, it turned out, had been the organizers' plan from the start. There they would hold what they called a Yip-in, which would shut the train station down. Exactly how shutting down the main train station into and out of New York City would help end the war was never explained. Nevertheless, excited, the crowd marched uptown.

Don McNeil, a reporter for the *Village Voice*, was on the scene. He had followed the story from the moment when the Yip-in had been announced at a press conference at the Americana Hotel and several thousand handbills had been passed out. In his *Voice* piece, he described how a huge crowd of young people showed up, most coming by subway so that they could get off the train and walk up the stairs into the station. Others marched up from downtown. He wrote that it was "a sea of heads and it was hard to move.... [A]n estimated six thousand people were jammed together under the vaulted ceiling."[12]

At first they gathered peacefully in the station surrounded by cops, but as the hours went by both the police and the Yippies lost patience. Then two demonstrators climbed the information booth that stood in the center of the vast room. There were four great clocks on top of the information booth and the kids removed the hands from them. When they took down the hands of the clocks the police moved in, surrounding the information booth. The demonstrators moved back but evidently not quickly enough, because the police pressed in on them. The two forces clashed like opposing armies. The riot police shut the area down, closing off the side streets to prevent the demonstrators from escaping, and waded into them with clubs and tear gas. It was a riot, quickly and completely growing out of control, one each side blamed on the other. Alan Levine of the New York Civil Liberties Union called it "the most extraordinary display of unprovoked police brutality I've seen outside of Mississippi."[13]

Reporter McNeil showed two policemen his press credentials and reports that they "looked at my credentials, cursed the *Village Voice,* grabbed my arms behind my back and, joined by two others, rushed me back toward the street, deliberately ramming my head into the closed glass doors, which cracked with the impact. They dropped me in the street and disappeared. My face, and my press card, were covered with blood. I went to the hospital to get five stitches in my forehead."[14] In its coverage of the event the *Village Voice* ran a photo of their lead reporter with blood flowing down his face. In his story on the riot McNeil blamed the situation on a lack of planning by both the Yippies and the police. When the Yip founders went to the city to arrange the Yip-in, the city told them they would have to go to the transit authority, since they intended to demonstrate in the train station. For some reason, Hoffman, Rubin, and Ochs did not take this step. Because there was no follow-up from either the Yippies or the city, Ochs was once again in the middle of a mass rally with no permit, an illegal gathering. There was no plan for crowd control on the part of the city. The police attack appeared to be spontaneous and was allowed to quickly spin into a full-fledged riot, on the side of both the police and the demonstrators. The Yip founders also lost control of their own people; they hadn't even brought a bullhorn to use in an effort to communicate with them. This characteristic lack of planning would lead to cracked heads, arrests, bad feelings on each side, and a further breakdown in cooperation between the authorities and the rebels. In just a couple of weeks, it would lead to another riot, another and bigger disaster that would serve to characterize the Democratic convention in Chicago and would later on influence the presidential election.

On to Chicago

Leftists were divided on whether to go to the Yip demonstrations in Chicago. The reasoning behind the division was simple: if Chicago's mayor and his police force were publicly, openly, and loudly stating that the situation was going to be violent, possibly winding up with fatalities, they saw no reason not to believe them. Mayor Daley was not known for his welcoming of dissent, and the Yippies had from their beginning appeared to be more interested in drawing attention to themselves than in ending the war. Their favorite strategy was to engage in deliberately provocative outrage in order to get the TV cameras running. When Abbie Hoffman threw money from the gallery onto the floor of the New York Stock Exchange he had not alerted the media. When he saw how much publicity he got without media attendance, he decided that from then on the cameras would roll whenever he pulled off a work of civil disobedience.[15]

Many members of the New Left didn't see any reason why they should risk their lives to be extras in one of Hoffman's TV productions. Linda, a young idealistic graduate student at Hunter College in New York City, was torn about whether or not she should participate. She knew that the demonstration could lead to trouble. Mayor Daley's public comments, as well as the Yippies' entire philosophy, indicated that the meeting between the two forces might not be peaceful. However, the demonstrators needed her on the line, she said, and she felt she had to go. The organizers needed all the bodies they could gather in order to stay safe; the more of them there were, the lesser the chance of anyone's being hurt. She bought into the safety in numbers idea, not realizing that the larger the number the bigger the threat the Chicago establishment would perceive. She had a more complicated motivation, also: her younger brother was in prison for dodging the draft and if the war ended he might be able to get his sentence commuted, maybe even get a pardon.

This was the American impatience. Even though everything the New Left had done to date had not ended the war, a massive gathering in Chicago might. The New Left, ever optimistic and ever naive, always seemed to feel that they were one demonstration away from success. No matter how many negative outcomes they experienced, they expected the next one to be the one that would radicalize the people, give the New Left a majority, and bring down the establishment. Chicago could do the trick.

The stage was set for violence and disruption from the beginning. For weeks before they came, the Yippies had been open about their intentions, promising to disrupt the convention. They sent out fliers by the thousands, wrote articles, made speeches, and held Yip-ins in Grand Central Station and Central Park to announce that they were coming to Chicago. They threatened to throw nails from overpasses to block traffic, block intersections and streets with parked cars, and block access to police precinct houses. They said they would lace the city's water supply with LSD, take over the convention, and nominate a pig for president.[16] What they announced sounded like the fantasies of middle school boys, so it was no wonder many of their allies had trouble taking their plans seriously and were reluctant to join them.

The Chicago police department, however, took them seriously and promised to stop them. Mayor Daley put his police on twelve-hour shifts, which effectively gave him 50 percent more manpower on the streets. He borrowed riot control equipment from the federal forces, loaded potential trouble spots like Lincoln Park with police in full riot gear, and had the national guard on alert for reinforcements.[17] As Dylan had written, you didn't need a weatherman to know which way the wind blew. A clash between the two forces was inevitable. That clash would be televised; the Yippies would see to that. Since Hoffman, Rubin, Krassner, Ochs, and the others were by now committed to street theater—Hoffman once said the first duty of a revolutionary was to know where the cameras were—they paid more attention to the media than to winning their point. Rubin, especially, was intrigued by the possibility of becoming famous through television.

When the hundreds of thousands of demonstrators the Yip leaders had decided in their heads were coming failed to show up, Hoffman and his other leaders were forced to improvise. Everything came to a head over a flatbed truck. The music festival promised by the Yippies failed to materialize when only the Detroit band MC5 came to the park for the gig, but the organizers decided the show would go on despite the lack of musicians. Their idea was to use a flatbed truck for a stage. The Chicago police, however, would not allow a truck to be driven into the park to serve as a stage or for any other purpose—once again, the Yippies had failed to get permits—so the band

17. Impatience Leads to Escalation

used the electric lines that led to a concession stand to plug in their equipment. The owner complained, demanding they stop using his outlets. While Rubin tried to get another source for sound, Hoffman decided to take matters into his own revolutionary hands by sneaking the truck into the park. The police stopped him and a period of frantic negotiation began that culminated in a compromise; the truck could be parked in the street, next to the park but not in it. When Hoffman went to move the vehicle, the crowd, not having been told that a deal had been made, rushed the truck to prevent its being moved, leaving the police pinned in. Hoffman declared that the police had stopped the festival and the riot that the Chicago gathering had been inevitably headed for broke out.[18] This was on Friday night. Both the police and the demonstrators ran wild in the streets until order was restored Monday morning.

Unlike the Grand Central Station debacle, the Chicago riots were televised. Linda's friends saw her in close-up being beaten to the ground by cops with clubs. The camera caught a tight shot of her face; she looked as though she could not believe what was happening to her.

Chapter 18

The Chicago Seven Get Famous

Because of their actions in Chicago, Yippie founders and anti-war activists Jerry Rubin, Abbie Hoffman, Dave Dellinger, Rennie Davis, John Froines, Lee Weiner, Tom Hayden, and Black Panther Party cofounder Bobby Seale were all arrested for conspiracy and inciting to riot and were ordered to trial in Chicago. The media referred to them as the Chicago Eight until Seale's trial was removed from the others; then they acquired the name they are remembered by today: the Chicago Seven.

In court, the Yippies did what they did best: they turned the trial into a media circus, in which they were the clowns. They made Judge Julius Hoffman the butt of their jokes, insulting him, toying with him, and denigrating him in every way possible. According to Rubin, their treatment of Judge Hoffman was deliberate and planned: "Our strategy was to give Judge Hoffman a heart attack. We gave the court system a heart attack, which is even better."[1] Hoffman and Rubin's antics were increasingly juvenile. When he was sworn in, for example, Abbie Hoffman's raised hand would have his middle finger extended. As a protest against the proceedings he dropped the use of his last name. He called Judge Hoffman a disgrace, saying he would have served Hitler better than he did the defendants, and claimed that Hoffman's "idea of justice is the only obscenity in this room."[2]

William Kuntzler, the attorney for the defense, tried to portray his clients as idealistic victims of police violence, His witness list was frontloaded with celebrities; in a two-week period he called the folk singers Judy Collins and Arlo Guthrie, novelist Norman Mailer, poet Allen Ginsberg, LSD guru Timothy Leary, and, of course, Phil Ochs.[3] Phil Ochs appeared as a "cultural witness." Defense attorney William Kuntzler was anxious to have Ochs testify, feeling his testimony would nail down his defense, which was that people had a right to congregate together, to sing and dance in the streets. At the time of the trial, Ochs' biographer Marc Eliot reports, Ochs was not in great

18. The Chicago Seven Get Famous

shape; he'd been eating Valium pills like M&Ms, having prescriptions from many doctors that he filled in many different drug stores. He thought he was fighting off anxiety attacks but in reality his bipolar illness was getting more pronounced. As his day to testify inched closer, his attacks became more frequent and more severe.

When Ochs was sworn in, Kuntzler asked questions designed to establish that he was a singer. When he asked if Ochs had ever written a song with President Kennedy in it, the prosecutor objected and Judge Hoffman sustained it. Trying another tack, Kuntzler asked if he'd ever appeared on television. Again the prosecutor objected and the judge sustained it. Since Judge Hoffman had not wanted Phil Ochs to participate in the trial at all, he did everything he could to limit the role the singer would play. Ochs did manage to get into the trial record the fact that he had been involved in the formation of the Youth International Party, saying "the idea of Yippie was to be a form of theater politics, a form of theatrically dealing with what seemed to be an increasingly absurd world and trying to deal with it in other than just a straight moral level. They wanted to be able to set out fantasies in the streets to communicate their feeling to the public.[4] Judge Hoffman sustained an objection to that testimony also.

Ochs and Kuntzler had to fight like MMA heavyweights to get any of Ochs' testimony into the record. Finally, Kuntzler turned the topic to Phil's music, wanting Ochs to sing for the court. Handing Ochs his guitar case, Kuntzler established to Judge Hoffman's satisfaction that Phil's guitar was in it. After eliciting testimony that this was the guitar on which Phil had written and sung "I Ain't Marchin' Anymore," Kuntzler asked him sing the song. Judge Hoffman responded as though the defense attorney had asked Ochs to strip naked, absolutely refusing to let Ochs sing. If he had a recording of the song, Hoffman said, then maybe—if they could also prove it was the song that was sung in the park on that occasion—then maybe it would be admissible, but he did not intend to allow any live singing. The witness was prepared to sing it exactly as he sang it that day, Kuntzler claimed. "I am not prepared to listen, Mr. Kuntzler," Judge Hoffman said. Kuntzler did not go down easily. He asked Phil to recite the lyrics, which Ochs did.[5]

Outside the courtroom Ochs found a receptive audience for his song: the gathered media reporters. He was interviewed, sang the song for them, and then rushed back to hotel room to watch himself on the evening news. He was thrilled as he saw himself on *CBS Evening News with Walter Cronkite*. Cronkite was the most popular anchorman in the country and had recently been named as the most trusted man in America. To be on his newscast, Ochs felt, was to reach the pinnacle. His song also made it onto the ABC and NBC newscasts. There he was, singing an anti-war song on the evening news on all three of the network broadcast channels. Ochs could not have been happier.[6]

On February 18, 1970, Abbie Hoffman, Jerry Rubin, Dave Dellinger, and Rennie Davis were found guilty of intent to cross state lines in order to incite a riot. All seven were acquitted on the conspiracy charges. At the sentencing, Abbie Hoffman suggested Judge Hoffman try LSD and offered to hook him up with a dealer. Never a fan of Hoffman's humor, the judge sentenced him and his codefendants to five years and fined them $5,000 each.[7]

Since Judge Hoffman, in his zeal to convict the defendants, had made dozens of legal errors, the court of appeals overturned the convictions. The Chicago Seven walked. All the trial had accomplished was what they had wanted it to: make celebrities of them.

Chapter 19

The New Left Loses Its Credibility

The police riots at the march on Grand Central Station and the Chicago convention had shown the ugly and brutal side of the anti-war debate. By 1968 those qualities had become dominant; the movement was fractured, coming apart. Impatience had driven many activists away and adult hypocrisy had taken its toll.

Lyndon Johnson's vice president, Hubert Humphrey, had wound up with the Democratic nomination as a compromise candidate—by the time the convention rolled around none of the peace candidates who had stepped up against Lyndon Johnson were seen as credible. Eugene McCarthy was perceived as too closely associated with the anti-war movement to maintain any credibility; George McGovern had leaped in late and was seen not as a genuine anti-war advocate but as an opportunist.[1] The only credible alternative candidate, Robert Kennedy, was in the grave, shot down by the assassin Sirhan Sirhan as Kennedy walked through the kitchen of the Ambassador Hotel in Los Angeles where he was holding a rally.[2]

Humphrey was the favorite of the old guard and they still had the clout to see to it that he won the nomination. After the complete mess the Yippies and the police had made of their convention in Chicago, the establishment Democrats had no more sympathy for the New Left. This attitude counted Hubert Humphrey among its adherents. At first, he'd been sympathetic to the youth movement, but Humphrey was a politician, capable of seeing which way the wind was blowing. He had become one of those leaders who discovered the direction in which the people were going, placed himself out in front of the line, and convinced himself they were all following him.

By the 1968 elections, the antics of the Yippies had turned off many of the New Left's previous sympathizers. As the crowd turned against the anti-war movement, Humphrey did, too. He had once been a strong supporter of civil rights but now, as a presidential candidate, he presented himself as the conservative Democrat in the race in order to secure the support of the southern states.[3] At the same time Humphrey had worked inside the hall to nail down the nomination at the convention, the city of Chicago had been exploding outside. The parks and streets of the city overflowed with protestors. In response, Mayor Daley brought 6,000 federal troops and 18,000 members of the Illinois National Guard to subdue them.[4] Humphrey saw his future when he secured the nomination to almost no media coverage because all of the cameras and microphones were out in the streets. The news, both visual and print, was dominated by footage of the police riots going on outside the convention hall.

Life on the campaign trail was no better. When he was introduced at a solidarity march for civil rights, the crowd of 50,000 booed him.[5] Ironically, Humphrey had long been a forceful advocate for civil rights and was the man responsible for adding the civil rights plank to the party platform. Now the very people whose rights he had fought for had turned against him.[6] When he tried to pitch himself as a peace candidate, the booing crowds always reminded him that he was Lyndon Johnson's vice president, tied to the war by his binds to Johnson, who objected whenever Humphrey tried to step out of his shadow. Johnson saw Humphrey's role as a candidate as one of publicly validating Johnson's approach to the war, and the media had a hard time separating the two members of the administration. Humphrey said, "The vice president of the United States is one of the president's advisors, he is not president. And that's the first thing he needs to learn."[7]

The media constantly pointed out the irony of Humphrey's situation; he was being booed by civil rights organizations when, back at the 1948 convention, he was booed by the Dixiecrats for pushing through a civil rights plank in the party platform. By 1968, though, he was being booed by the left because he had muscled in a plank supporting the Vietnam War. That move cost him the support of the anti-war forces, who showed up at his rallies to jeer him. He responded by accusing the young people of using the war issue as "escapism," a move that did not endear him to them.[8]

That remark showed the real problem with Humphrey; since his ambition appeared to the voters to be larger than his convictions and he was losing to Nixon, who claimed to have a secret strategy for ending the war and had succeeded in developing a "southern strategy" that moved the Dixiecrats into the Republican party, Humphrey decided he would be whoever he needed to be to win. He turned solidly against the anti-war movement until his advisers convinced him that he needed their votes to take California and New York. Upon hearing that, he declared in a nationally televised speech that, if elected, he would immediately end the bombing of North Vietnam and arrange a cease-fire.[9]

Humphrey lost, Nixon took the presidency—and under Nixon the war went on for another six years.

The Year That Killed the New Left

Often spoken of as the year that changed everything, 1968 destroyed the dream. The year began with the Tet offensive in Vietnam, an event that was followed by the death of any hope of electing a progressive Democrat who would end the war. That dream was killed when Robert Kennedy was shot. The already split civil rights movement took another, bigger hit when Martin Luther King, Jr., was shot on a hotel room balcony in Memphis. Used to being the underdogs, the New Left suddenly found themselves declared the enemy by the Nixon administration. News that the newly elected president kept an ongoing and growing enemy's list and the fact that many of the New Left as well as the people they respected were named on it caused kids who had already lost faith in their government to feel even further estranged from it.

The election had empowered the forces of what Nixon and his vice president, Spiro Agnew, called the Silent Majority; these were the ordinary middle-class working people the New Left had hoped to radicalize. Instead the Nixon administration radicalized them by successfully painting these leftist kids as the enemy of all things American.[10] If it ever had been, Nixon's majority was no longer silent and its members could not abide the kids who identified with and participated in the anti-war movement. Now, when they mounted a protest or a rally, the New Left did not just have to fear out-of-control policemen; they were just as likely to be attacked by ordinary citizens who did not agree with them. The very people they tried to win over were turning violently against them. The New Left felt that a darkness had fallen upon the land. The already-fractured movement began coming apart like the shell of a soft-boiled egg.

The Music Reflects the Times

If the political scene was becoming dark and dangerous, so was the music. In 1966, at the University of California, Berkeley, where the Free

Part II. "Hey, Hey, LBJ, How Many Kids Did You Kill Today?"

Speech movement had begun, two San Francisco bands, Jefferson Airplane and Mystery Trend, performed at a benefit for the Vietnam Day Committee. The advertising poster shows a war scene, featuring black and white sketches of soldiers trying to escape the exploding bombs being rained down on them from airplanes above. The poster contains the word "Vietnam" at its top, while beneath that the word "peace" has been scrawled. The Airplane and Mystery Trend played psychedelic music in its first association with the movement.[11]

Psychedelic music had evolved from the drug culture. As LSD experimentation spread through the sixties, a music developed that attempted to replicate the visions, hallucinations, and other altered states that acid produced. Often played while accompanied by light shows that flashed almost random images on a screen behind the players, it was an assault on the senses. The guitars were amped up, producing a deliberate distortion and feedback, as screeching electric sounds became part of the musical palate. Eastern instruments, such as the Indian sitar and tabla, were frequently used and the song development relied on extended improvised solos. Structures were more complicated, with frequent modulations and lyrics drug-related. In their song "White Rabbit," the Jefferson Airplane urged its audiences to feed their heads, reminding them that different pills had different effects—some made you grow, others shrank you, but the ones your mother made you take were ineffective.[12] Studio technological effects were extensive.

In 1964 the progressive folk group Holy Modal Rounders probably became the first folkies to apply psychedelic techniques to their music when they recorded a psyched-up version of Charlie Poole's "Hesitation Blues."[13] But it took the work of the Beatles to give the new sound impact in America. They used distortion and feedback in "I Feel Fine" and ladled drug references into their lyrics. The *Sgt. Pepper's Lonely Hearts Club Band* album, especially the track "A Day in the Life," remains a strong example of the form. Where the Beatles led, the Beach Boys followed, and their "Pet Sounds" tried to capture an acid experience on record. But psychedelic music hit a peak with a completely unknown band from Austin, Texas. In 1968 the Thirteenth Floor Elevator captured the zeitgeist with their record "You're Gonna Miss Me." They followed that one up with a string of songs that virtually defined the psychedelic sound. By 1968 anti-war music had become psychedelic. The Chambers Brothers contributed "Time Has Come Today," which in live performance often ran more than nine minutes long, due to its improvised solos. Edwin Starr recorded "War: What Is It Good For?" There were also the Byrds'

19. The New Left Loses Its Credibility

aforementioned "Draft Morning," which for its coda descends into a cacophony of war sounds and distorted instruments, and Jimi Hendrix's guitar workout of "The Star-Spangled Banner."

The psychedelic sound reached a dead end and faded out for two major reasons. One was that the music itself was too repetitive, dependent on electronic effects that soon grew overly familiar, so that it became formulaic and predictable. The second was that an already troubled mind could be blasted into a permanent state of schizophrenia by the use of LSD, which happened in too many cases. Brian Wilson of the Beach Boys, Brian Jones of the Rolling Stones, Roky Erickson from the Thirteenth Floor Elevator, Peter Green from Fleetwood Mac and Syd Barrett from Pink Floyd were among the many who became acid casualties and found their lives shattered by the drug.[14] Thousands of ordinary citizens had their minds dismantled by it also.

Despite the failure of psychedelic music, the very nature of the protest song changed. The West Coast Pop Art Experimental Band applied psychedelic influences to their weirdly odd "Suppose They Gave a War and Nobody Came," which they described in a spoken introduction as an African tribal chant that they wrote. Over African drumbeats, a throbbing bass line, and drone-like electric guitars, they chanted the title continually through the song and wrapped it up with the sound of a crying baby. Creedence Clearwater contributed "Fortunate Son," the lyrics of which spoke about the way the rich got draft deferments while the poor had to go off to fight the war. Joan Baez took a poem by Nina Dusheck and wrote music for it. The result was "Saigon Bride," about a young soldier forced to say good-bye to his Saigon bride to go fight the enemy. Why? The narrator says the reasons won't matter when they are dead. As she usually did, Baez discussed the war in terms of the people it affected rather than as an act of policy. Jazz singer Nina Simone also found inspiration in a poem. Taking Langston Hughes' "Backlash Blues" as her model, she changed it from a civil rights poem into an anti–Vietnam War song. All of these songs were electric folk-rock, several of them exhibiting strains of psychedelic effects, which it turned out were perfect for replicating the sounds of war.

In 1964 Buffy Sainte-Marie had written "Universal Soldier," a song about how each of us is responsible for war and how the old way of thinking about international issues leads to death and destruction. Released on her first album, the recording of the song became very well known among a small circle of folk singers and their followers but never generated a large following among the general public, remaining no more than a minor hit that failed to break though to mass acclaim. A year later, the British folk singer Donovan released a cover of the song as a single and this time the mass record-buying audience was more receptive. Donovan's version became a major hit, reaching number fifty-three on the Billboard charts.

"Universal Soldier" is unique in that its lyrics claim that we are all responsible for war. Instead of being the innocent victims of out-of-control governments, we are actually coconspirators—we support the wars. Even if we oppose them, our silence and our refusal to act on our beliefs prove that we, when we get right down to it—and contrary to our words—actively support them. We fight the wars, and when we attempt to refuse to fight we run to another country instead of standing and fighting for our right to resist. And we refuse to accept the consequences of our attitudes and behaviors. Buffy Saint-Marie says that we can't just sit back and blame our elders. Before we can change the situation, we have to recognize our part in it.[15]

By 1968, though, the New Left had lost the ability to make that distinction. Instead of taking responsibility, the various groups blamed each other. It appeared as if they had decided that if they could not win over the public at large and could not demand that the government stop the war, then they would fight each other. They had learned that, although they had freedom of speech, America at large had no responsibility and little desire to listen. The right to free speech also guaranteed the listener the right to ignore what was being said. The New Left did not know how to handle that knowledge and many of its members were too impatient to learn to live with it. Taking a cue from the Yippies, the New Left got the enemy plainly in its sights but then turned their guns on themselves. From then on, protestors who had lost their sense of direction would have to listen to music that had also lost its way.

Chapter 20

The Shift in Academia
What Is Relevant?

As we have seen, 1968 was a year of change. All of the various threads that made up radicalism in America seemed to coalesce at the same time and the result was a society far from what it had been. As a result of the murders of leaders such as Malcolm X and Dr. Martin Luther King, Jr., riots were erupting in our major cities. The Black Power movement, which included Black Panthers and other African-American movement groups, successfully stole the thunder from SDS and the other white radical groups. That movement, with its emphasis on self-reliance, encouraged a shift away from any alliances with any white groups and empowered African Americans:

> The Black Power movement instilled a sense of racial pride and self-esteem in blacks. Blacks were told that it was up to them to improve their lives. Black Power advocates encouraged blacks to form or join all-black political parties that could provide a formidable power base and offer a foundation for real socioeconomic progress. For years, the movement's leaders said, blacks had been trying to aspire to white ideals of what they should be. Now it was time for blacks to set their own agenda, putting their needs and aspirations first. An early step, in fact, was the replacement of the word "Negro" (a word associated with the years of slavery) with "black."
>
> The movement generated a number of positive developments. Probably the most noteworthy of these was its influence on black culture. For the first time, blacks in the United States were encouraged to acknowledge their African heritage. Colleges and universities established black studies programs and black studies departments. Blacks who had grown up believing that they were descended from a backwards people now found out that African culture was as rich and diverse as any other, and they were encouraged to take pride in that heritage. The Black Arts movement, seen by some as connected to the Black Power movement flourished in the 1960s and 1970s. Young black poets, authors, and visual artists found their voices and shared those voices with others. Unlike earlier black arts movements such as the Harlem Renaissance, the new movement primarily sought out a black audience.[1]

The movement itself, for all of its effects as a positive force, was riddled with factions; the more radical members saw their more conservative members who advocated nonviolence and negotiation as sell-outs and "Uncle Toms." Many of them, it appeared, would rather be pure than successful. Some observers, however, view these schisms more as categories than divisions:

> "I would see them as complementary more so than anything else," says Gerald Horne, the John J. and Rebecca Moore Chair of History and African American Studies at the University of Houston. The prolific historian is author of over 30 books, including the upcoming "Facing the Rising Sun: African Americans, Japan and the Rise of Afro-Asian Solidarity." While noting the limited analytical value of such a conventional two-tiered construct, Horne says, "I think they both played a role" and both had "their assets and their liabilities."
>
> "They are interrelated struggles and the one grows out of the other," says Paul Coates, owner of Black Classic Press, one of the oldest Black-owned publishing institutions in the country. The former black power leader notes how the civil rights movement recedes in the late '60s as "what we look at as the Black Power movement really comes in to fore" with the "more confrontational extension of demands" for Black liberation and human rights. Coates clarifies "they are connected and part of the same struggle."[2]

While the Black Power movement was rising, SDS itself was splintering. New members, younger and more aggressive than the old hands, were splitting the group apart, creating a crisis of factionalism and therefore causing many of its leaders to wonder whether they were even relevant anymore.

Todd Gitlin, an SDS leader, wrote to Carol McEldowney, another leader, that he had been talking with other members about the end of the movement. McEldowney replied, describing what Gitlin called a mix of desperation and bravado and saying that all of the action now was coming from African-American radicals and she did not know if there was a place for white people anymore.[3] Having nowhere else to go, the young white radicals turned on the universities. At this time, Tom Hayden says, "Campuses around the world exploded with spontaneous and uncoordinated student occupation of campus buildings, the only method by which students might gain leverage against their uncaring administrations. The revolt made the Port Huron Statement seem mild. This was the lunch counter sit-in extended to the liberal north and the free speech movement gone global, exposing the complicity of the universities within the larger system."[4]

It is questionable how spontaneous and uncoordinated the student strike at Columbia really was. In March of 1967 Columbia law student and SDS organizer Bob Feldman, while doing research in the college library, came across some documents that struck him as interesting. What he found was a sheaf of papers describing Columbia's work with the Institute for Defense Analysis, a weapons research think tank that reported to the Defense Department. SDS made the connection public by submitting articles by Feldman to left-wing publications. The group also led a series of protests that continued for a solid year, demanding that Columbia shed the affiliation. The university responded by placing six ringleaders of the demonstrations on probation.[5]

At this same time, Columbia—which had a history of callous treatment of the African-American population who lived in the neighborhood (a few years earlier they had evicted 7,000 Harlem residents from properties the college owned)—made another move that was widely viewed as insensitive and deliberately racist: they planned to build and operate a whites-only gym in Morningside Park.[6] This time, instead of banning people of color from the buildings the college owned, they would ban them from a property that belonged to the city in which they all lived. Although not much help in doing it was necessary, SDS helped stir up outrage about this plan. For months the park and the campus overflowed with protestors. In the face of massive protests, Columbia altered their plans; they would add a basement community facility that Harlem residents could enter from the Harlem side of the building. Local residents would be able to use the lower level of the building without a white person ever seeing them. Neighborhood residents did not see this compromise as much of a solution. They referred to the building as "Gym Crow" and continued to picket the construction site.[7]

After police arrested demonstrators who tried to stop the construction of the gym, members of SDS and Student Afro Society marched on, and occupied, Hamilton Hall, where the Columbia administration had its offices. Together the two groups held the building overnight, but in the morning the SAS shocked the white protesters by demanding that they leave. Tensions rose between the groups and for a while they occupied separate areas of the building. But finally the white protesters left, taking over Low Library, which housed the president's office, and immediately occupied it.[8]

Mason, Barry's former roommate and the man who prompted my involvement in the Woolworth demonstration many years back, was a student at Hunter College when Columbia was taken over. At a Jefferson Airplane concert on his campus, mimeographed fliers were passed around—take advantage of other people's crowds, Abbie Hoffman had said, to get your own message across. The fliers asked that, as a display of solidarity, students come and join the protesters at Columbia. Mason decided to go. When he arrived at Low Library he saw what looked more like a fraternity party than a serious demonstration. Students lounged everywhere in the president's office. New SDS leader David Shapiro propped his feet up on the president's desk while he smoked a cigar from the collection he found in a desk drawer and toyed with the stuff he found on top of it. A couple of dozen people sat on the floor and a young man was snoring loudly, stretched out on the carpet like a corpse. Someone had brought in beer and many occupiers were drinking from cans. Other protestors were giggling like twelve-year-olds as they passed joints around.

The crowd was not all Columbia students—or students from any college. Street hippies, older activists, and neighborhood people were there, as well as an actor from an afternoon soap opera. A Village folkie tried unsuccessfully to lead the crowd in singing "We Shall Not Be Moved," and Tom Hayden, who was equally unsuccessful in trying to whip up the emotions of the crowd, tried to organize them into a coherent, unified band instead of the lackadaisical mob Mason felt they were rapidly becoming. He said later it was as if they'd been caught up in Oz's poppy fields and could not stay awake.

Acting dean Henry S. Coleman came to the building to negotiate with the demonstrators but told the protestors he had no control over the demands they were making and even if he had he was not about to give in to any demand under conditions like these. He was taken hostage, held in his office for twenty-four hours, and then released.[9] Most Columbia students shared the goals of the takeovers but despised the tactics. Three hundred students called themselves the Majority Coalition and formed a living chain around Low Library. Anyone who wanted to, they said, could leave under their protection, but no one could go in and no supplies would be allowed past them. When a group of protestors tried to crash through their line, fights broke out. That was the administration's and the New York government's last straw. Police were called in to clear the buildings. During the police siege the SAS was treated differently from the white SDS. African-American lawyers waited outside Hamilton Hall to represent the departing SAS protestors and a squad of African-American police officers cleared the building peacefully. White demonstrators, though, faced police violence, which led to student-police battles. Four faculty members, one hundred thirty-two students, and twelve cops were injured. Seven hundred protestors were hauled off to jail.[10] For the rest of the semester, no regular classes were held at Columbia. Instead, the school offered "Liberation classes," featuring celebrities such as Allen Ginsberg, the Grateful Dead, and Country Joe and the Fish.

The rebellion spread and appeared at other colleges at about the same time. Students occupying administration buildings and marching through the streets in front of their campuses became a familiar sight. These rebellions

20. The Shift in Academia

generally centered on the fact that the curriculum appeared to be irrelevant to the lives students were living. The driving word became "relevance," as students demanded a curriculum that actually made a difference to alienated lives in a nihilistic time: what they studied now seemed to have nothing to do with life as it was actually lived. On their own, English majors were reading Vonnegut, Brautigan, Fitzgerald, Faulkner, and the rest of the twentieth-century texts, but the most modern author their coursework studied was the early American Gothic author Charles Brockton Brown. Psychology students studied B.F. Skinner, a man who, as educator James Herndon said, could make a pigeon do anything he wanted it to but didn't know a damn thing about pigeons.[11] Cutting-edge psychologists like Carl Rogers were ignored. Art students were being forced to paint representative landscapes at a time when light shows, "happenings," and multimedia extravaganzas ruled and artists like Jackson Pollock, Andy Warhol, Roy Lichtenstein, and Willem de Kooning showed a new way. Modern poetry was challenging the assumptions of what poetry was and where it came from, but the departments were still arguing about whether T.S. Eliot should be considered American or British.

Most people said that time travel was impossible but that to set foot in a major college was to travel back to the nineteenth century. Students felt they deserved better and began to demand better. Songs advocating personal freedom bloomed like weeds. The Rascals caught the tenor of the times when they sang "People Got to Be Free," while Steppenwolf declared we were all "Born to Be Wild." Jim Post, singing with his wife as Friend and Lover, made the top ten with a pro-peace song, "Reach Out of the Darkness," while the Animals came out with a powerful psychedelic diatribe about the futility of war: "Sky Pilot." The Beatles tried to bring a little sanity to the table with their song "Revolution," which pointed out how wrongheaded the self-styled revolutionary approach was.

Other than their themes, what did these songs have in common? They all used elements of psychedelic sounds, like feedback and fuzztone guitars, all were progressive, and all were as fragmented as the movement they both described and spoke to. The movement was not only splitting into two racially divided forces, it was also losing its focus, as a result losing not only its supporters but its direction and purpose.

Part III
Burn, Baby, Burn

Chapter 21

Radicalism in Both Politics and Music Dies

By the end of the turning point year, conditions had changed for the most prominent folk musicians who were widely associated with the movement. Joan Baez was trying to build a marriage with anti-draft activist David Harris, who a year earlier had formed the Resistance, a group that tried to get young men to fight the draft by returning their draft cards, refusing to be inducted. Harris's concentration was on attempting to end the war. As his efforts met with some degree of success, the federal law enforcement agencies began paying more attention to him. Baez at this time supported Harris's actions and tried to meld a marriage with radical politics. Soon Harris was serving a prison sentence because of his political activities.

Bob Dylan, having been off the scene for eighteen months due to his motorcycle accident, returned with a new persona as a country crooner, issuing *Nashville Skyline,* which included a duet on "Girl from the North Country" with his friend Johnny Cash. He followed that up with *John Wesley Harding*, another country-themed album. Joan Baez recorded a song urging him to give the crooning up and return to protest writing and singing, a request Dylan ignored.

Peter, Paul and Mary, faced with declining record sales and having learned from their failed attempt to sway the nomination to McCarthy that their power was more an existential illusion than a real factor, broke up. Mary Travers did solo albums that avoided politics. Paul Stookey, who had over the years returned to his religion, formed a Christian band and recorded praise songs. Peter Yarrow married Eugene McCarthy's daughter and remained a familiar sight at anti-war demonstrations, playing and singing without his partners.

Phil Ochs claimed not to be interested in topical songs any longer and moved from New York to Los Angeles, signing with A&M Records, which gave him an opportunity to pursue a goal he'd stated he'd made back in 1965: "I'm at the point in my songwriting where I give much more consideration to the art involved in my songs rather than the politics. I'm trying to weld sharper, more cogent, and more original use of language and music. The messages in my songs are now secondary to that part of my mind that creates."[1]

The riots in Chicago, the trial of the Chicago Seven, the assassinations of Martin Luther King, Jr., and Robert Kennedy, and Richard Nixon's election had worn Ochs out and made him despondent, convincing him that people no longer even listened to the type of protest songs he had specialized in. Ochs lost his political focus, moved to Los Angeles, and recorded *Pleasures of the Harbor* in 1967, following it with *Tape from California* in 1968. Both albums used a full orchestra and elements of folk rock to put across songs that were far more personal and private than his New York protest material. Ochs described the albums as "baroque-folk."[2] They neither sold well nor were well received critically. Critic Robert Christgau said *Pleasures of the Harbor* "epitomized the decadence that has infected pop since Sergeant Pepper. The gaudy musical settings inspire nostalgia for the three chord strum."[3] The commercial and critical failure of what he considered his most important work to date affected Ochs greatly. Creatively lost and precariously balanced mentally, he was drinking too much and his bipolar disorder was acting up. His lifestyle had packed the pounds on him and he was embarrassed by the weight he had gained, which caused him to retreat even more deeply into alcohol.

The New Left Loses Its Way

The movement was having as much trouble with its own identity as Phil Ochs was with his. In fact, it shattered like a dropped light bulb. SDS after Columbia split into factions. The more conservative members wanted to continue the protests, while the ones who identified with radicalism declared that protesting was a dead and ineffective policy and wanted to escalate. The two groups tried to coexist for a while but that strategy didn't work. Soon the more radical of the factions dubbed themselves the Weather Underground, or the Weathermen—inspired by a line about a weatherman in Bob Dylan's song "Subterranean Homesick Blues"—and started on a course of violent confrontations. In 1970 alone the Weather Underground and their followers detonated more than 330 bombs inside the United States.[4] America's own citizens were blowing up other Americans' property. It was a long ride from peaceful protests to almost daily acts of terrorism. What had happened to cause young activists to board that train?

There is no single answer. A partial explanation can be found in the Nixon administration's attitude toward protest groups, both black and white. In a 1994 interview John Erlichman, Nixon's chief domestic affairs adviser, remembered the following:

> The Nixon campaign in 1968, and the Nixon White House after that, had two enemies: the anti-war left and black people. You understand what I'm saying? We knew we couldn't make it illegal to be either against the war or black, but by getting the public to associate the hippies with marijuana and blacks with heroin, and then criminalizing both heavily, we could disrupt those communities. We could arrest their leaders, raid their homes, break up their meetings, and vilify them night after night on the evening news. Did we know we were lying about the drugs? Of course we did.[5]

Not only did the administration know it was lying, but the movement knew it also. Nixon's attitude was another betrayal. New Left paranoia increased; the people who had adopted as a mantra "never trust anyone over thirty" now lost the ability to trust anyone at all, including each other. As Todd Gitlin wrote, the Chicago convention had exposed the Democrats as Democrats; it had shown that the two-party system was frozen against reform and that the movement was essentially arguing with itself.[6]

Growing less, rather than more, popular, having failed in its attempt to radicalize the middle class, the people of the movement were, according to Gitlin, either blind to the negative effects they were having on the public at large or convinced that losing the support of the people was a good thing, proof of what Gitlin called "our revolutionary mettle."[7] The radicals decided, by some Orwellian logic, that failing was winning. By 1969 SDS, having been driven into the wilderness by the riots at the 1968 Democratic convention, crumbled like stale cake. The members of the movement had been forced to watch helplessly as the Democrats, whom they had previously thought of as allies, sent forth Hubert Humphrey, a candidate who promptly turned against them until he needed them, using his candidacy to advocate for Lyndon Johnson's policies. The two peace candidates, Eugene McCarthy and George McGovern, both more friendly toward the young radicals, were ignored like the working class under Nixon. At the October 1968 SDS convention in Boulder, Colorado, John Jacobs argued for direct violent action, introducing a resolution entitled "The Elections Don't Mean Shit—Vote Where the Power Is—Our Power Is in the Street."[8] The resolution was adopted and the split of the organization into competing factions was now complete.

When Gitlin argued for organizing over mobilizing, Weatherman Mark Rudd, demonstrating characteristic impatience, declared that organizing was

21. Radicalism in Both Politics and Music Dies

just another word for going slow. By the end of 1968 the fact that an action was dangerous became a badge of seriousness. "Chaos in the streets was an arguable strategy for the not-so-modest purpose of ending the war; now it was being touted as more: a prologue to revolution."[9] The idea that an armed resurrection against the government would succeed in overthrowing it and replacing it with a left-leaning regime was, of course, patently absurd. Yet the Weather Underground took it seriously, believing that the revolution was within reach and that just a few more firebombs were needed for it to come into existence. Those SDS people advocating direct action joined the Weathermen, and the few remaining members who stuck with organizing tried to coexist with the ones advocating immediate violent action. Like so much else with the New Left, the cooperation between the two factions ended in Chicago, this time in October of 1969.

The Black Power movement had given birth to the Black Panthers, a group given to wearing paramilitary uniforms, carrying firearms, and monitoring the activities of the police. At first the core activity of the Panthers was organizing programs to help African-American citizens. They were known for sponsoring free breakfasts for children and providing security in their neighborhoods. J. Edgar Hoover, though, could see nothing noble in the group and declared them to be "the greatest threat to the internal security of the country."[10] He set out to destroy the party and, although the effort took him almost ten years, he succeeded. Meanwhile, though, the sight of armed uniformed black men patrolling the ghetto streets and holding rallies to teach the African-American poor armed self-defense created a sense of excitement in young white radicals, who by now had self-styled themselves as revolutionaries. They admired the Panthers and, like children looking up at their fathers, wanted to be just like them.

The Weathermen decided to bring Lyndon Johnson's tactic home: they would end the war by escalating the war on our shores. They reasoned that only when America experienced what Vietnam had gone through and had seen their cities burning would they understand. Then they would not only stop the war, the middle class would also rise up and overthrow the government. To understand this reasoning it has to be understood that these men and women were young and had been taught in their colleges and universities—the site of most of their experiences—that ideas were primary. They could quote left-wing philosophers but had not learned the critical thinking necessary to see through empty abstract notions. Most of them were still, although they would not have been able to recognize the trait in themselves, believers in magical thinking.

Part III. Burn, Baby, Burn

The rallying cry of the Weather Underground became "bring Hanoi to America" and they began building and detonating bombs in banks, corporate headquarters, government buildings, and even private homes, thinking those actions would bring about their goal of creating a revolutionary party that would overthrow the United States government. In 1970 they officially declared themselves the Weather Underground Organization and issued a declaration of war against the United States. Their founding document described them as a white fighting force connected to the Black Liberation Movement and other radical movements with the goal of the destruction of U.S. imperialism and the achievement of a classless world: world communism.[11] John Jacobs stated the goals of the weather underground this way: "Weathermen would shove the war down their dumb, fascist throats and show them, while we were at it, how much better we were than them, both tactically and strategically, as a people. In an all-out civil war over Vietnam and other fascist U.S. imperialism, we were going to bring the war home. 'Turn the imperialists' war into a civil war,' in Lenin's words. And we were going to kick ass."[12] They saw "the onset of a sustained armed struggle against the state as the best means of creating revolutionary consciousness among the mass of American people."[13]

Origins of the Weather Underground Organization

This group did not come about by accident or impulse. As noted, by 1969 the Weathermen, seeing SDS as ineffectual and unwilling to take direct action and beyond contempt, had split from them, going off on their own. Their first major action took them back to Chicago's Lincoln Park. Earlier they had blown up the statue commemorating the policemen killed in the 1886 Haymarket Riots. At this point, the group had not gained much firsthand knowledge about explosives, and the blast was too big. In addition to destroying the statue, it blew out 100 windows, scattering debris from the statue onto the Kennedy Expressway.[14] Declaring the action a success, the group decided to build upon it by bringing thousands of demonstrators back to Chicago in an effort to overwhelm the police and local officials.

As Burroughs reports, the gathering was a disaster. A disappointing crowd of 800 showed up, but 2,000 policemen attended. Badly outnumbered, the casual demonstrators promptly left. The next day the Weathermen's crowd size was down to 300, while the law enforcement crew still numbered 2,000. Tom Hayden spoke, assuring the crowd that the Chicago Seven stood behind them, but Abbie Hoffman and John Froines, two other members of the Chicago Seven, showed up, viewed the situation and quietly disappeared. It was one of the few times Hoffman was able to resist a microphone and a crowd.

At ten-thirty at night, event organizer John Jacobs gave a signal and the crowd started toward their destination, the Drake Hotel, where Chicago Seven judge Julius Hoffman lived. The Weathermen flowed over the Gold Coast like baseball fans after the Cubs won the World Series. However, their purpose was not to celebrate but to destroy. They smashed car windows and shop windows, trashing the houses and businesses of the very people they wanted to radicalize and win to their side. The crowd hit the police barricades but by now they were so pumped with adrenaline that they didn't even slow down. It was like the Charge of the Light Brigade. Three hundred protestors attacked 1,000 armed riot police and were wiped out. One contingent managed to reach the hotel, where they encountered unmarked cars of policemen who began firing into the crowd. The cops waded into the Weathermen and beat them with clubs. Within 30 minutes the riot had been put down. Twenty-four policemen were injured, six Weathermen were shot, and 68 were arrested. No one knows how many were beaten and injured.

When he got out of jail, John Jacobs said the night was a great victory. They didn't have to win. Just the fact that they were willing to fight the police made it a success.[15]

How Could the Impulse to Revolution Have Happened?

At this point, 50 years later, the entire transformation from protesters to revolutionaries appears to be completely illogical and perhaps more rooted in fantasy than in politics. How could otherwise intelligent people buy into the pulp fiction cliché that the American people would rise up en masse against their government and overthrow it violently? It has to be understood that those were crazy times. The nation was fighting an illegal war, one that everyone knew was being lost although the government every day declared the nation to be within minutes of winning it. Che Guevara, who had helped Fidel Castro overthrow the Baptista regime in Cuba, was now in the mountains of South America leading armed revolts against other governments. He had become a role model for young American revolutionaries, their symbol of rebellion. When the Cuban revolution became successful, Guevara became a leader of the new government, establishing a program of land reform and a campaign to spread literacy among the peasants. His books *The Motorcycle Diaries* and *Guerrilla Warfare* became best sellers and were widely read by America's New Left activists,

Guevara was a complicated man. During the Cuban revolution, he would read the works of Robert Louis Stevenson and the Spanish lyric poets to his men between firefights. When he discovered that 40 percent of the Cubans were illiterate, he began teaching literacy classes and the members of his army who could read taught the others. Yet he could also execute an enemy or an AWOL soldier without compunction.[16] This man inspired the Weather Underground.

The emergence of the youth counterculture, which was in full bloom, also contributed to the move toward revolution. Strange and odd cults and religions were springing up everywhere. The Beatles became followers of Maharishi Yogi, founder of Transcendental Meditation. Gurus flocked to America, setting up ashrams throughout the country. Chicago Seven member Rennie Davis was a follower of Guru Raj, a fifteen-year-old boy, of whom he said during the trial, "All I want to do is lay my head on his foot for as long as he'll let me. Sometimes he lets me."[17] Admired musicians such as Carlos Santana were joining ashrams.

LSD, peyote, and other hallucinogens were as common as seaweed in the ocean and everyone was convinced Richard Nixon was tapping their phone. On top of this, the Cold War was raging and John Lennon and his new wife Yoko Ono held a "bed-in" for peace, during which they lay in their bed for a couple of weeks, spending their honeymoon entertaining the press by trying to explain how occupying a bed in a hotel room in Canada could end the Vietnam War. While in that bed, they recorded "Give Peace a Chance."[18] It was a world gone mad, and in that context the actions of the Black Panthers and the Weathermen seemed almost normal.

From Demonstrators to Criminals

The appearance of normality disappeared when the violence escalated from symbolic protest to crime. In September two members of the Weather Underground, Katherine Ann Power and William Saxe, joined two ex-convict Black Panthers, William Gilday and Robert Valerie, in robbing the State Street Bank and Trust in Newbury, Massachusetts. Emboldened by their success, they raided a national guard armory. They stole weapons and ammunition and set fire to the building, causing $125,000 in damages, then used their new weapons a few days later to rob another bank. This time, Gilday killed a policeman who tried to break up the robbery.[19] In November members of the Weather Underground fired shots into a Cambridge police station but no one was injured in that attack.[20] These actions were intended to win young people over to the Weather Underground Organization (WUO). They did not. Many of the attempts to win over the young, when they were not criminal, were childish and silly. Weathermen led what they called "jailbreaks" in which they invaded high schools and ran through the halls shouting anti-war slogans.[21] They did this without any embarrassment or irony. When it wasn't murderous, the movement was filled with look-at-me bravado. In many ways it was schizophrenic.

Music Can't Capture the Times

The times were too crazy to be summed up in song. The music reflected the craziness. King Crimson recorded "21st Century Schizoid Man," while Steppenwolf celebrated the "Draft Resister." The Rolling Stones protested the war with "Gimme Shelter" and cheered on the revolutionaries with "Street Fighting Man." Even bluesman John Lee Hooker sang against the war in "I Don't Wanna Go to Vietnam." Poet Ed Sanders recognized that music had power that printed poetry did not, so he formed a band, the Fugs, who captured the Orwellian use of language that had crept into vogue with "Kill for Peace." Avant garde rocker Lou Reed offered up "Kill Your Sons," and Tom Paxton checked in with "Talkin' Vietnam Pot Luck Blues." Those songs pointed out the absurd side of Vietnam, saying we had reached a point where the truth could be grasped only through fantasy.

Yet, even while the music became more existential, the more traditional anti-war songs could still be heard, if from surprising sources. Melanie gave us "Lay Down (Candles in the Rain)" and "Peace Will Come (According to Plan)." Bobby Darin reached the sophisticated nightclub audience with "A Simple Song of Freedom." The music, then, was all over the place—as fragmented and scattered as the movement was. Todd Gitlin laments the turn away from radicalism that he found in the music as the revolution went on, saying Bob Dylan had "slid over to Tin Pan Alley pieces ('Love is all you need/it makes the world go round') in the 1969 *Nashville Skyline*, including a duo with no less a mainstream idol than Johnny Cash. To partisans who remembered his acoustic heartfelt period, Dylan's calm sounded smug, tranquilized. To settle his quarrel with the world, he had filed away his passions. Joan Baez also borrowed the sweet twang of country and western guitars; so did Arlo Guthrie, who by 1972 had removed himself from the no-man's-land of 'Alice's Restaurant' to the heartland 'City of New Orleans.'"[22]

What happened to cause a shift from serious topical music, either electric or acoustic, to a more mundane style of rock to the rise of the singer-songwriter genre in the seventies? There is, of course, no single answer. Like the movement itself, it was the result of a confluence of events. However, looming high on the list was the British Invasion of the mid-sixties, which brought to the American airwaves and record shops acts like the Beatles, the Rolling Stones, Chad and Jeremy, Peter and Gordon, Manfred Mann, the Troggs, Donovan, the Kinks, and Wayne Fontana & the Mindbenders. Even though the members of most of these bands had begun as acoustic folk singers or, in England, skiffle artists, their emergence as self-contained rock bands who wrote, played, sang, and produced their own records severely damaged the acoustic movement in the States. It wasn't really Bob Dylan who killed traditional unamplified folk music; it was the exciting new music from England.

Perhaps because the Vietnam War wasn't as all-consuming in England, fewer items of anti-war protest material emerged from the British Invasion. British musicians were more likely to attack the class system that held so much power in Europe. The Animals' "We've Got to Get Out of This Place," about a young couple slowly being beaten down by the rough conditions of their lives, serves as an example. The psychedelic culture was dominant among the musicians and their working-class followers. As strong in England as it was here, the psychedelic culture created bands—like the Animals, the Who, Cream, and Pink Floyd—who became known for performing in that genre and kept the dead end going longer than it would have had it been just a domestic scene.

The British Invasion brought all of the elements that would become folk-rock to the forefront. Until their music crossed the Atlantic, rock was considered dead in America and folk flourished. The music of women played a minor role; they were confined by male producers to singing trivial songs about trivial events, like Leslie Gore's "It's My Party (and I'll Cry if I Want To)" and Connie Francis's "Stupid Cupid." Emboldened by the new and different sounds emanating from freeform FM radio, female artists fought to enlarge their musical palette. By 1969 they had established themselves as serious folk-rock singer-songwriters. *Newsweek* ran a feature called "The Girls—Letting Go," which covered Joni Mitchell, Laura Nyro, Lotti Golden, and Melanie, all of whom were writing and singing songs shrouded in private symbolism and mystery, songs with depth and meaning, all with one thing in common: they explored the artists' heads as much as they did society at large. These songs were more internal than external.[23] While the revolution took place in the streets, these songs took place in the heart.

When the psychedelic experiments led nowhere, the bands that had relied on the effects either broke up or changed their approach so that by the end of the decade, roots rock had taken hold. This genre blended rock, country, the blues, and folk music into a new whole, one that covered a wide range and spread in as many directions as the movement itself did.

Once again, Bob Dylan is credited with beginning it. He had gone to Nashville against his record company's wishes and made *Blonde on Blonde* with that city's best studio musicians, including Hargus "Pig" Robbins, Kenneth Buttrey, Charlie McCoy, Bill Aikens, and Joe South. Al Kooper, who played organ throughout the album, was the only musician brought down from New York. Dylan later told *Playboy* magazine that the songs on *Blonde on Blonde* were the closest he ever came to matching the sound he heard in his mind.[24] Dylan's songs were as private and mysterious as he once had been public and straightforward, exploring his mind and heart instead of commenting on issues. To show the degree of his influence, consider this. A few months before the album was released a member of a well-known New York band was asked what his group was up to. He responded that, just like everybody else, they were waiting to see what Dylan was going to do next.

One thing was for certain, what Dylan did next would have nothing to do with fighting the police in the streets, breaking car and shop widows, or blowing up buildings. Few strong artists wanted to be associated with activities like those. Not only had the movement lost the support of the American people, it had also lost the musicians who used to inspire it.

The Art of Opposites

Neil Postman, in his book, *Teaching as a Conservative Activity*, claimed that in order to preserve homeostasis and stability in a culture "education tries to conserve tradition when the rest of the environment is innovative. Or it is innovative when the rest of society is tradition-bound.... [T]he function of education is always to offer the counterargument, the other side of the picture.... Its aim at all times is to make visible the prevailing biases of a culture and then, by employing whatever philosophies of education are available, to oppose them."[25] His argument might be applied to art in general. Therefore, as the culture came apart, as the center refused to hold and chaos became the norm, as the movement grew more violent, the music became quieter, more introspective, as if it were rejecting the politics of the day and expressing the peaceful calm that was missing from society at large. The New England folk singer Tom Rush is credited with starting the singer-songwriter movement by releasing his album *The Circle Game* in 1968. On it, he recorded for the first time songs by Joni Mitchell, Jackson Browne, and James Taylor, paving the way for those artists to be able to record their own first albums. *The Circle Game* became Rush's most popular album and the interest it generated caused record companies to rush to sign folkies.

As usual, the Beatles were out in front. Having formed the Apple Corporation to handle their business affairs, as one of the first acts of their new company they issued the debut album by James Taylor, a calm and laid-back affair that consisted mostly of folk and countrified ballads such as "Carolina in My Mind," a song about the singer's longing to be back home, "Sunshine, Sunshine," and "Something in the Way She Moves," love songs both previously sung by Rush on *The Circle Game*, and "Rainy Day Man." The *Rolling Stone* reviewer called the album "the coolest breath of fresh air I've inhaled in a long time. It knocks me out."[26] There was no way, though, that the album could have been considered a political statement.

Taylor's friend Carole King, who had written songs protesting the nothingness of suburban life ("Pleasant Valley Sunday") released *Tapestry,* an album of quiet, introspective material that contained songs like "You've Got a Friend," "Where You Lead," "So Far Away," and "Beautiful," as well as her own versions of songs she'd written for artists like Aretha Franklin ("You Make Me Feel Like a Natural Woman," and the Shirelles ("Will You Love Me Tomorrow?"). The only thing political about the album was its complete lack of politics, almost like a rejection. *Tapestry* won critical raves. Richard Goldstein called it an album that would, because of its lack of technical decorum, liberate female singers.[27] It sold well from the beginning and has become one of the biggest sellers of all time, moving 25,000,000 copies to date.

By the late sixties and early seventies the resurgence of folk music was complete. Singer-songwriters dominated FM radio and the charts. Artists such as John Stewart, Cat Stevens, Carly Simon, Jesse Winchester, Hoyt

21. Radicalism in Both Politics and Music Dies

Axton, Gene Clark, Nick Drake, Van Morrison, Laura Nyro, Neil Young, the Eagles, the Nitty Gritty Dirt Band, Jim Croce, Linda Ronstadt, J.D. Souther, and Paul Simon all put out important and exciting records exploring contemporary life from a point of view that eschewed rigid and dogmatic political positions.

Chapter 22

The Death of Music as Revolution

One band that did not desert the movement was Detroit's MC5. Founded in 1964, it consisted of singer Rob Tyner, guitarists Wayne Kramer and Fred Smith, bassist Michael Davis, and drummer Dennis Thompson. The MC5 labored in obscurity as just another bar band for five years until they signed with Electra Records and their first album, *Kick Out the Jams*, was released. The title of the album indicates the type of music they played: loud, raucous, undisciplined, basic, high-energy rock that today is often described as proto-punk. The MC5, once they hit, blazed onto the scene like a tornado, and just like a tornado they passed through and disappeared quickly. By 1972 they were gone.

While they existed, though, they made a splash like a lunar capsule landing in the Atlantic. In Detroit they regularly drew crowds of 1,000 or more, and when they toured they frequently drew a better response than the bands they opened for.[1] Politically they made just as big of a splash. Band manager John Sinclair was an admirer of the Black Panthers. Panther Huey P. Newton suggested that he form the White Panthers, a militant organization of white people that would raise funds for the Black Panthers. Sinclair soon involved the others in the movement and their live show evolved into a blend of music and political theater. They carried rifles on stage and at the end of the show Tyner would fake being shot by an unseen assassin.[2]

They played a lot of anti-war rallies, including the gathering at the Democratic convention in Chicago in 1968, where other acts, reading the situation, either did not show up or, as in the case of Neil Young and Country Joe and the Fish, showed up but refused to enter the chaos that was happening in the park and did not play. The MC5 was the only scheduled band to go on, and they played for eight hours.[3]

Like so much of the revolutionary movement, the MC5 was self-destructive. On the song "Kick Out the Jams," the title song of their first album, recorded for Electra Records, they sang the line, "Kick out the jams, mother-fucker." Hudson's, a major retail chain headquartered in Detroit, refused to stock the record. In retaliation, the band took out a full-page ad in the Detroit underground paper, the *Fifth Estate*, that read, "Stick alive with the MC5 and fuck Hudson's." The ad contained the Electra Records logo, which the band used without permission. Hudson's retaliated against this retaliation by withdrawing all Electra products, including the classical Nonesuch subsidiary, from their stores.[4]

Electra promptly dropped the band from the label. Although MC5 signed with Atlantic Records, ironically a subsidiary of Electra, the best part of their career was over. Electra had known that the band was strongest live and therefore had been careful to record them in concert. Atlantic put them into the studio with Jon Landau (who later became Bruce Springsteen's manager) as producer. According to the band, Landau did not understand their music and pushed them in a direction they were not comfortable with, trying to get the sound he wanted instead of the one they had pioneered. Their manager John Sinclair was not there to protect them, since he was at the time serving a prison sentence for drug possession. The resulting album was widely ignored. Neither critics nor the public responded to it, so it lay there like an overly big breakfast that would not digest. If the second album sold poorly, the third tanked completely.[5] Atlantic dropped the band, which struggled on for a few more years. However, eventually drugs took their toll. Wayne Kramer went to prison for drug offenses. In prison in Kentucky, Kramer ran into bassist Michael Davis, who was also serving time for drug crimes. MC5 could never come back from this dissolution and had disappeared by 1972.

Rock took a conservative turn after the fall of the MC5, returning to folkie sounds. This trend can be seen in the sudden burst into mass popularity of the West Coast aggregation the Eagles. Aggressively nonpolitical in their music, the Eagles were formed by veterans of Linda Ronstadt's band and very quickly became one of the most successful bands in America. Over the course of their career, they had five number-one singles, six Grammies, and six number-one albums and sold more than 150,000,000 albums. *Their Greatest Hits* became the best-selling album of the twentieth century.[6] Like most of the singer-songwriter acts, the Eagles music had a touch of mystery to it, with private, open symbolism that was put across in three- and four-part harmony. Their music, rather than being directly political, told a different story of America, describing a country where love was the most sought after and hard to find value. The Eagles explored the life they lived: the bewildering

Los Angeles underground, mysterious women who can neither be understood nor told good-bye, love sought, found, and lost, the drug culture, life beneath the surface in America, the craving for freedom.

The Eagles found the zeitgeist. The direction of their music perfectly matched the direction the country was going in, so they became the most popular folk-rock band in America. Their first few singles told the story of where music was going. Relying on acoustic guitars, the songs demonstrated a basic satisfaction with life. The turmoil of the New Left and the violence of the Weather Underground seemed far away from the world the Eagles sang about. "Take It Easy," co-written by Jackson Browne and Eagles member Glen Frey, urges its listeners to relax, to give up trying to make sense, and to just find a comfortable place and stay there—hardly a call to revolution. "Peaceful Easy Feeling," their first single and first hit, was about the love the singer had for his partner and the joy he finds in the certainty he has that she will not let him down. This was followed by "Witchy Woman," a song acknowledging the dark side, exploring the mystery of a woman who went mad, possibly from hard drugs, possibly from a privileged upbringing since a silver spoon, both a symbol of wealth from birth and hard drugs, is mentioned prominently. The mysterious and dark lyrics are presented with a soft folk-rock beat and pretty harmonies that make the words seem lighter and more welcoming than they are. These songs appeared on their first album, *Eagles*, and sent a clear signal that the days of the MC5 were over.

The Eagles only overtly political song was "Hotel California." Because the lyrics are cryptic and obscure, they have been interpreted in ways that the band might not have intended. The Eagles were accused of advocating Satanism, which they denied. Don Henley explained the lyrics, saying it was "basically a song about the dark underbelly of the American dream and about excess in America, which was something we knew about."[7]

Fleetwood Mac was as important as the Eagles to the changing musical paradigm. Originally formed as a British blues band by veterans of John Mayall's band in 1967, Fleetwood Mac at first played the same type of music they had performed with Mayall: hard-driving rocking blues. Although they were successful in Europe and England, a series of unfortunate circumstances prevented them from reaching the top or from breaking through in America. Much of their lack of American success might have had to do with their bad luck with lead guitar players. Peter Green, the band's first guitarist, succumbed to schizophrenia after taking LSD; his increasing instability caused him to become unreliable, so he had to leave the band. While the band was touring,

22. The Death of Music as Revolution

Green's replacement, Jeremy Spencer, went out one night for a magazine and never came back. A few days later, the band learned that Spencer had joined a cult, the Children of God. Bob Welch joined in Jeremy Spencer's place. He decided the reason they could not break out of the pack in America was that their headquarters in London were simply too far from their record label in Southern California, Warner Brothers. Being an ocean away, they were overlooked and received little attention from the company. He convinced the band to move to Los Angeles, where they could get more support from Warner. As soon as they were set up in L.A., he too left the band to try a solo career.[8] Fleetwood Mac's guitarists tended to drop like the exploding drummers in Rob Reiner and Christopher Guest's psuedo-documentary, *This Is Spinal Tap*.

Each of the lineup changes caused Fleetwood Mac to move away from their blues background and toward a more popish, folk-rock sound. Searching for a replacement guitarist once again when Bob Welch left, John McVie and Mick Fleetwood heard Lindsay Buckingham and invited him to take the Fleetwood Mac vehicle for a spin. Buckingham agreed but only if his singing partner and girlfriend, Stevie Nicks, could climb aboard. They agreed and finally, nine years after they formed, Fleetwood Mac had a stable lineup.[9]

Buckingham's folk background—he had learned guitar by studying John Stewart's playing with the Kingston Trio—added a new dimension to their music. With pianist and blues-based singer Christine McVie, the ethereal vocals and mystical songwriting of Stevie Nicks, Lindsay Buckingham's brilliant guitar, adventurous writing, and strong voice, and a solid rhythm section in John McVie and Mick Fleetwood, the band was capable of going in any direction it chose. The directions it chose were definitely not political. Fleetwood Mac specialized in exploring the interior, rather than society or politics. Their songs were about lost love, found love, entanglements—topics the remnants of the revolutionary left would consider trivial and escapist. The fact was, though, that at the point in time when Fleetwood Mac emerged as a commercial force, America, having been through the revolutionary years of the sixties, was ready to escape.

Fleetwood Mac, the first album by this lineup, took these various influences and melded them into a solid and original whole, to which audiences responded by buying 5,000,000 copies. The album reached number one and produced four hit singles.[10] Finally, Fleetwood Mac had fulfilled their promise without sabotaging themselves. But behind the scenes, it appeared that the band was about to repeat the old pattern. John and Christine McVie's marriage ended, as did Mick Fleetwood's. Buckingham and Nicks broke up. All succumbed in some way to the pressures and tensions of big-time success; drugs and alcohol became daily staples in their diet. They managed to hold it all together in order to make *Rumours,* their follow-up album, which is widely thought of as the album in which they explored all of the domestic horrors they'd been experiencing. If *Fleetwood Mac* pushed them up the mountain, *Rumours* had them soaring through the air above it. With songs based on every twist and turn of the personal relationships the band had endured, songs that explored divorce, betrayal, drug use, and a determination to go their own way, *Rumours* was a much darker album than its predecessor, a fact that could cause one to wonder why it was so much more successful. It won a Grammy award for the 1977 album of the year, generating seven hit singles and selling 19,000,000 albums in the United States alone.[11] It remains a best seller, having moved to date more than 40,000,000 copies, and is one of the biggest-selling albums of all time.[12]

After *Rumours,* Lindsay Buckingham felt free to explore, so under his leadership they made *Tusk,* an unpredictable and frankly experimental two-album set filled with more challenging music than the band was associated with. *Tusk* did not sell as well as the previous albums, topping out at around three million copies. Having released a 5,000,000-selling record, followed by one at 40,000,000, Fleetwood Mac and their record company suffered from a set of unrealistic expectations and, even though most bands would be ecstatic over sales of 3,000,000 units, they all saw Buckingham's experiment as a failure. They had reached a point where both Fleetwood Mac and their record company were disappointed in albums that merely went multi-platinum, selling "only" a couple of million copies. Other albums followed and, while they were not as successful as *Rumours,* 40,000,000 being a hard number to top, they still sold very well.

It is worth noting that the domestic dramas explored in Fleetwood Mac's albums were released to a huge and waiting young public at the same time the Weather Underground was trying to radicalize that same population, to turn them into revolutionaries by committing bank robberies and murder and by blowing up government buildings. In 1987 Buckingham, saying that the felt his creative juices were curdling by being in the band, quit. Stevie Nicks, by now having established a strong solo career, also departed. Once again, Fleetwood Mac had to rebuild. They soldiered on with different lineups until Bill Clinton used "Don't Stop (Thinking About Tomorrow)" as a theme song for his presidential campaign. The Buckingham-Nicks Fleetwood Mac reunited to play his inauguration and this time they stayed together. It is ironic that Fleetwood Mac, which was not at all a politically oriented group of musicians, recording primarily love and loss songs with the occasional foray into mysticism, were able to reunite because of a political campaign. When they did become associated with politics, however, it was within the existing system and it was with a song about a generalized sense of optimism.

The Postman Hypothesis

Again, the Postman hypothesis seems appropriate. As long as Fleetwood Mac's music matched the dominant paradigm—heavy, psychedelic-based blues during the anti-war years, they could not reach the peak their talent suggested they were capable of reaching. Only when they opposed the paradigm, adopting a more conservative approach when the dominant paradigm was exploding into violence, could they fulfill all of their promise.

We can then assume several points about the Postman hypothesis. One is that it can only partially explain the fact that music quite often goes into a different direction than the mainstream of society. Music is rebellious, and when artists agree with the rebellion they tend to write songs that support it. When they cannot support the dominant movement, then, of course, they write songs that go in another direction. Two is that eventually these very artists come to realize that music cannot change anything and rarely solves anything. It can reinforce ideas and can, occasionally, alter the thinking of listeners. But the change the young radicals seek does not come from people who are in power, as their power leads them to crave and develop more power. The third point is that people who are a part of the system have a problem seeing flaws in the system. The way things are done, they say, is the way things have always been done; therefore, it is the way things are *supposed* to be done. This logic operates from a basic a priori assumption that things are pretty much what they should be, that the system is basically fine and simply needs a little tinkering. It is like the old saw that doctors suffer through medical school because their teachers suffered through medical school. The syllogism says candidates become good doctors if they suffer. We want to create good doctors. Therefore we'll make them suffer. The basic assumption—that suffering makes good doctors—is never challenged.

If the government's role has been to wage and end wars, then an attempt by ordinary citizens—civilians, if you will—to end the war has to be wrongheaded and possibly even criminal. No, change rarely comes from the government. Being connected to a system is what veins are to a body—something taken so much for granted that it is never explored. The solutions proposed by members of the system are, in themselves, systemic; they tend to advocate doing more of the same, only harder. The results are rarely satisfactory. That logical structure carries with it the clear implication that if years of action in the street did not end the war then escalating those actions will not do it either.

Does this mean that the New Left wasted years of their lives fighting against the war? Not at all. Their actions turned America against the war and eventually led to its end. For the ones who were deeply committed to their system of opposition, however, the problem lies in that word "eventually." Peace didn't happen quickly enough for these impatient young people, so their impulse was to escalate, to do more of the same thing harder and longer. Such an action could not succeed; its basic assumption was never challenged.

Artists eventually recognize that change comes from within each individual rather than from the three branches of government, so they use their art to explore their feelings and emotions, the Michael Jackson "Man in the Mirror" concept. The Eagles describe a society gone to hell in "Hotel California," but, more important, they concentrate on their reactions to it. They imply that the conditions in the hotel can be changed, saying that just because things are this particular way does not mean they must be this way. On the surface, the music is as different as oatmeal and prime rib. Beneath the surface, though, it's still the same. Fleetwood Mac urges us to go our own way; ten years earlier Bob Dylan recommended we not follow leaders. The Eagles said rely on yourself, and Dylan, even when he supposedly abandoned politics, as in "Maggie's Farm," continued to issue paranoid warnings that few people can be trusted, that you have to save yourself first. By the end of the decade, Dylan had, as we've discussed, abandoned touring with the band and played sweet, good-natured country music, in which the only thing he protested was his relationship with his manager Al Grossman in "Dear Landlord."

Joan Baez also took a turn for the country, starting with *David's Album*, which she did for her husband, a huge country music fan. She recorded the album while he was serving time for draft evasion. Although she never abandoned political music, its dominance in her repertoire receded.

But regardless of where the music was going, on the political front the Weather Underground continued to dominate the scene.

Chapter 23

You Don't Need a Weatherman...

The Weathermen drove the SDS out of business exploiting the split they had created in the organization by claiming to be the genuine SDS. The Weather Underground pressured the larger group to turn to violent action, demanding that they become literal as well as cultural outlaws. Only by "bringing Hanoi to America"—that is, by blowing up American cities the way the military did Hanoi—could we end the war. The theory was that as they saw these acts of sabotage and violent resistance the Great American Middle Class, starting with the young, would become radicalized and rise up against the government, overthrowing it and establishing a utopia in its place.

Exactly how robbing banks, opening fire on police stations, blowing up government buildings and corporate headquarters, as well as rioting in the streets would lead to the middle class turning off their TVs and going out to overthrow the government was never explained. In philosophical terms, it was a priori, something that just had to be accepted as the starting point of the argument. The fact was, these young people were just that—young—and many of them came from privileged backgrounds. As noted earlier, most of them grew up in prosperous suburban homes and went directly from good high schools into colleges. All they had ever known was school. As Tom Rush once said, "We had to go out and make our own depression. But we always knew we could call home for money."[1] Living in a world of privilege and illusion and suffering from a feeling of nothingness make it easy to go over the line into delusion—even if its main effect and underlying, unspoken purpose is simply to make the person who went over the edge feel something.

The Weathermen, then, determined they would own the streets. They committed some daring acts, like breaking the LSD pioneer Timothy Leary out of prison.[2] Leary, a psychologist who had begun conducting experiments with LSD at Harvard University before the substance was declared illegal, took the drug himself and experienced visions that caused him to develop a new personal philosophy of consciousness expansion and move from experimenter to advocate, coining the phrase, "Turn on, tune in, drop out." According to writer Jesse Walter, the phrase came from a conversation with another guru of the day: "What's fascinating is Leary's relationship to that panic. Leary has written that his best-known slogan—'tune in, turn on, drop out'—was inspired by a lunch with the media theorist Marshall McLuhan, who told him, 'You call yourself a philosopher, a reformer. Fine. But the key to your work is advertising.... You must use the most current tactics for arousing consumer interest.' According to Leary, McLuhan even broke into a jingle: 'Lysergic acid hits the spot/Forty billion neurons, that's a lot.'"[3] Leary became a proselytizer for the drug, publicly advocating its use as both a consciousness-raising experience and a good high. Even after it was outlawed, he continued to advocate for it, lecturing on its benefits, and urging people to break the law, use acid, and voluntarily become outsiders.

Since the federal government was, at best, misinformed about the effects of marijuana and peyote and, at worst, as Nixon's cabinet member John Erlichman admitted, deliberately lying about their dangers, few hippies, radicals, and other young people believed their warnings about LSD. Its use increased dramatically, with Leary at its center as spokesman. President Nixon declared him to be the most dangerous man in America,[4] and due to his frequent arrests he served short periods of time in thirty-six different prisons.[5] Leary made his living from LSD, not by selling it but by forming the League for Spiritual Discovery (LSD) to promote the use of acid, and toured the country doing lectures and using light shows to replicate the LSD experience for his audiences, which were primarily made up of college students.[6] He was arrested for smuggling marijuana from Mexico into the United States. The drug was found on his girlfriend but Leary took responsibility for it and was sentenced to ten years for that offense with another ten tacked on for a previous arrest.

The Brotherhood of Eternal Love, an acid-based group that claimed Leary as a leader, hired the Weathermen for $25,000 to break him out of jail. The arrangement was simplicity itself: Leary would climb the fence that surrounded his minimum security prison, then the Weather Underground would smuggle him out of the country. The plan succeeded. They picked Leary up after he'd made it over the fence and drove him away from the prison in a pickup truck. They then helped him and his girlfriend leave the country for Algiers.[7]

The Weather Underground considered action like freeing Leary as mere fundraising and would accept funds from whoever offered them—they even took money to cover their operations and training in guerrilla warfare from Fidel Castro's government. Their real goal was bigger, though, suggested to them by North Vietnamese officials they met in Cuba. The North Vietnamese convinced them that armed action against the U.S. government would stop the war. The Weathermen were young and naive enough to believe them.[8] John Jacobs stated the real goals of the group, as well as their level of political sophistication: "Weatherman would shove the war down their dumb, fascist throats and show them, while we were at it, how much better we were than them [the federal government], both tactically and strategically, as a people. In an all-out civil war over Vietnam and other fascist U.S. imperialism, we were going to bring the war home. 'Turn the imperialists' war into a civil war,' in Lenin's words. And we were going to kick ass."[9]

In his book, *Days of Rage*, historian Brian Burroughs traces the young radicals' new fondness for firebombs. In February of 1970 members of the Weather Underground firebombed the Golden Gate Park precinct of the San Francisco Police Department, killing one officer and wounding several others. Later in the month, a group indulged in a Molotov cocktail rampage through Manhattan, tossing simple but deadly homemade explosives into the second floor of the Columbia University Law Library, at police cars parked at the Charles Street Precinct, and at military recruiting booths at Brooklyn College. All of this activity was leading up to the evening's prime target, the home of New York Supreme Court justice John M. Murtagh, who was presiding over the trial of a group of Black Panthers. The Weathermen intended to send him a warning. Painting slogans like "Free the Panther Twenty-one" on the sidewalk outside his house, they tossed three firebombs at it, blowing out the front windows.

Two weeks later, the four Weathermen who bombed the judge's house were at it again. They chose as a firebombing target a dance at the noncommissioned officer's club at Fort Dix across the Hudson River in New Jersey. Deciding to escalate the results by using nail bombs—a type of shrapnel-throwing explosive that scatters nails over a large area—instead of Molotov cocktails, the group spent the afternoon of the dance building the bombs in their rented Greenwich Village townhouse. One of the bombs exploded, killing WUO members Ted Gold, Terry Robbins, and Diana Oughton. Cathy Wilkerson and Kathy Boudin made it safely out of the house. Actor Dustin Hoffman, who lived next door, came home to find the house next to his blown to pieces and still on fire. He told the *New York Times* how odd it felt to see the carnage and to be interviewed by TV reporters who wore full makeup while the fire blazed behind them. The FBI claimed the group had enough explosives in their townhouse to blow up both sides of the street.

The explosion was the effective end of the organization. Their numbers decimated by deaths and desertions, the remaining handful of WUO members went truly underground to escape prosecution. Instead of simply hiding out, however, they continued their acts of domestic terrorism, only this time concentrating on symbolic bombings in which properties, rather than people, were to be the targets.[10] Even as members were being indicted and arrested, the WUO continued its activities. The roundup by officers of the law had intensified. In April the FBI arrested fugitives Linda Sue Evans and Dianne Donghi. The numbers continued to dwindle, but those still on the run still robbed banks and other businesses and set off bombs. On June 9, 1970, the remnants of the group planted a bomb in the headquarters of the New York City Police Department at 240 Center Street. About six minutes before it went off the WUO issued a warning, and no one was injured. The WUO officially claimed responsibility.[11]

On Ho Chi Minh's birthday the Weather Underground placed a bomb in the women's bathroom in the Pentagon. The damage caused flooding that destroyed computer tapes holding classified information. Again, the WUO claimed credit. Bombing had become an everyday occurrence, a favorite tactic. As the war wound down and their level of violence rose, the Weather Underground lost the support of other leftist organizations and in a manifesto, *Prairie Fire: The Politics of Revolutionary Anti-Imperialism*, they called for a violent overthrow of the federal government, which would be replaced with a "Dictatorship of the Proletariat." It also called for renouncing other left-wing groups and operating as a self-contained underground group.[12]

By 1974 the war was over and the Weather Underground lost its main purpose, but that fact made no apparent difference to them. By then, their goals had changed. War or no war, they wanted the government overthrown. By then they had learned that going it alone was futile and self-defeating, so they reissued *Prairie Fire* in a revision that called for cooperation with other, above-ground groups. This move split them into two competing factions. The May 19th Communist Organization wanted to remain underground, while the Prairie Fire Collective wanted to come out of hiding and work on building a mass movement that included a wider range of American citizens.[13] The Prairie Fire Collective members surfaced and surrendered to authorities. The May 19th group, however, refused to quit and continued its program of attacking American institutions.[14]

By 1977 the Weathermen were finished. Five members were arrested for attempting to plant a bomb in California state senator John Briggs' office. They were convicted and sent to prison. That case was the tipping point. Weathermen began turning themselves in to the authorities and the movement was effectively ended. A few members remained underground, refusing to give up the fight. In 1981 former WUO members Kathy Boudin, Judith Alice Clark, and David Gilbert joined up with members of the Black Liberation Army to rob a Brinks truck in Nanuet, New York, that contained $1.6 million. The robbery went bad and three people were killed. The three WUO members were captured, convicted, and sentenced to long terms in prison. It was the dying gasp of the organization.[15]

The Dying Gasp of Meaningful Music

Not only did the movement die, the music that had inspired it and pushed it along died also. Folk music entered one of its hard-to-find periods. It appeared that the long war had killed America's ideals along with its fighting forces, and the music grew as cold and selfish as the movement had. As far back as 1970 a fragmentation in the songs America was listening to could be discerned: Simon & Garfunkel could sing of love and friendship and always being there in "Bridge Over Troubled Water," but they soon afterward broke up due to internal dissension. The Beatles advocated a laid-back spiritual approach that urged listeners to "Let It Be," but the Guess Who attacked the values this country showed in "American Woman," a blistering attack on American hypocrisy. If there was a split, it was resolved during the seventies when escapism had become the staple of the music. Three Dog Night wished "Joy to the World," and John Denver offered up "Rocky Mountain High." The songs that weren't sheer escapism were trivial, speaking of feelings without feeling them. The Bee Gees wondered "How Can You Mend a Broken Heart," and Carole King claimed "It's Too Late." Folk no longer seemed to matter.

As Paul McCartney was fond of pointing out, by the seventies people wanted "Silly Love Songs." Captain & Tennille had the number one song of 1975 with "Love Will Keep Us Together," while Redbone urged us to "Come and Get Your Love." Where these performers led, others followed. "Love's Theme" was put on the charts by the Love Unlimited Orchestra and Frankie Valli charted with "My Eyes Adored You." As far as the dying embers of folk music went, John Denver explored solipsism with "Sunshine on My Shoulders" and offered the ultimate escapism with "Thank God I'm a Country Boy." Denver's success enabled other folk-country artists to make the pop charts, most prominently Glen Campbell, whose "Rhinestone Cowboy" was one of the biggest hits of the decade.

Many of these were good songs done by popular and respected artists who were simply reflecting the times they were living in, as folk music in all its manifestations had always done. America had just endured more than ten years of an unjust and unwinnable war. During the previous decade the country had been split down the middle like a pig on a spit, its government having lied to its own citizens about the war, made enemies of its own young, and ordered its policemen and national guardsmen to beat, shoot, and kill innocent college students who protested the war and racism. Alienation and a sense of nothingness had become as normal as television, and the country was sick at heart. People wanted to escape what they had been through, to be able to ignore what their lives had become and the conditions under which they had been living. Every war in our history had been followed by a period of escapism and this one was no exception. America's citizens felt a psychic need to lighten up.

The Ultimate Musical Escapism

The music simply reflected this need, culminating in the ultimate escapism: disco. By the mid-seventies dance music had captured the hearts of America's young as well as its charts. Among the earliest of disco records to seize the public need to bust a move on the dance floor was Van McCoy's "The Hustle," a song designed specifically for dancing. The Hustle was a dance invented in the early seventies by Puerto Rican teens in the South Bronx that spread as quickly as a virus. By 1976 it had been formalized into a six-step partner dance called the New York Hustle, which McCoy's record popularized. Featured in the 1977 movie *Saturday Night Fever,* the Hustle became a national pastime and brought the disco form to the forefront.[16] Walter Murphy's "A Fifth of Beethoven" became the next huge disco hit. Exactly what its title made it sound like, the song used a theme from Beethoven set to a dance beat. Revolutionary for the time, the record boosted the disco trend.[17]

In his book, *Turn the Beat Around: The Rise and Fall of Disco,* Peter Shapiro traces the growth of the form and relates how performers of all stripes felt compelled to issue disco recordings. Johnny Taylor contributed "Disco

23. You Don't Need a Weatherman...

Lady." Ron Stewart abandoned the blues-based rock he'd been doing and released "Do You Think I'm Sexy?" The Miracles did "Love Machine," and Abba burst onto the scene with "Dancing Queen." K.C. and the Sunshine Band had a steady stream of dance songs that hit including "Get Down Tonight."

The Bee Gees, reading the tea leaves, saw a chance to raise their profile by turning their backs on the folk-rock that had made them famous and morphing into the kings of disco. It appeared that disco was going to become the exclusive music of America. The form dominated the airwaves the way the bands of the British Invasion had a decade earlier. It reached its apex in the late seventies when Chic offered up "Le Freak," Gloria Gaynor recorded "I Will Survive," and the Bee Gees' younger brother Andy Gibb joined the family business by releasing "Shadow Dancing." Even soul singer Lou Rawls was compelled to join the disco revolution, with songs like "You'll Never Find Another Love Like Mine" and "Let Me Be Good to You."[18]

Its fans defended disco from its numerous attacks by rockers by saying that many of the lyrics might be trivial and meaningless but it was good to dance to. Few songs made this argument better than A Taste of Honey's "Boogie Oogie Oogie" and the Village People's "YMCA." Like so many others in the genre, these songs were as devoid of content as a politician's stump speech. The music, producer rather than artist driven,[19] became mechanical and emphasized the dance rhythms over other values. Soon it took on an aura of satire, mocking itself, reducing itself to sheer silliness. Like psychedelic music before it, disco hit its inevitable dead end and had nowhere else to go.

Just as the New Left had done, disco eventually ran its course. It could not adapt to changing conditions, so it disappeared.

Conclusion

How could the people in the movement have changed from idealistic civil rights workers to violent outlaws in less than a decade? How could the best and brightest of America's young people possibly delude themselves into thinking that the middle- and working-class people of this country could be inspired by terrorist acts to rise up and violently overthrow their government? How could such an idea have possibly made sense to them?

Singer-songwriter Vince Martin believes that the Weather Underground was simply a small and statistically insignificant portion of the New Left and were anomalies not representative of the movement. According to Martin, the Weathermen did not actually become criminals: they already were, using the movement as a cover. "Every movement has dishonesty and deceit in it," he says. "The New Left was no different. The dishonesty was in the ones who came into the movement for less than honorable reasons." Martin is correct to a point, but the fact remains that the New Left's reasoning was to a large degree a product of their education. Most of them became radicals in college, having studied political systems and ideas there. Movement people were accustomed to theorizing, having been trained to discuss ideas in the universities that spawned them. All action sprang from theory, they believed, and their theories were based on the prevailing Aristotelean logic that their classrooms made them experts in.

Two-Valued Orientation

Alfred Korzibski, one of the creators of the field of general semantics, described the type of logic that characterized his field as non–Aristotelian. Aristotelian logic is based on a two-valued orientation, which can best be defined as the inability to hold two contradictory ideas in the mind at the same time. A two-valued thinker divides all of reality into two opposing camps that generally boil down to things he approves of and things he does not. Statements such as "you're either for us or against us" or "my friend or my enemy" or the slightly more complex "the friend of my enemy is my enemy" are two-valued. In fact, any either-or choice is an example of two-valued orientation.[1]

All sets of opposites are two-valued: Good or evil, heaven or hell, love or hate. All of these claim that there are only two possible positions that can be taken and these two are polar opposites. When the Johnson and Nixon administrations divided American citizens into two camps—those who agreed with their policies and the enemy—and used that division as an rationale for its law enforcement agencies to spy on groups and individuals they saw as being on the opposite side, adopting a "America: love it or leave it" or "my country, right or wrong" attitude, that was two-valued. Two-valued orientation is absolute; the in-between disappears. The comedian Mitch Hedburg satirized this position by joking that he was once in a band that people either loved or hated—unless they were indifferent to them. A true two-valued orientation removes the possibility of indifference, reducing the question to love or hate, which become the only possibilities.

This attitude is prevalent among many different groups. Some extreme and radical religious denominations believe an individual is either saved or damned, that one is either a Christian or a heathen and that Christians are going to heaven and all others are going to hell. To them, all things are judged according to whether they are Christian or not. Good and evil are absolutes, good being godly and evil covering the satanic bases.[2] In two-valued orientation, all behavior falls into one of these two camps. In the political climate we currently inhabit, two-valued orientation dominates. Many Republicans think of Democrats as the enemy, while many Democrats believe all Republicans are heartless fanatics who want to take everyone's money away from them and give it to their millionaire contributors. As a result, we have spent the past decade in a stalemate that has rendered Congress completely ineffective.

To this day, then, many people still live in a two-valued "us" and "them" world where other people either agree with them or become the enemy. Some Republicans proclaim that all "liberals" endanger "America," and some Democrats consider all "conservatives" to be right-wing fanatics. Neither perspective leads to the compromise essential in passing effective legislation or creating a country that can live up to its stated values. Without respect or a willingness to look for a middle ground, debates among the citizenry devolve into hateful shouting matches.

Conclusion

It might be said that my analysis is unfair because it fails to tell both sides of the story. That very objection is two-valued. After all, those who offer that criticism say there are two sides to every story, which is the reason why formal debates and classroom essays are divided into pro and con structures, where the two identified sides can be examined. That is a classic structure that offers only one of two ways of looking at a subject: the so-called right way and the way that is declared wrong. The members of the New Left graduated from universities that taught Aristotelian logic. They were trained in the two-valued orientation these institutions taught. Being able to see only two sides was convenient for them because they could more easily perceive the evil forces that they were fighting. Their goal was to smash the opposite side.

When we are dealing with something like the white supremacist movement in Mississippi in the early sixties, it is easy to view it in a two-valued way. In fact, it is hard to see it any other way. However, ease of apprehension does not address the major problem of two-valued orientation: it oversimplifies. Few things are that simple. When people insist there are two sides to every story, they are looking at these stories in a two-valued way. In truth, there are as many sides to a story as there are people examining the story. In the case of the white supremacists, the hard-to-grasp truth is that many of the citizens of Mississippi were as appalled and repulsed by the behavior of the Klan and its racist sympathizers as the people who came to Freedom Summer were. Many Mississippians did not share the Klan's hatred. When Phil Ochs had his song "Here's to the State of Mississippi" in his repertoire, his friend, the blues singer and guitarist Mississippi John Hurt, suggested to him that the song—since it generalized its attack to include all of the citizens of the state—wasn't fair. After all, Hurt said, "People like me live in Mississippi, too."[3] Ochs got Hurt's message and stopped singing the song.

Two-valued orientation was most fully discussed by linguist and general semantics expert S.I. Hayakawa in his book, *Language in Action* (reissued in an expanded edition coauthored by Alan R. Hayakawa as *Language on Thought and Action*). Unfortunately, in his later years, when he was made acting chancellor of the University of California, Berkeley, during the student strikes, Hayakawa fell victim to the very condition he had written about so cogently, coming to see the demonstrators as the enemy and the administration as the good guys.

In his book, however, in order to demonstrate that two-valued orientation was the product of a closed mind Hayakawa pointed to the Nazis, who under Hitler's lead, divided everything into two categories: Aryan and not-

Aryan. Things they approved of were Aryan; things they opposed were not-Aryan. All living things could be placed in one of those two categories. And they were. Chickens, for example, were either Aryan or not, depending on how many eggs they laid. Lions were Aryan, bunny rabbits were not. Polish people, Jews, and blacks were not-Aryan, while tall, lean, blonde people with good muscle tone, whether male or female, were Aryan. The Nazis, of course, embarked on a program of exterminating everything that was not-Aryan.[4]

Two-Valued Orientation Leads to Problems

The dangers of a two-valued orientation, then, become obvious. It is a mode of thinking that creates more problems than it solves. Before Hayakawa succumbed to it, though, he lined out the alternative to the two-valued paradigm: multi-valued orientation. Multi-valued orientation resolves many of the problems two-valued modes cause. It is important to note that multi-valued thinking is not simply a two-valued approach that recognizes how complicated things are. A common logical error is to adopt a mode of thinking that ultimately there are only two sides, one true and one untrue, but that one has to wade through a massive amount of complications to arrive at the true one. The shades of grey idea oversimplifies. No, multi-valued thinking recognizes that most things are relative, that each person's idea of what is true is true for that person and that thinking does not lead to *the* truth but to *a* truth.

Multi-Valued Orientation

As an example, consider this statement from theologian Robert V. Thompson:

> If I'm being asked about whether or not I believe in some supreme being with an extreme ego who insists that people conform to a rigid dogma, I say, "No, I don't believe in that God."
> If I'm asked if I believe in a God whose abode is in a heaven, separated from the earthly domain, the answer is, "No, I don't believe in that God."
> If the question is whether I believe in a God that uses coercive power to get his way, I reply, "No, not that one either."[5]

Does this mean that Thompson is an atheist? No, it simply means he is operating from a multi-valued position. He recognizes the complexity and that more than one way of examining every problem exists. As he says, "Here's to a God who giggles with delight, who tickles creation in order to waken it to the pleasures of life and the joys of living, who gets under your skin and who wants to get up close and personal."[6]

This is not to say that multi-valued orientation is about religion. It isn't necessarily; theology just serves as an excellent example. What multi-valued orientation is about is an approach to reality. We use a religious question as an example because it illustrates the subjective aspect to all questions concerning the world we occupy. We do not have to dive into the area of faith to see that a multi-valued approach to thinking, acting, and being pays dividends. It widens our picture of reality.

People who are committed to two-valued orientation think this more complex approach to cognition is evasive. Either-or believers take comfort in two-valued approaches because within those parameters they can feel certain. They can determine that they know the truth and sometimes come to believe that they have a duty to spread that truth. That feeling of certainty is denied multi-valued thinkers. The multi-valued are always aware of the fact that they are walking the edge of uncertainty, that they can never escape the possibility that they might be wrong.

Two-valued orientation is, in David Reisman's words, other-directed. In a two-valued society, the most important value is conformity. As long as everyone thinks the same way, harmony can prevail. When people begin stepping out of line and dissenting, social and political unrest appears and the ruling classes far too often interpret this unrest to mean that order has broken down and must be restored by any means necessary. Innovation, creativity, and progress all suffer, as do the people caught in this system.

Two-Valued Orientation in Politics

The late fifties, the time that spawned the New Left, was a two-valued time. The young radicals came out of two-valued homes with two-valued governments and went to two-valued schools where they were taught two-valued modes of reasoning. When they saw injustice, it offended their ideals and they felt they were faced with two opposing ways of responding: to ignore it or to take direct action. They chose the idealistic approach, taking action, and, as a result many enlarged their way of thinking, moving closer to a multi-valued approach, one that saw breaking the law in order to help the disenfranchised as merely one of many possible ways to achieve their goals. Others did not make that jump. The Weather Underground, with its us-versus-them mentality remained aggressively two-valued. To them, violent, revolutionary action was the only way.

Of course, certain situations are, at least on their surface, two-valued. White supremacists in Mississippi denying African Americans the right to vote that the Constitution gives them boils down to essentially a basic question of right and wrong, to which the proper answer is that it is wrong. The folk singers who went to Mississippi for Freedom Summer operated from a two-valued orientation. The white supremacists were evil and needed to be stopped; the artists were willing to put their lives on the line to stop them. It was an us-versus-them proposition. History has, of course, shown that the artists were correct.

Two-Valued Songs

Most topical songs written from a two-valued perspective, however, fail as art. Having been written to a specific situation, they have a very short shelf life. They serve a propaganda purpose and when the situation being sung about is no longer current, neither is the song. In 1964 Malvina Reynolds, the San Francisco folk singer, wrote "It Isn't Nice,": which sets up a duality: your way or my way. It then claims that the singer's way is actually the only way because the alternative, the nice way advocated by the person being addressed in the song, never works but *always* fails. "It Isn't Nice" had quite a run, being recorded by Reynolds herself, Judy Collins, Barbara Dane, Annie Patterson, Cyril Paul, Carolyn Hester, and Jackie Washington, among others. It was a powerful song, speaking directly to the civil rights movement and, for a while, appeared to be headed for a long life. But then the situation that inspired it changed and it all but disappeared. Its two-valued nature caused it to be applicable only to the times; as the times changed, it grew less appropriate and therefore less heard.

Phil Ochs faced the same situation with "Here's to the State of Mississippi." When Dave Van Ronk told Ochs he was wrong to focus on Mississippi when just as much racial hatred could be found down the block in Greenwich Village, he was pointing out the two-valued nature of the song, which postulated that the people of the Village and the North were the home of the good guys, and the southern state of Mississippi was the home of every racial evil.[7]

Conclusion

Ochs couldn't see the problem in dividing the problem into two opposing camps and placing all the blame on the southern camp until a few years after he'd written the song when Mississippi John Hurt objected it. On hearing Hurt, Ochs had a click moment and realized that both Van Ronk and Hurt were correct in their objections.[8] He stopped singing the song and began turning his attention inward in his writing, exploring not just politics but everyone's responsibility for the way things were in songs like "Outside a Small Circle of Friends" and "Pleasures of the Harbor."

This recognition of the complexity of situations explains why the music got so much more complex and unfocused. Musicians were learning that the two-valued songs they'd been writing could neither capture the truth nor qualify as the truth, and most writers are not as interested in being applicable to a political situation as they are in creating a work of art. Take Ed McCurdy's classic anti-war song "Last Night I Had the Strangest Dream" Ed McCurdy was not typical of the Greenwich Village folkies. Born in rural Pennsylvania, he left the family farm at the age of eighteen to become a singer. What kind of singer, what genre he sang, didn't make any difference to him. What counted was performing. He sang gospel in Oklahoma but then became a traveling singer of the Great American Songbook in clubs. The stripper Sally Rand hired him to sing romantic ballads to her as she peeled off her clothing. Working with her introduced him to the dying but still pulsing vaudeville circuit, and he toured the remaining vaudeville palaces as a straight man to comedians.[9] Ever restless, in 1948 he moved to Canada, where he hosted his own network radio show. There he met and befriended the folk singers Pete Seeger, Josh White, and Oscar Brand, all of whom appeared as guests on his program. They introduced him to folk music, which he came to love, and he recorded his first album of folk songs in 1949.[10]

That album brought him back to America. He settled in Greenwich Village and gained prominence due to a string of albums released on Electra Records, many of which featured the bawdy songs first done by traveling minstrels in Elizabethan England. McCurdy also wrote and recorded original songs, including his most famous composition, "Last Night I Had the Strangest Dream," which has become an enduring classic. That song has been recorded in almost eighty different languages and by a variety of artists ranging from jazz singers to country stars to folkies.[11] In addition to McCurdy, artists such as the Weavers, Pete Seeger, the Chad Mitchell Trio, Simon & Garfunkel, Donal Leace, Joan Baez, the Kingston Trio, Johnny Cash, Serena Ryder, Garth Brooks, and jazz saxophonist Charles Lloyd have covered it. As recently as 2016 Carolyn Hester released a version of the song.

Conclusion

When the Berlin wall came down, Tom Brokaw was there covering the event on live TV. He had his cameras pick up school kids on the East German side of the wall, singing the song as the wall was taken down. When it was recorded by Josh White, Jr., "Last Night I Had the Strangest Dream" became the official theme song of the Peace Corps.[12]

When hundreds of anti-war songs or, if one prefers, pro-peace songs, have been written, recorded and forgotten, why does this one endure? Why is it still sung when most of the others are now historical relics? At least a part of the answer is that "Last Night I Had the Strangest Dream" is a multi-valued song. It does not attack. It does not divide the world into good guys and bad guys, claiming that those who agree with us are good and those who oppose us are evil. Listening to the song or reading its lyrics, you cannot locate an enemy in its lyrics. Rather than an attack, the song is a celebration. It does not say anyone is at fault but instead takes pleasure in the fact that war has ended, thereby implying that all of us are responsible for the condition of war and for the necessity of ending it. It does this in a joyous and celebratory manner, substituting dancing and singing in the streets for shooting and killing. In short, because it is multi-valued, it is art in the service of a larger cause, rather than two-sided us-versus-them propaganda.

The Death of the New Left

The New Left died out because it was two-valued, us against the war, and the war ended, leaving the forces of us with no opponent. The movement people tried to substitute the federal government for the war on the grounds that the government makes war and therefore is the enemy, but that approach was entirely two-valued. The public at large could see its flaws and were unable to buy into the fantasy of revolution.

The bombings and robberies of the Weather Underground instead of recruiting the young repelled them. The Weathermen had become deluded by their own two-valued thinking and came to believe that since they were morally right their actions were right. They had become incapable of seeing beyond their preconceived assumptions and were unable to see what would happen as a result. As Weather leader Bernadette Dorhn said, "We never expected to spend twenty-five years in prison."[13]

Anyone who was capable of seeing more than one viewpoint would have known that prison was a very definite possibility. In fact, the novelist Norman

Mailer, in his book about the 1966 march on Washington, *The Armies of the Night*, wrote eloquently of his realization that anti-war protestors might have to spend years in prison.[14] As a novelist, accustomed to examining rather than judging, Mailer had the perspective of seeing more than two sides of the story, something too many movement people lacked. Two-valued orientation was a major reason for the collapse and disappearance of the New Left.

The Fate of the Folkies

So what became of the folk singers most associated with trying to end the war when the war ended and the movement collapsed?

Phil Ochs was affected most dramatically. Eliot reports that his bipolar disorder got the best of him and he took on a second personality that he named John Trane. Trane was at best an unpleasant person, a snarling drunk who alienated everyone he came in contact with and continually claimed that Phil Ochs was dead. Ochs quit writing and was unable to perform. Occasionally he'd book a gig and take the stage, but it was more often John Trane who showed up and not Phil Ochs. The results were not pretty. After a long period of suffering, he moved into his sister's home and hung himself, leaving a note that said the songs would not come anymore.[15]

Bob Dylan, as he always had, maintained his own direction, went his own inner-directed way. He mounted loose-knit collaborative tours, like the Rolling Thunder Revue—Joan Baez accompanied him on that one—and made underground movies like *Reynaldo and Claire*, as well as studio pictures. He had a prime supporting role in *Pat Garrett and Billy the Kid*. He recorded what he wanted to record when he wanted to record it and after 1976's "Hurricane" never cut another protest song. Continuing to fight his unwanted designation as the voice of a generation, he decided the best way he could escape that title was by building a new audience, so he embarked on his never-ending tour, which still goes on, and won himself a new set of fans.

Peter, Paul and Mary broke up and went their separate ways, but after almost a decade they reunited for a PBS special. Enjoying the reunion, they continued to work together and won their audience back through touring and appearances on public television. They continued as a group until Mary Travers died. As of this writing, Peter and Paul tour together, keeping the memories alive.

Carolyn Hester continues to record and tour, still playing clubs and con-

Conclusion

certs around the world. Now that her two daughters are grown, they have become her touring band.

In San Francisco, during the weeks leading up to Donald Trump's inauguration, citizens held a rally on the steps of city hall to protest the Republican plans to repeal Obamacare.

Who better to be there than Joan Baez? She sang for them.

Chapter Notes

Preface

1. Richard Just, "Why Phil Ochs Is the Obscure '60s Folk Singer America Needs Today," *Washington Post*, Jan 24, 2017.
2. *Ibid.*
3. *Ibid.*
4. Thomas Fuller, and Christopher Mele, "Berkeley Cancels Milo Yiannmopoulis, and Donald Trump Tweets Outrage," *New York Times*, Feb 1 2017.
5. *Ibid.*
6. Robie Gray, "How Milo Yiannopoulis's Berkeley 'Free Speech Week' Fell Apart," *The Atlantic*, Sept. 22, 2017.
7. Alexandra Rosenmann, "Robert Reich Has a Chilling Theory About Those Berkeley Protestors," www.alternet.com, 2017.
8. Peter Stone Brown, "Where Is Phil Ochs When We Need Him?" Counterpunch.org. 2017.
9. David Hinkey, "Forty Years Later, We Still Need Phil Ochs," *Huffington Post*, 2017.
10. Rob Young, "Folk—The Music of the People—Is Hip Again," theguardian.com, 2010.

Introduction

1. "Freedom Struggle," americanhistory.si.edu.
2. Colin Wilson, *Lingard: A Novel by Colin Wilson* (New York: Crown, 1970), endnotes.
3. A.E. Van Vogt, *The Violent Man* (Pocket Books, 1962), p. 96.
4. *Ibid.*, p. 9.
5. Colin Wilson, *The Essential Colin Wilson* (Berkeley, CA: Celestial Arts, 1986), p. 9.
6. *Ibid.*
7. Van Vogt, *The Violent Man*, p. 9.
8. Kirkpatrick Sale, *SDS: Students for a Democratic Society* (New York: Vintage, 1974), p. 7.

9. Will Kaufman, *Woody Guthrie's Modern World Blues* (Norman: University of Oklahoma Press, 2017), p. 32.
10. *Ibid.*, p. 31.
11. *Ibid.*
12. *Ibid.*, 32.

Chapter 1

1. Todd Gitlin, *The Sixties* (New York: Bantam Books, 1996), p. 13–15.
2. Rick Crawford, "What Lincoln Foresaw: Corporations Being 'Enthroned' After the Civil War and Re-Writing the Laws Defining Their Existence," radicalorg.com, 2016.
3. Peter Ustinov Quotes, BrainyQuote.com, https://www.brainyquote.com/quotes/peter_ustinov_103982, BrainyMedia Inc., 2019.
4. "The Fifties," schmoop.com.
5. Richard H. Rovere, *Senator Joe McCarthy* (New York: Harcourt, Brace,1959), p. 79.
6. "Joseph R. McCarthy," history.com.
7. Joyce Oh, and Amanda Latham, "Senator Joseph McCarthy: McCarthyism and the Witch Hunts," The Cold War Museum, 2008, coldwar.org.
8. *Ibid.*
9. Jack Mirklinson, "60 Years Ago, Edward R. Murrow Took Down Joseph McCarthy," *Huffington Post*, 2014.
10. Michael Newton, "The Invisible Empire: The Ku Klux Klan in Florida," *The Journal of Southern Religion*. Review, 2010, jsr.fsu.edu.
11. "HUAC," history.com.
12. David L. Dunbar, "The Hollywood Ten: The Men Who Refused to Name Names," *The Hollywood Reporter*, 2015. hollywoodreporter.com.
13. Paul Goodman, *Growing Up Absurd* (New York: Random House, 1962), p.19.

Chapter Notes

Chapter 2

1. David A. DeTurk, and A. Poulin, eds. *The American Folk Scene* (New York: Dell Books, 1967), p. 110–117.
2. *Ibid.*, p105.
3. Tony Russell, *Country Music Records: A Discography, 1921-1942* (Oxford: Oxford University Press, 2008), p. 826.
4. DeTurk, and Poulin, p. 107.
5. *Ibid.*
6. Denisoff, R. Serge, *Great Day Coming: Folk Music and the American Left* (Urbana: University of Illinois Press, 1971), p. 89.
7. *Ibid.*, p. 183.
8. DeTurk, and Poulin, *American*, p. 126–27.
9. Donald Brown, *Bob Dylan: American Troubadour* (Lanham, MD: Rowman & Littlefield, 2014).
10. Martin Luther King, *Why We Can't Wait* (New York: New American Library, 2006).
11. www.learning.blogs.nytimes.com.
12. Marc Eliot, *Death of a Rebel* (New York: F. Watts, 1989), p. 23.
13. Robert Christgau, "Phil Ochs: 1940–1976," www.robertchristgau.com
14. Eliot, *Death of a Rebel*, p. 52.
15. *Ibid.*, p. 277.
16. www.songsandhymns.org.

Chapter 3

1. Michael Schumacher, *There but for Fortune: The Life of Phil Ochs* (New York: Hyperion, 1996) p., 226.
2. voicesofthecivilrightsmovement.com.
3. "Peter Paul and Mary Talk About the March on Washington," Youtube.

Chapter 4

1. https://en.wikipedia.org/wiki/Bob_Moses_(activist).
2. *Ibid.*
3. Bruce Watson, *Freedom Summer: The Savage Season That Made Mississippi Burn and Made America a Democracy* (New York: Viking, 2010), p. 6–7.
4. *Ibid.*, p. 26.
5. *Ibid.*, p. 226.
6. https://en.wikipedia.org/wiki/Bob_Moses_(activist).
7. "Plessy v. Ferguson," https://www.oyez.org/cases/1850–1900/163us537.
8. "Morgan v. Virginia," https://www.loc.gov/item/usrep328373/
9. John Lewis, and Michael D'Orso, *Walking with the Wind: A Memoir of the Movement* (New York: Simon & Schuster, 1996), p. 7.
10. William A. Nunnelley, *Bull Connor* (Tuscaloosa: Univ. of Alabama Press, 1991), p. 93.
11. Watson, *Freedom Summer*, p. 128.
12. http://archivesspace.lib.miamioh.edu/repositories/2/resources/624.
13. www.jfklibrary.org.
14. Watson, *Freedom Summer*, p. 53.

Chapter 5

1. Watson, *Freedom Summer*, p.63–65.
2. Gitlin, *The Sixties*, p. 135.
3. Watson, *Freedom Summer*, p. 6–7.
4. "Phil Ochs Biography," SonnyOchs.com. Retrieved April 17, 2009.
5. Eliot, *Death of a Rebel*, p.20.
6. Robert Shelton. "64 Folk Festival Ends in Newport; Weekend Event Presented Music and Workshops," *New York Times*, 1964.
7. Watson, *Freedom Summer*, p. 24.
8. *Ibid.*
9. Gitlin, *The Sixties*, p. 137.
10. Watson, *Freedom Summer*, p. 37.
11. *Ibid.*, p. 94.
12. *Ibid.*, p. 26–27.
13. *Ibid.*
14. Eliot, *Death of a Rebel*, p. 301–08.
15. Les Bayless, "Three Who Gave Their Lives: Remembering the Martyrs of Mississippi Freedom Summer, 1964," *People's Weekly World*, 25 May 1996.
16. Eliot, *Death of a Rebel*, p. 82–83.
17. *Ibid.* p. 83.

Chapter 6

1. "Village History," *The Greenwich Village Society for Historic Preservation*.
2. Watson, *Freedom Summer*, p. 231.

Chapter 7

1. Joan Baez. *And a Voice to Sing With* (New York: Simon and Schuster, 1987), p. 104.
2. *Ibid.*, 105.

Chapter Notes

3. Watson, *Freedom Summer*, p. 218.
4. *Ibid.*
5. *Ibid.*, p. 219.
6. Baez, *and a Voice to Sing With*, p. 105.
7. *Ibid.*, p. 103.
8. *Ibid.*, p. 104.
9. *Ibid.*
10. *Ibid.*
11. *Ibid.* p. 57–58.
12. Bob Gibson, and Carole Bender, *Bob Gibson: I Come for to Sing: The Stops Along the Way of a Folk Music Legend* (Naperville, IL: Kingston Korner, 1999), p. 143.
13. Baez, *And a Voice to Sing With*, p. 67–68.
14. *Ibid.* p. 68.
15. *Ibid.* p. 120.
16. *Ibid.* p.
17. David Hajdu, *Positively 4th Street: The Lives and Times of Joan Baez, Bob Dylan, Mimi Baez Farina and Richard Farina* (New York: Picador, 2001), p. 201.

Chapter 8

1. Folklib Index: A Library of Folk Music Links: http://www.folklib.net/
2. rankly.com/item/mary-travers.
3. William Ruhlman. "A Song to Sing All Over This Land." peterpaulandmary.com.
4. *Ibid.*
5. *Ibid.*
6. *Ibid.*
7. Coretta King. "Remembering the Twentieth Anniversary March in 1983" irehr.org.
8. Ruhlman, "A Song to Sing All Over This Land."

Chapter 9

1. Donald Brown, *Bob Dylan: American Troubadour* (Lanham, MD: Rowman & Littlefield, 2014).
2. Marc Hogan, "Bob Dylan's 'Da Vinci Code' Cracked in New Book," Spin.com., May, 19, 2014.
3. John Pareles, "Critic's Notebook: Plagiarism in Dylan, or a Cultural Collage?" *New York Times*, 2003.
4. Hogan, "Bob Dylan's 'Da Vinci Code' Cracked in New Book."
5. Eliot, *Death of a Rebel*, p. 66.
6. Claudia Driefus, "Bob Dylan in the Alley: The Alan J. Weberman Story," *Rolling Stone*, 1971.
7. Kevin Gosztola, "Fifty Years Ago: The Music of the March on Washington Rally." Shadowproof.com. 2013.
8. *Ibid.*
9. Brown, *Bob Dylan: American Troubadour*, p. xx.
10. "Bobby Vee and Bob Dylan: 5 Fast Facts You Need to Know," Heavy.com.
11. *Ibid.*
12. Brown, *Bob Dylan: American Troubadour*, p. 4.
13. *Ibid.* p. 2.
14. *Ibid.* p. 4.
15. Bob Dylan, *Chronicles, Volume 1* (New York: Simon and Schuster, 2005), p. 247.
16. Hank Reineke, *Arlo Guthrie: The Warner/Reprise Years* (Lanham, MD: Rowman & Littlefield, 2012).
17. Liam Clancy, *Liam Clancy: The Mountain of the Women: Memoirs of an Irish Troubadour* (New York: Doubleday, 2002).
18. Robert Shelton, "Bob Dylan: A Distinctive Stylist," *New York Times*, 1961.
19. Brown, *Bob Dylan: American Troubadour*, p. 10.
20. Dylan, *Chronicles, Volume 1.*, p. 46.
21. Baez, *And a Voice to Sing With*, p. 83–84.
22. Brown, *Bob Dylan: American Troubadour*, p. 11.
23. *Ibid.*, p. 12.
24. "Bob Dylan and the Civil Rights Movement," www.aboutentertainment.com.

Chapter 10

1. "Freedom Summer," History.com.
2. Watson, *Freedom Summer*, pp. 296–97.
3. Gitlin, *The Sixties*, pp. 149–150.
4. *Ibid.*, p. 151.
5. *Ibid.*, pp. 149–150.

Chapter 11

1. Tom Hayden, *The Long Sixties* (Boulder: Paradigm Publishers, 2009), p. 9.
2. *Ibid.*, p. 22.
3. *Ibid.*, p. 25.
4. Students for a Democratic Society (U.S.), *The Port Huron Statement* (New York, N.Y.: Students for a Democratic Society, 1962).
5. Watson, *Freedom Summer*, p. 126.
6. *Ibid.*
7. "Platform of the States Rights Democratic Party, August 14, 1948," *Political Party Platforms*,

Parties Receiving Electoral Votes, 1840–2004. The American Presidency Project.
8. "Port Huron Statement Draft," sds.1960s.org.
9. Nina Baym, and Robert S. Levine, eds. *Norton Anthology of American Literature* (New York: Norton, 1962).
10. Students for a Democratic Society (U.S.), *The Port Huron Statement.*
11. Gitlin, *The Sixties*, p. 116.

Chapter 12

1. Gitlin, *The Sixties*, p. 164.
2. *Ibid.*
3. "Police Crack Down on Free Speech Movement Protest,"www.americanrhetoric.com.
4. *Ibid.*
5. Online Archive of California, *Vietnam Day Committee,* retrieved on April 5, 2007.
6. *Ibid.*
7. Ed Denson, "1968 Country Joe and the Fish: How the Band Got Started," people.well.com.
8. Bruce H. Franklin, "The Anti-War Movement We're Supposed to Forget," *Chronicle of Higher Education*, 10-20-2000.
9. Peter Brush, "Rise and Fall of the Dragon Lady," *Vietnam* 22, no. 3, 2009.
10. Fendell W. Yerxa, "Goldwater Says Generals Have a Nuclear Authority," *New York Times*, 1964.
11. Woody Guthrie, "Letter to Alan Lomax," in Roy Pratt, *Rhythm and Resistance: Explorations in the Political Uses of Popular Music* (New York: Praeger, 1990), p. 115.
12. Anthony Scaduto, *Bob Dylan: A Biography* (New York: Helter Skelter, 2001), p. 161.
13. Pratt, *Rhythm and Resistance: Explorations in the Political Uses of Popular Music*, p. 208.
14. Eliot, *Death of a Rebel*, p. 24.
15. Allen Guttmann, "Protest Against the War in Vietnam," *Annals of the American Academy of Political and Social Science*, 382, 1969, pp. 56–63.
16. Wikileaks.com.
17. Paul Nelson, *The Little Sandy Review,* 1964.
18. *Ibid.*

Chapter 13

1. Elijah Wald, *Dylan Goes Electric: New-port, Seeger and the Night That Split the Sixties* (New York: Day Street Books, 2015).
2. Marshall McLuhan, and Lewis Henry Lapham, *Understanding Media the Extensions of Man* (Cambridge (Mass.): The MIT Press, 1994).
3. Marshall McLuhan, *The Medium and the Message: Understanding the Information World* (CG Books, 2016).
4. "Eisenhower Gives Famous 'Domino Theory' Speech," History.com.
5. Michael Novak, *The Experience of Nothingness* (New York, Harper and Row, 1970), p. 10–11.
6. Friedrich Nietzsche, *The Will to Power* (New York: Random House,1967), p. 11.
7. Novak, *the Experience of Nothingness*, p. 10.

Chapter 14

1. Margaret Mead, *Culture and Commitment* (New York: Doubleday, 1970), p. 1.
2. See John Holt, *Instead of Education;* George Dennison, *The Lives of Children;* Paul Goodman, *Compulsory Miseducation;* and James Herndon, *How to Survive in Your Native Land.*
3. Paul Simon, "Kodachrome," *Paul Simon's Greatest Hits, Etc.* New York: Charing Cross Music, 1977.
4. Watson, *Freedom, P. 281.*
5. Jeannie C. Riley, "Generation Gap," 1970.
6. Gitlin, *The Sixties*, p. 102.

Chapter 15

1. Carl Boggs, "Marxism, Prefigurative Communism, and the Problem of Worker's Control," *Radical America,* November, 11, 1977., p. 100.
2. Baez, *And a Voice to Sing With*, p. 124.
3. www.metrolyrics.com.

Chapter 16

1. "U.S. Orders 50,000 Troops to Vietnam," 1965, news.bbc.co.uk,
2. "1968 United States vs. O'Brien, 391 U.S. 367," supreme.justia.com.
3. Hank Reineke, *Arlo Guthrie: the Warner/Reprise Years* (Lanham, MD: Rowman & Littlefield, 2012),p. 48.
4. Mary Travers, azquotes.com.

5. See Michael Scott Cain, *The Americana Revolution* (Lanham, MD: Rowman & Littlefield, 2017).
6. ACLU, Southern California Branch, *Day of Protest, Night of Violence: The Century City Peace March* (Los Angeles: Sawyer Press, 1967).
7. Baez, *And a Voice to Sing With*, p. 124.
8. Herman Graham III., *The Brothers' Vietnam War: Black Power, Manhood and the Military Experience* (Gainesville: University of Florida Press, 2003), p. 16–17.
9. David Anderson, and Ernst, John, eds. *The War That Never Ends: Student Opposition to the Vietnam War* (Lexington: University of Kentucky, 2014), p. 228.

Chapter 17

1. Peter Gessner, and Yom, Hurwitz, directors, *Last Summer Won't Happen*, 1968.
2. Don McNeil, *Moving Through Here* (New York: Knopf, 1967), p. 225.
3. Eliot, *Death of a Rebel*, p. 127.
4. *Ibid.*, p. 129–130.
5. *Ibid.*, p. 160.
6. McNeil, *Moving Through Here*, p. 225.
7. *Ibid.*, p. 227.
8. *Ibid.*, p. 227.
9. *Ibid.*, p. 228.
10. Anderson, and Ernst, p. 230.
11. McNeil, *Moving Through Here*, p. 225.
12. Eliot, *Death of a Rebel*, p. 128.
13. *Ibid.*, 128.
14. McNeil, *Moving Through Here*, p. 226.
15. *Ibid.*, p. 224.
16. *Ibid.*, p. 226.
17. Eliot, *Death of a Rebel*, p.141.
18. *Ibid.*, p. 181.

Chapter 18

1. "The Chicago Eight Trial: In Their Own Words," https://famous-trials.com/chicago8/1374-ownwords.
2. J Anthony Lucas, "Judge Hoffman Is Taunted at Trial of the Chicago 7 After Silencing Defense Council," *New York Times*, 2/6/1970.
3. Douglas O. Linder, "The Chicago Eight Conspiracy Trial," www.law2.unkc.edu.
4. Eliot, *Death of a Rebel*, p.177.
5. *Ibid.*, p. 168–175.
6. *Ibid.*, p. 168–177.
7. Linder, "The Chicago Eight Conspiracy Trial."

Chapter 19

1. Joe Allen, "1968: The Democrats and the Antiwar Movement," *International Socialist Review*, isreview.com, 2015.
2. Kenneth T. Walsh, "How Robert Kennedy's Death Shattered the /Nation," *U.S. News and World Report*, usnews.com, 2015.
3. Gore Vidal, "The Best Man, 1968," *Esquire*, 2008.
4. Frank Kusch, *Battleground Chicago: The Police and the 1968 Democratic National Convention* (University of Chicago Press, 2008).
5. Stephen Smith, and Kate Ellis, *Campaign '68: Hubert H. Humphrey*, American Radio Works Documentary.
6. Eliot, *Death of a Rebel*, p. 187–88.
7. Smith and Ellis, *Campaign '68*.
8. *Ibid.*
9. "Lyndon Johnson and Hubert Humphrey on 30 September 1968," Presidential Recordings Digital Edition: prde.upress.virginia,edu.
10. "Silent Majority," nixonlibrary.gov.
11. www.SFMSEUM.ORG.
12. www.metrolyrics.com.
13. M. Hicks, *Sixties Rock: Garage, Psychedelic and Other Satisfactions* (Urbana: University of Illinois Press, 2000), p. 59–60.
14. Alan Travis, and Sally James Gregory, "How Rock'n'roll Fell Out of Love with Drugs," *The Guardian*, 2003.
15. "In Depth: Universal Soldier," buffysaintemarie.com.

Chapter 20

1. "Black Power Movement," law.jrank.org.
2. Amari D. Jackson, "Examining the Movements for Civil Rights and Black Power," *Atlanta Black Star*, 2017.
3. Gitlin, *The Sixties*, pp. 244–245.
4. Tom Hayden, *The Long Sixties* (Boulder, CO: Paradigm Press, 2009), p. 63.
5. Jeff Smith, "This Day in Resistance History: 1968 Columbia Student Uprising, " Grand Rapids Institute for Information Democracy, 2012.
6. *Ibid*.
7. Stefan Bradley, "Gym Crow Must Go!" Black Student Activism at Columbia University,

Chapter Notes

1967–1968," *The Journal of African American History*. Vol. 88, No. 2 (Spring, 2003), pp. 163–181.
  8. Frank Da Cruz, "Columbia University 1968," columbia.edu., 1998.
  9. "Henry S. Coleman, Popular Dean Held Captive During 1968 Protests, Dies at 79," *Columbia Magazine*, 2017.
  10. "1968: Columbia in Crisis," exhibitions.cul.columbia.edu.
  11. James Herndon, *How to Survive in Your Native Land* (New York: Simon and Schuster, 1971), p. 47.

Chapter 21

  1. DeTurk and A. Poulin, eds. *The American Folk Scene*, p. 153–54.
  2. David Cohen, "Phil Ochs: Pleasures of the Puzzle," *Columbus Free Press*, 12-4-97.
  3. Altrockchick, "Phil Ochs—Pleasures of the Harbor—Classic Music Review," www.altrockchick.com, 2013.
  4. Brian Burroughs, *Days of Rage* (London: Penguin Books, 2015).
  5. Tom LoBianco, "Report: Aide Says Nixon's War on Drugs Targeted Blacks and Hippies," cnn.com, 2016.
  6. Gitlin, *The Sixties,* pp. 335–336.
  7. *Ibid.,* p. 393.
  8. Carol Taylor, "History: Student for a Democratic Society Was Top 1968 Story in Boulder," Daily Camera, dailycamera.com, 2011.
  9. Gitlin, *The Sixties*, p. 415.
  10. "Black Panther Greatest Threat to U.S. Security," July 16, 1969, California Digital Newspaper Collection, cdnc.eur.edu.
  11. Burroughs, *Days of Rage.*
  12. Harold Jacobs, "Weatherman," www.sds-1960s.org.
  13. *Ibid.*
  14. Burroughs, *Days of Rage.*
  15. Jacobs, "Weatherman."
  16. "Che Guevara," *New Left Review*,1967, newleftreview.org.
  17. "Rennie Davis—Spokesman for the Lord of the Universe." prem-rawat-bio.org.
  18. Margot Adler, "After 40 Years, the Bed-In Reawakens," National Public Radio, npr.org, 2009.
  19. Burroughs, *Days of Rage.*
  20. Dan Berger, *Outlaws of America: The Weather Underground and the Politics of Solidarity* (Oakland, CA: AK Press, 2005), p. 95.

  21. Burroughs, *Days of Rage.*
  22. Gitlin, *The Sixties,* p. 428.
  23. Herbert Saal, "The Girls—Letting Go," *Newsweek,* 1969.
  24. Bob Dylan interview, *Playboy,* March 1978, reprinted in Jonathan Cott, *Dylan on Dylan: The Essential Interviews* (Hodder and Stoughton, 2006), p. 204.
  25. Neil Postman, *Teaching as a Conservative Activity* (New York: Delacorte Press, 1979), pp. 13–14.
  26. Jon Landau, "James Taylor: James Taylor Album Review," *Rolling Stone,* 31.
  27. Joe Levy, and Stephen Van Zandt, "Tapestry: Carole King," in *Rolling Stone's 500 Greatest Albums of All Time* (New York: Wenner, 2006), p. 36.

Chapter 22

  1. Don McLeese, *MC5's Kick Out the Jams* (London: Continuum International Pub, 2005).
  2. Mathew J. Bartkowiak, *The MC5 and Social Change: A Study in Rock and Revolution.* (Jefferson, NC: McFarland, 2009).
  3. "The MC5 Performs at the 1968 Chicago Democratic National Convention Just Before All Hell Breaks Loose," openculture.com.
  4. Raul Rossel, "The MC5 Kick Out the Jams Album & 'F*#K Hudson's' Ad Controversy," feelnumb.com, 2011.
  5. "MC5 Bio," rollingstone.com.
  6. "Chart History: Eagles," Billboard.com.
  7. Steve Kroft, "Eagles: Dark Days," *Sixty Minutes*, 11/25/07.
  8. Mark Taurnicht, "History," fleetwoodmac.net.
  9. Tshepo Mokoena, "Fleetwood Mac's Stevie Nicks: 'Lindsey Buckingham and I Will Always Be Antagonizing Each Other,'" the guardian.com, 2015.
  10. "1970s Timeline," goyourownway.com.
  11. *Ibid.*
  12. "Top Ten Best Selling Albums Worldwide (All Time.)" rankings.com.

Chapter 23

  1. Tom Rush, *Got a Mind to Ramble*, Liner Notes: Prestige Records, 1961.
  2. Jesse Walker, "The Acid Guru's Long Strange Trip," Theamericanconservative.com, 2006.

3. *Ibid.*
4. Bill Minutaglio, *Most Dangerous Man in America: Timothy Leary, Richard Nixon and the Hunt for the Fugitive ... King of LSD* (New York: Grand Central Pub, 2018).
5. "Dr. Timothy Leary Archives," tekgnostics.com.
6. Walker, "The Acid Guru's Long Strange Trip."
7. Mark Walston, "The Brotherhood of Eternal Love, Timothy Leary and the Rise of LSD," markwalston.com, 2012.
8. Senate Judiciary Committee (1975). *Report of the Subcommittee to Investigate the Administration of the Security Act and Other Internal Security Laws of the Committee of the Judiciary.* Government Printing Office. pp. 5, 8–9, 13, 18, 137–147.
9. Kevin Gillies, *Vancouver Magazine*, November, 1968.
10. Burroughs, *Days of Rage*.
11. *Ibid.*
12. Weather Underground Organization. *Prairie Fire: The Politics of Revolutionary Anti-Imperialism: Political Statement of the Weather Underground.* [San Francisco]: Communications Co, 1976, p. 76.
13. Nefant 12, "The Weather Underground: Communication and Social Change in American History," blogs.evergreen.edu.
14. "Weather Underground," revolvy.com.
15. Nefant 12, "The Weather Underground: Brink's Robbery: The End of the Underground," blogs.evergreen.edu.
16. Alan Jones, and Jussi Kantonen, *Saturday Night Forever: The Story of Disco* (Chicago, Illinois: A Cappella Books, 1999).
17. Tom Bentkowski, "Ludwig on the Charts," New York Magazine, Vol. 10 no. 13, March 28, 1977, p. 65.
18. Peter Shapiro, "Turn the Beat Around: The Rise and Fall of Disco," Macmillan, 2006.
19. "Disco Music," shsu.edu.

Conclusion

1. "Korzibski's Non-Aristotellian Systems," Korzibwski Institute for the Study of General Semantics, kortzibskiinstitute.blogspot.com.
2. Two-valued orientation is discussed more thoroughly in S.I. Hayakwa and Alan R. Hayakawa's *Language in Thought and Action* (San Diego, CA: Harcourt Brace Jovanovich, 1990).
3. "Here's to the State of Mississippi," Shadows That Shine, philochsthing.com, 2014.
4. Hayakawa and Hayakawa, *Language in Thought and Action.*
5. Robert V. Thompson, *A Voluptuous God* (Kelona, BC: Copper House, 2007), pp. 21–22.
6. *Ibid.*, p. 23.
7. www.elyrics.net.
8. "Here's to the State of Mississippi," Shadows that Shine, philochsthing.com, 2014.
9. Bruce Eder, "Ed Mccurdy: Artist Biography," allmusic.com.
10. *Ibid.*
11. "The Lyrics Connection." Arlo.Net, 2010.
12. *Ibid.*
13. Burroughs, *Days of Rage*.
14. Norman Mailer, *The Armies of the Night: The Novel as History, History as a Novel* (New York: Plume, 2017).
15. Eliot, *Death of a Rebel*, pp. 260–275.

Bibliography

Adler, Margot. "After 40 Years, the Bed-In Reawakens." https://www.npr.org/templates/story/story.php?storyId=112082796. August 25, 2009.

Allen, Joe. "1968: The Democrats and the Antiwar Movement." *International Socialist Review.* no. 60 (2008). https://isreview.org/issue/60/1968-democrats-and-antiwar-movement.

American Civil Liberties Union. *Day of Protest, Night of Violence, the Century City Peace March: A Report.* Los Angeles: Sawyer Press, 1967.

Anderson, David, and John Ernst, eds. *The War That Never Ends: Student Opposition to the Vietnam War.* Lexington: University of Kentucky, 2014.

Baez, Joan. *And a Voice to Sing With: A Memoir.* New York: Simon & Schuster, 1987.

Bartkowiak, Mathew J. *The MC5 and Social Change: A Study in Rock and Revolution.* Jefferson, NC: McFarland, 2009.

Bayless, Les. "Three Who Gave Their Lives: Remembering the Martyrs of Mississippi Freedom Summer, 1964." *People's Weekly World.* 25 May 1996.

Baym, Nina, and Levine, Robert S., eds. *Norton Anthology of American Literature.* New York: Norton, 1962.

Bentkowski, Tom. "Ludwig on the Charts." *New York Magazine* 10. no. 13 (1977).

Berger, Dan. *Outlaws of America: The Weather Underground and the Politics of Solidarity.* Oakland, CA: AK Press, 2005.

"Black Panther Greatest Threat to U.S. Security." July 16, 1969. *California Digital Newspaper Collection.* https://cdnc.ucr.edu/cgibin/cdnc?a=d&d=DS19690716.2.89.

"Black Power Movement." http://law.jrank.org/pages/4776/Black-Power-Movement.html.

Blair, Cynthia. "1967: Hippies Toss Dollar Bills Onto NYSE Floor." In Fran Capo and Frank Borzellieri, eds. *It Happened in New York.* Guilford, Conn: TwoDot, 2007.

"Bob Dylan Interview," *Playboy.* March 1978. Reprinted in Jonathan Cott, ed. *Dylan on Dylan: The Essential Interviews.* London: Hodder and Stoughton, 2006.

"Bobby Vee and Bob Dylan: 5 Fast Facts You Need to Know." https://heavy.com/entertainment/2016/10/bobby-vee-bob-dylan-velline-influences-nobel-prize-dead-alive-tribue-to-suzie-baby-music-chronicles-volume-one/.

Boggs, Carl. "Marxism, Prefigurative Communism, and the Problem of Worker's Control." *Radical America.* November 11, 1977.

Bradley, Stefan. "'Gym Crow Must Go!' Black Student Activism at Columbia University, 1967–1968." *The Journal of African American History* Vol. 88, No. 2 (Spring, 2003).

Brown, Donald. *Bob Dylan: American Troubadour.* Lanham, MD: Rowman & Littlefield, 2014.

Brown, Peter Stone. "Where Is Phil Ochs When We Need Him?" February 18, 2011. https://www.counterpunch.org/2011/02/18/where-is-phil-ochs-when-we-really-need-him/.

Brush, Peter. "Rise and Fall of the Dragon Lady." *Vietnam* 22, no. 3 (2009).

Burroughs, Bryan. *Days of Rage.* London: Penguin Books, 2015.

"Che Guevara." *New Left Review,* 1967. https://newleftreview.org/I/46/new-left-review-che-guevara.

Christgau, Robert. "Phil Ochs 1940–1976." www.robertchristgau.com

Clancy, Liam. *Liam Clancy: The Mountain of the Women: Memoirs of an Irish Troubadour.* New York: Doubleday. 2002.

Cohen, Dave. "Phil Ochs: Pleasures of the Puzzle." *Columbus Free Press.* 1997. http://freepress.org/Backup/UnixBackup/pubhtml/culture/philochs.html.

Corbett, Ben. "Bob Dylan and the Civil Rights Movement." https://www.thoughtco.com/bob-dylan-and-civil-rights-movement-1322012.

Bibliography

Crawford, Rick. "What Lincoln Foresaw: Corporations Being "Enthroned" After the Civil War and Re-Writing the Laws Defining Their Existence." 2016. https://ratical.org/corporations/Lincoln.html.

Da Cruz, Frank. "Columbia University 1968." 1998. http://www.columbia.edu/cu/computing history/1968/.

Denisoff, R. Serge. *Great Day Coming: Folk Music and the American Left*. Urbana: University of Illinois Press, 1971.

Denson, Ed. "Country Joe and the Fish: How the Band Got Started." https://people.well.com/user/cjfish/begin.htm, 1968.

DeTurk, David A., and Poulin, A., eds. *The American Folk Scene*. New York: Dell Books, 1967.

"Disco Music." Sam Houston State University. http://www.shsu.edu/~lis_fwh/book/hybrid_children_of_rock/Disco2.htm.

"Dr. Timothy Leary Archives." http://www.tekgnostics.com/leary.htm.

Driefus, Claudia. "Bob Dylan in the Alley: The Alan J. Weberman Story." *Rolling Stone*, 1971.

Dunbar, David L. "The Hollywood Ten: The Men Who Refused to Name Names." *The Hollywood Reporter*, 2015. https://www.hollywoodreporter.com/lists/hollywood-ten-men-who-refused-839762.

Dylan, Bob. *Chronicles, Volume 1*. New York: Simon & Schuster. 2005.

_____. *The Freewheeling Bob Dylan*. Liner notes. 1963.

Eder, Bruce. "Ed Mccurdy: Artist Biography." https://www.allmusic.com/artist/ed-mccurdy-mn0000134952/biography.

"Eisenhower Gives Famous 'Domino Theory' Speech." http://www.history.com/this-day-in-history/eisenhower-gives-famous-domino-theory-speech. 2009.

Eliot, Marc. *Death of a Rebel*. New York: F. Watts, 1989.

"Eugene McCarthy." http://www.retrocampaigns.com/clean-for-gene.html.

Folklib Index: A Library of Folk Music Links: http://www.folklib.net/

Franklin, Bruce H. "The Anti-War Movement We're Supposed to Forget." *Chronicle of Higher Education*, 10–20–2000.

"Freedom Struggle." Smithsonian Institution. http://americanhistory.si.edu/brown/history/6-legacy/freedom-struggle-1.html/.

"Freedom Summer." http://www.history.com/topics/black-history/freedom-summer.

Fuller, Thomas, and Christopher Mele. "Berkeley Cancels Milo Yiannopoulis, and Donald Trump Tweets Outrage." *New York Times*, Feb 1, 2017.

Gessner, Peter and Hurwitz, Yom, directors. *Last Summer Won't Happen*. Documentary, 1968.

Gibson, Bob, and Carole Bender. *Bob Gibson: I Come for to Sing : The Stops Along the Way of a Folk Music Legend*. Naperville, IL: Kingston Korner, 1999.

Gillies, Kevin. Vancouver magazine, November, 1968.

Gitlin, Todd. *The Sixties*. New York: Bantam Books, 1993.

Goodman, Paul. *Growing Up Absurd*. New York: Random House. 1962.

Gosztola, Kevin. "Fifty Years Ago: The Music of the March on Washington Rally," 2013. https://shadowproof.com/2013/08/28/fifty-years-ago-the-music-of-the-march-on-washington-demonstration/.

Graham, Herman, III. *The Brothers' Vietnam War: Black Power, Manhood and the Military Experience*. Gainesville: University of Florida Press, 2003.

Gray, Robie. "How Milo Yiannopoulis's Berkeley 'Free Speech Week' Fell Apart." *The Atlantic*, Sept. 22, 2017.

The Greenwich Village Society for Historic Preservation.

Guthrie, Woody. "Letter to Alan Lomax." In Roy Pratt, ed., *Rhythm and Resistance: Explorations in the Political Uses of Popular Music*. New York: Praeger, 1990.

Guttmann, Allen. "Protest Against the War in Vietnam." *Annals of the American Academy of Political and Social Science*. 382. 1969.

Hajdu, David. *Positively 4th Street: The Lives and Times of Joan Baez, Bob Dylan, Mimi Baez Farina and Richard Farina*. New York: Picador, 2001.

Hayakawa, S. I., and Alan R. Hayakawa. *Language in Thought and Action*. San Diego: Harcourt Brace Jovanovich, 1990.

Hayden, Tom. "Henry S. Coleman, Popular Dean Held Captive During 1968 Protests, Dies at 79." *Columbia Magazine*. columbia.edu. 2017.

_____. "Here's to the State of Mississippi." *Shadows That Shine*. 2014. philochsthing.wordpress.com.

_____. *The Long Sixties*. Boulder: Paradigm Publishers, 2009.

Herndon, James. *How to Survive in Your Native Land*. New York: Simon & Schuster, 1971.

Hicks, M. *Sixties Rock: Garage, Psychedelic and*

Bibliography

Other Satisfactions. Urbana: University of Illinois Press, 2000.

Hinkey, David. "Forty Years Later, We Still Need Phil Ochs." *Huffington Post*, 2017.

Hoffman, Abbie. "1988 Speech to the First National Student Convention," Rutgers University. onthiosidety.com.

———. Hubert Humphrey Presidential Campaign, 1968.

Hogan, Marc. "Bob Dylan's 'Da Vinci Code' Cracked in New Book." Spin.com. 2014.

Hoover and the FBI. LunaRay films, 1971, PBS.org,

Hughes, Ken, Matthews, Kieran K., and Selverstone, Marc J. eds. Lyndon Johnson and Hubert Humphrey on 30 September 1968. prde.upress.virginia,edu.

———, In Depth: Universal Soldier. buffysaintemarie.com. No date listed.

Jackson, D. Amari. "Examining the Movements for Civil Rights and Black Power." *Atlanta Black Star*. 2017.

Jacobs, Harold. "Weatherman." www.sds-1960s.org.

Jones, Alan, and Jussi Kantonen. *Saturday Night Forever: The Story of Disco*. Chicago, IL: A Cappella Books, 1999.

Just, Richard. "Why Phil Ochs Is the Obscure '60s Folk Singer America Needs Today." *Washington Post*. Jan 24, 2017.

Kaufman, Will. *Woody Guthrie's Modern World Blues*. Norman: University of Oklahoma Press, 2017.

King, Coretta. "Remembering the Twentieth Anniversary March in 1983." irehr.org.

King, Martin Luther. *Why We Can't Wait*. New York: New American Library, 2006.

"Korzibski's Non-Aristotellian Systems." Korzibwski Institute for the Study of General Semantics. kortzibskiinstitute.blogspot.com.

Kosareff, Steve. "'Dreamers on the Rise': Tribute to Robert and John Kennedy." johnstewartdocumentary.wordpress.com.

Kroft, Steve. "Eagles: Dark Days." *Sixty Minutes*. 11/25/07.

Kusch, Frank. *Battleground Chicago: The Police and the 1968 Democratic Convention*. Chicago: University of Chicago Press, 2008.

Landau, Jon. "James Taylor: James Taylor Album Review." *Rolling Stone*, 31. learning.blogs.nytimes.com.

Levy, Joe, and Van Zandt, Stephen. "Tapestry: Carole King." In *Rolling Stone's 500 Greatest Albums of All Time*. New York: Wenner, 2006.

Lewis, John, and D'Orso, Michael. *Walking with the Wind: A Memoir of the Movement*. New York: Simon & Schuster, 1996.

Linder, Douglas O. "The Chicago Eight Conspiracy Trial." www.law2.unkc.edu.

LoBianco, Tom. "Report: Aide Says Nixon's War on Drugs Targeted Blacks and Hippies," 2016. cnn.com.

Lucas, J. Anthony. "Judge Hoffman Is Taunted at Trial of the Chicago 7 After Silencing Defense Council." *New York Times*, 2/6/1970.

Mailer, Norman. *The Armies of the Night: The Novel as History, History as a Novel*. New York: Plume, 2017.

"The MC5 Performs at the 1968 Chicago Democratic National Convention Just Before All Hell Breaks Loose." openculture.com.

McLeese, Don. *MC5's Kick Out the Jams*. London: Continuum International Pub, 2005.

McLuhan, Marshall. *The Medium and the Message: Understanding the Information World*. CG Books, 2016.

———, and Lewis Henry Lapham. *Understanding Media the Extensions of Man*. Cambridge (Mass.): the MIT press, 1994.

McNeil, Don. *Moving Through Here*. New York: Knopf. 1970.

Mead, Margaret. *Culture and Commitment*. New York: Doubleday, 1970.

Minutaglio, Bill. *Most Dangerous Man in America: Timothy Leary, Richard Nixon and the Hunt for the Fugitive … King of LSD*. New York: Grand Central Pub, 2018.

Mirklinson, Jack. "60 Years Ago, Edward R. Murrow Took Down Joseph McCarthy." *Huffington Post*. 2014.

Mokoena, Tshepo. "Fleetwood Mac's Stevie Nicks: 'Lindsey Buckingham and I Will Always Be Antagonizing Each Other." The guardian.com, 2015.

Muni, Scott. "Abbie Hoffman: Interview." https://www.pastemagazine.com/articles/2008/10/abbie-hoffman-interview-part-1.html.

Nefant 12. "The Weather Underground: Brink's Robbery: The End of the Underground." blogs.evergreen.edu.

———. "The Weather Underground: Communication and Social Change in American History." Prairie Fire. blogs.evergreen.edu.

Nelson, Paul. *Little Sandy Review*, 1964.

Newton, Michael. "The Invisible Empire: The Ku Klux Klan in Florida." *The Journal of Southern Religion*, Review. jsr.fsu.edu. 2010.

Nietzsche, Friedrich. *The Will to Power*. New York: Random House. 1967.

Bibliography

"1968: Columbia in Crisis." Columbia University Archives. https://exhibitions.cul.columbia.edu/exhibits/show/1968.

"1970s Timetine." http://www.fleetwoodmac-uk.com/timeline/1970-timeline.htm.

Novak, Michael. *The Experience of Nothingness*. New York: Harper and Row. 1970.

Nunnelley, William A. *Bull Connor*. Tuscaloosa: Univ. of Alabama Press, 1991.

Oh, Joyce, and Latham, Amanda. "Senator Joseph McCarthy: McCarthyism and the Witch Hunts." The Cold War Museum. coldwar.org., 2008.

Online Archive of California. *Vietnam Day Committee*. Retrieved on April 5, 2007.

Pareles, John. "Critic's Notebook: Plagiarism in Dylan, or a Cultural Collage?" *New York Times*, 2003.

"Peter, Paul and Mary Talk About the March on Washington." Youtube.

Peter Ustinov Quotes. BrainyQuote.com, https://www.brainyquote.com/quotes/peter_ustinov_1 03982, BrainyMedia Inc., 2019.

"Phil Ochs—Pleasures of the Harbor—Classic Music Review." altrockchick.com. September 17, 2013. https://altrockchick.com/2013/09/17/classic-music-review-pleasures-of-the-harbor-by-phil-ochs/.

"Platform of the States Rights Democratic Party." *Political Party Platforms, Parties Receiving Electoral Votes, 1840–2004*. The American Presidency Project, August 14, 1948.

"Police Crack Down on Free Speech Movement Protest." www.americanrhetoric.com.

Postman, Neil. *Teaching as a Conservative Activity*. New York: Delacorte Press. 1979.

Pratt, Roy. *Rhythm and Resistance: Explorations in the Political Uses of Popular Music*. New York: Praeger, 1990.

Reineke, Hank. *Arlo Guthrie: The Warner/Reprise Years*. Lanham, MD: Rowman & Littlefield, 2012.

"Rennie Davis—Spokesman for the Lord of the Universe." http://www.prem-rawat-bio.org/renniedavis.html.

Riley, Jeannie C. *The Generation Gap*. [Nashville, Tenn.]: Plantation Records, 1970.

Rosenberg, Jennifer. "Robert Kennedy Assassination." thoughtco.com, 2017.

Rosenmann, Alexandra. "Robert Reich Has a Chilling Theory About Those Berkeley Protestors." www.alternet.com, 2017.

Rossel, Raul. "The MC5 Kick Out the Jams Album & 'F*#K Hudson's' Ad Controversy." feelnumb.com, 2011.

Rovere, Richard H. *Senator Joe McCarthy*. New York: Harcourt, Brace, 1959.

Ruhlman, William. "A Song to Sing All Over This Land." peterpaulandmary.com.

Rush, Tom. *Got a Mind to Ramble*. Liner Notes. Prestige Records, 1961.

Russell, Tony. *Country Music Records: A Discography, 1921–1942*. Oxford: Oxford University Press, 2008.

Saal, Herbert. "The Girls—Letting Go." *Newsweek*, 1969.

Sale, Kirkpatrick. *SDS: Students for a Democratic Society*. New York: Vintage, 1974.

Scaduto, Anthony. *Bob Dylan: A Biography*. New York: Helter Skelter, 2001.

Schreider, Jason. *Whispering Pines: The Northern Roots of Folk Music ... From Hank Williams to the Band*. ECW Press, 2009.

Schumacher, Michael. *There but for Fortune: The Life of Phil Ochs*. New York: Hyperion, 1996.

Senate Judiciary Committee. *Report of the Subcommittee to Investigate the Administration of the Security Act and Other Internal Security Laws of the Committee of the Judiciary*. Government Printing Office, 1975.

Shapiro, Peter. *Turn the Beat Around: The Rise and Fall of Disco*. London: Faber & Faber, 2005.

Shelton, Robert. "Bob Dylan: A Distinctive Stylist," *New York Times*, 1961.

_____. "64 FOLK FESTIVAL ENDS IN NEWPORT; Weekend Event Presented Music and Workshops," *New York Times*, 1964.

Simon, Paul. "Kodachrome." *Paul Simon Greatest Hits, Etc.* New York: Charing Cross Music, 1977.

Smith, Jeff. "This Day in Resistance History: 1968 Columbia Student Uprising." Grand Rapids Institute for Information Democracy, 2012.

Smith, Stephen, and Ellis, Kate. *Campaign '68: Hubert H. Humphrey*. Documentary. American Radio Works.

SonnyOchs.com. Retrieved April 17, 2009.

Stien, David Lewis. *Living the Revolution: Yippie in Chicago*. Indianapolis, Bobbs-Merril Co., 1969.

Students for a Democratic Society (U.S.). *The Port Huron Statement*. New York, N.Y.: Students for a Democratic Society, 1962.

Taurnicht, Mark. "History" fleetwoodmac.net.

Taylor, Carol. "History: Student for a Democratic Society Was Top 1968 Story in Boulder." *Daily Camera*. dailycamera.com, 2011.

Thompson, Robert V. *A Voluptuous God*. Kelowna, BC: CopperHouse, 2007.

Bibliography

"Top Ten Best Selling Albums Worldwide (All Time.)" rankings.com.

Travis, Alan and Gregory, Sally James. "How Rock'n'roll Fell Out of Love with Drugs." *The Guardian*. 2003.

"U.S. Orders 50,000 Troops to Vietnam." news.bbc.co.uk.,1965.

"United States Vs. O'Brien, 391 U.S. 367." supreme.justia.com, 1968.

Wald, Elijah. *Dylan Goes Electric: Newport, Seeger and the Night That Split the Sixties*. New York: Day Street Books, 2015.

Walker, Jesse. "The Acid Guru's Long Strange Trip." theamericanconservative.com, 2006.

Walsh, Kenneth T. "How Robert Kennedy's Death Shattered the Nation." *U.S. News and World Report*, 2015. usnews.com.

Walston, Mark. "The Brotherhood of Eternal Love, Timothy Leary and the Rise of LSD." markwalston.com, 2012.

Watson, Bruce. *Freedom Summer: The Savage Season That Made Mississippi Burn and Made America a Democracy*. New York: Viking, 2010.

Weather Underground Organization. *Prairie Fire: The Politics of Revolutionary Anti-Imperialism: Political Statement of the Weather Underground*. [San Francisco]: Communications Co, 1976.

Wilson, Colin. *The Essential Colin Wilson*. Berkeley, CA: Celestial Arts, 1986.

_____. *Lingard: A Novel by Colin Wilson*. New York: Crown, 1970.

Van Vogt, A. E. *The Violent Man*. New York: Pocket Books, 1962.

Vidal, Gore. "The Best Man, 1968" *Esquire*. 2008 esquire.com.

Yerxa, Fendell W. "Goldwater Says Generals Have a Nuclear Authority." *New York Times*, 1964.

Index

Abba 165
Agnew, Spiro 129
Aikens, Bill 149
"Alice's Restaurant" 148
"Alice's Restaurant Massacree" 111–112
"All My Trials" 108
All the News That's Fit to Sing 41
Allison, Mose 48
The Almanac Singers 3, 25
American Civil Liberties Union 113
"American Woman" 163
Americans for Democratic Action 88
Andersen, Eric 43–45, 57, 97, 102
Anderson, Marian 66
The Animals 137, 148
Any Day Now 56
The Armies of the Night 174
Atlantic Records 153
Axton, Hoyt 150–151

"Backlash Blues" 131
Baez, Joan 3, 27–29, 43, 50, 52–58, 65–66, 70–71, 78, 84, 89–90, 106, 108, 114, 115, 131, 140, 148, 158, 172, 174, 175
Baldry, Long John 78
Barrett, Syd 131
Beach Boys 130–131
The Beatles 130, 137, 146, 148, 150, 163
The Beau Brummels 33
"Beautiful" 150
Beck, Jeff 78
The Bee Gees 163, 165
Belafonte, Harry 33, 52–53, 56–57
Bendix, Regina 12
"Beyond the Horizon" 64
Bikel, Theodore 44, 66, 71, 89–90
Birchers, John 6
Bitter End 61
Black Arts movement 133
Black Classic Press 134
Black Liberation Army 163
Black Liberation Movement 144
Black Panther Party 124, 143, 146, 152, 161
Black Power movement 133–134, 143
Blair, Ezell 7

Block, Lawrence 95
Blonde on Blonde 149
"Blowin' in the Wind" 28, 33, 49, 62, 65–66, 70–71, 87, 107–108
Blue, David 33
Blue Dog Cellar 48
Bob Dylan 69–71
"Bob Dylan's Dream" 70
Bodenheim, Maxwell 47
Boggs, Carl 105
"Boogie Oogie Oogie" 165
Bootleg Series 70
"Born to Be Wild" 137
Bottom Line 47
Boudin, Kathy 163
Bound for Glory 68
'Bout Changes and Things 97–98
Bradstreet, Anne 81
Brand, Oscar 27, 172
Brando, Marlon 9
Brautigan, Richard 137
"Bridge Over Troubled Water" 163
Briggs, John 163
Broadside magazine 49
Brokaw, Tom 173
Brooks, Garth 172
The Brotherhood of Eternal Love 160
The Brothers Four 27
Brown, Charles Brockton 137
Brown, Donald 67, 70
Brown, Peter Stone 2
Brown, Rita Mae 5
Browne, Jackson 150
Brunswick 46
Buckingham, Lindsay 155–156
Buckley, William F. 81
Burroughs, Brian 161
Butterfield, Paul 91
Buttrey, Kenneth 149
Byrd, Charlie 47–48
The Byrds 33, 78, 86, 97, 111–113, 130

Cafe Au Go Go 47
Cafe Wha 47
Calypso King 52

Index

Camp, Hamilton 60, 62
Campbell, Glen 164
Campbell, Ian 86
Capitol Records 26
Captain & Tennille 163
Carawan, Guy 57
"Carolina in My Mind" 150
"Carry It On" 49
Carson, Sandra 77
Cash, Johnny 5, 41, 67, 69, 140, 147, 172
Castro, Fidel 117, 145, 161
Cerri, Dick 48
Chad and Jeremy 148
Chad Mitchell Trio 61, 172
Chambers Brothers 130
Chandler, Len 43, 78
Chaney, James 44, 50, 73
"Changes" 29
Chic 165
Chicago Eight 124
Chicago Seven 126, 141, 144–145, 146
Children of God 155
"Chimes of Freedom" 89, 105
Christgau, Robert 29, 141
Chronicles 64, 70
"Cindy, Oh Cindy" 32
The Circle Game 150
Circle in the Square Theater 47
"City of New Orleans" 148
Clancy, Liam 69
Clancy Brothers 69
Clancy Brothers' Tradition 48
Clark, Gene 151
Clark, Judith Alice 163
Clark, Atty. Gen. Ramsey 114
Clifton, Bill 89
Clinton, Bill 156
Club 47 55, 70
Club Passim 55
Coates, Paul 134
Coffin, William Sloane 114
Coleman, Henry S. 136
Collins, Judy 33, 50, 106, 124, 171
Columbia Records 48, 55, 69
"Come and Get Your Love" 163
Committee for a Sane Nuclear Policy (SANE) 94, 105
Confessions of a Yakuza 64
Congress of Racial Equality (CORE) 37–38, 42, 71, 83
Connor, Bull 37, 42, 53
Cooper, Clarence 89
"Copper Kettle" 26
Coral Records 46
Cosby, Bill 62
Council of Federated Organizations (COFO) 35, 37–38, 44, 73
Country Joe and the Fish 30, 84–85, 136, 152

Cousins, Norman 105
Cream 148
Creedence Clearwater Revival 131
Croce, Jim 151
Cronkite, Walter 125
Crosby, Stills and Nash 78
"Crucifixion" 29

Daley, Richard 118, 121–122, 128
"Dancing Queen" 165
Dane, Barbara 171
Darin, Bobby 147
Darling, Eric 89
"Darling Corey" 26
David's Album 158
Davis, Michael 152–153
Davis, Rennie 124, 126, 146
"A Day in the Life" 130
Days of Rage 161
Dean, James 67
"Dear Landlord" 158
Death of a Rebel 45
"The Death of Emmett Till" 65
Decca 46
de Kooning, Willem 137
Dellinger, Dave 124, 126
Dennison, George 100
Denver, John 163–164
"Disco Lady" 164–165
Dixiecrat Party 79–80, 128
Dixiecrat Revolution 80
"Do You Think I'm Sexy" 165
Dobson, Bonnie 78
Domino Theory 93
Donghi, Dianne 162
Donovan 30, 132, 148
"Don't Stop (Thinking About Tomorrow)" 156
"Don't Think Twice, It's All Right" 56, 62, 70, 108
Dorhn, Bernadette 173
"Draft Dodger Rag" 29, 89, 108, 111
"Draft Morning" 111, 131
"Draft Resister" 147
Drake, Nick 151
Duncan, Isadora 47
Dunhill Records 110
Dusheck, Nina 131
Dylan, Bob 3, 13, 27–28, 43, 44, 48, 49, 54–57, 59, 62–71, 78, 87–93, 97, 102, 105, 107–108, 113, 122, 140–141, 147–149, 158, 174

The Eagles 151, 153–154, 158
Eagles 154
Eisenhower, Dwight 18, 20, 47, 59, 93–94, 99, 102
"The Elections Don't Mean Shit—Vote Where the Power Is—Our Power Is in the Street" 142

Index

Electra Records 41, 152–153, 172
Eliot, Marc 124, 174
Eliot, T.S. 137
Elliot, Cass 62
Elston Gunn and the Rock Boppers 66–67; see also Dylan, Bob
Erickson, Roky 131
Erlichman, John 142
Evans, Linda Sue 162
"Eve of Destruction" 30, 32, 109–110
Evers, Medgar 43, 104
Evert, Chris 5
The Experience of Nothingness 95

"The Face of Folk Music" 43, 51
"Facing the Rising Sun: African Americans, Japan the the Rise of Afro-Asian Solidarity" 134
Faithful, Marianne 78
Farina, Richard 56
Feldman, Bob 134–135
Festival of Life 118
"A Fifth of Beethoven" 164
"50 Megatons" 79
Fleetwood, Mick 155–157
Fleetwood Mac 131, 154–156, 158
Fleetwood Mac 155–156
Flying Burrito Brothers 111
Folk City 70
"For What It's Worth" 110
Ford, Tennessee Ernie 26
Forman, James 52
"Fortunate Son" 131
"Forty Years Later, We Still Need Phil Ochs" 2
Fourteenth Amendment 36
Francis, Connie 148
Franklin, Aretha 150
Free Speech Movement 83–84
Freedom Libraries 72
Freedom Riders 30, 36–38, 40, 42–43, 52, 53, 77, 93
Freedom Riders of the South 11
Freedom Schools 72
Freedom Singers 57, 66, 71
Freedom Summer 35, 50–51, 62, 72, 82–83, 88, 93, 102, 106, 168, 171
The Freewheelin' Bob Dylan 70–71, 107
Friend and Lover 137
Froines, John 124, 145
The Fugs 147
"Fujiama Mama" 79

Gaslight 45, 47
Gaynor, Gloria 165
"Generation Gap" 102
Gerde's Folk City 47–49, 61, 69
Gershwin, George 47
"Get Down Tonight" 165

Getz, Stan 48
Gibb, Andy 165
Gibson, Bob 55, 60, 88, 107
Gil, Clarence 26
Gilbert, David 163
Gilday, William 146–147
Gilmore, Mikal 67
"Gimme Shelter" 147
Ginsberg, Allen 124, 136
"Girl from the North Country" 70, 140
"The Girls—Letting Go" 149
Gitlin, Todd 16, 74, 103, 134, 142, 147
"Give Peace a Chance" 146
Glory Records 32
Glover, Jim 41, 88
Goffin, Jerry 102
Gold, Ted 161
Golden, Lotti 149
Goldstein, Richard 150
Goldwater, Barry 86, 105
Goodman, Andrew 44, 50, 73
Goodman, Paul 23, 100
Gore, Leslie 148
Gorson, Arthur 88
Government Committee on Operations of the Senate 20
The Grapes of Wrath 68
Grateful Dead 78, 136
"Great Atomic Power" 78
Great Folk Scare 60
"The Great Mandala" 108
Green, Peter 131, 154–155
Gregory, Dick 106
Grossman, Albert 55, 60–63, 70, 88, 91, 158
Guerrilla Warfare 146
Guess Who 163
Guest, Christopher 155
Guevara, Che 117, 145–146
Gunnn, Elston *see* Dylan, Bob
Guthrie, Arlo 68, 111–112, 124, 148
Guthrie, Marjorie 12
Guthrie, Woody 3, 12, 27, 41, 59, 67–69, 87, 91
Guttman, Allen 89
"Gym Crow" 135

Haggard, Merle 5
Hammond, John 48, 69
"A Hard Rain's a-Gonna Fall" 70, 78, 107
Hardin, Tim 33
Harlem Renaissance 133
"Harper Valley PTA" 102
Harris, David 56, 115, 140
Harris, Gabriel 56
Harris, Rutha Mae 66
Harry Belafonte Singers 61
Havens, Ritchie 33, 78
Hayakawa, Alan R. 168–169
Hayakawa, S.I. 168

191

Index

Hayden, Tom 11, 76–82, 124, 134, 136, 144
Hayes, Lee 27, 61, 66
"Heartbreak Hotel" 41
Hedburg, Mitch 167
Hendrix, Jimi 131
Henley, Don 154
Henske, Judy 119
"Here's to the State of Mississippi" 45, 168, 171
Herndon, James 100, 137
"He's Got the Whole World in His Hands" 66
"Hesitation Blues" 130
Hester, Carolyn 3, 32, 43–44, 46–51, 57, 59–60, 69, 171–172, 174
Highlander Folk School 56
The Highwaymen 27
Hikmet, Zazim 86
Hinkey, David 2
Hitler, Adolf 124, 168
Hoffman, Abbie 84–85, 117–124, 126, 135, 145
Hoffman, Dustin 161
Hoffman, Judge Julius 124, 145
Hoffman, Judge William 125
Holly, Buddy 32, 33, 41, 46, 48, 67
Hollywood Ten 22
Holt, John 100
Holy Modal Rounders 130
Hooker, John Lee 147
Hoover, J. Edgar 143
Hope, Bob 89
Horn, Shirley 48
Horne, Gerald 134
"Hotel California" 154, 158
House Un-American Activities Committee (HUAC) 21–22, 27, 59
Houston, Cisco 27, 59
"How Can You Mend a Broken Heart" 163
"How I Got Over" 66
Hughes, Langston 131
Humphrey, Hubert 27, 109, 127–129, 142
"Hurricane" 174
Hurt, John 51, 168, 172
"The Hustle" 164

"I Ain't Marching Anymore" 29, 89, 106–107, 125
I Ain't Marchin' Anymore 41
"I Come and Stand at Every Door" 78, 86
"I Don't Wanna Go to Vietnam" 147
"I Feel Fine" 130
"I Feel Like I'm Fixin' to Die Rag" 85
"I Have a Dream" speech 53–54, 56
"I Shall Be Free" 70
"I Want Jesus to Walk with Me" 33
"I Was Born About 10,000 Years Ago" 61
"I Will Survive" 165
Ian, Janis 63
Ian and Sylvia 59
Ibsen, Henrik 47

"If I Had a Hammer" 33, 61–62, 66, 108
"If I Were Free" 108
"I'm Going to Say It Now" 102
"I'm on My Way" 66
Institute for Defense Analysis 134
Institute for the Study of Nonviolence 55, 106
"It Isn't Nice" 171
"It Makes the World Go Round" 147
"It's My Party (and I'll Cry If I Want To)" 148
"It's Too Late" 163
"I've Been 'Buked and I've Been Scorned" 66
Ives, Burl 26

Jackson, Mahalia 66
Jackson, Michael 158
Jackson, Wanda 79
Jacobs, John 142, 144–145, 161
Jefferson Airplane 30, 130, 135
"Jesus Hits Like the Atomic Bomb" 78
Jim Crow laws 42
"Jimmy Newman" 30
"Joe Hill" 108
John Wesley Harding 140
Johnson, Lyndon Baines 73, 82–90, 105, 109, 111–116, 127–128, 142–143, 167
Jones, Brian 131
"Joy to the World" 163
Just, Richard 1, 2

Kazee, Buell 26
K.C. and the Sunshine Band 165
Keating, Kenneth 25–28, 30, 59
Kennedy, John F. 38, 42, 59, 82, 88–89, 94, 117, 125
Kennedy, Robert 116–117, 127, 129, 141
Kerouac, Jack 76
"Kick Out the Jams" 152
Kick Out the Jams 152
"Kill for Peace" 147
"Kill Your Sons" 147
King, Carole 102, 150, 163
King, Coretta 62
King, Martin Luther, Jr. 29, 37–38, 42, 49, 52–54, 56, 62, 129, 133, 141
King Crimson 147
Kingston Trio 26, 60, 117, 155, 172
The Kinks 148
Kooper, Al 149
Korzibski, Alfred 166
Kramer, Wayne 152–153
Krassner, Paul 117–118, 122
Ku Klux Klan 21, 37–38, 42, 52–53, 168
Kuntzler, William 124–125

Lady Gaga 1
La Farge, Peter 63
La Follette, Robert, Jr. 19
Landau, Jon 153

Index

Langhorne, Bruce 48
Language in Action 168
Language on Thought and Action 168
"Last Night I Had the Strangest Dream" 172–173
"Lay Down (Candles in the Rain)" 147
"Le Freak" 165
Leace, Donal 172
Leadbelly 69, 91
League for Spiritual Discovery (LSD) 160
Leary, Timothy 124, 159–160
Lee, Bill 48
Lehrer, Tom 86
Lenin, Vladimir 144, 161
Lennon, John 146
"Let It Be" 163
"Let Me Be Good to You" 165
Levine, Alan 120
Lewis, John 37
Lichtenstein, Roy 137
Lincoln, Abraham 17
Little Richard 66–67
Living Theater 47
Lloyd, Charles 172
Lomax, Alan 87, 91–92, 98
London, Jack 64
The Lonely Crowd 18
"The Lonesome Death of Hattie Carroll" 65
"Lonesome Valley" 89
The Louvin Brothers 78
Love and Theft 64
"Love Is All You Need" 147
"Love Machine" 165
"Love Me, I'm a Liberal" 29, 104, 108
Love Unlimited Orchestra 163
"Love Will Keep Us Together" 163
"Love's Theme" 163
Lowell Blanchard and the Valley Trio 78
Lulu 78
Luther, Martin 30
Lynd, Straughton 11
"Lyndon Johnson Told the Nation" 30, 111

MacDonald, Country Joe 84–85
"Maggie's Farm" 102, 107, 158
Mailer, Norman 124, 173–174
Majority Coalition 136
Makem, Tommy 69
Malcolm X 104, 133
"Man in the Mirror" 158
Manfred Mann 148
March on Washington 53–54, 65–66, 87
Marlowe, Christopher 21
Marshall, Thurgood 37
Martin, Vince 32, 78, 166
"Masters of War" 70, 78, 87, 107
May 19th Communist Organization 162
Mayall, John 154

McCain, Franklin 6
McCarthy, Sen. Eugene 30, 109, 127, 116, 140, 142
McCarthy, Joseph 18–22, 59
McCartney, Paul 163
McCluhan, Marshall 101
McCoy, Charlie 149
McCoy, Van 164
McCurdy, Ed 172
McEldowney, Carol 134
MC5 122, 152–154
McGovern, George 127, 142
McGuinn, Roger 97
McGuire, Barry 30, 109
McLuhan, Marshall 92, 160
McNeil, Don 119–120
McVie, Christine 155
McVie, John 155
Mead, Margaret 99, 104
Melanie 147, 149
Melton, Barry 84–85
Mezzrow, Mezz 65
Million Man March on Washington 62, 109
Mills, C. Wright 18
The Miracles 165
Mississippi Democratic Party 73
Mississippi Freedom Democratic Party (MFDP) 73
Mississippi Summer 43, 45
"Mr. Tambourine Man" 89, 97, 113
Mitchell, Joni 149–150
The Monkees 102
The Monroe Brothers 26
Montauk, Paul 84
Monterey Folk Festival 70
Morgan, Irene 37
"Morning Dew" 78
Morrison, Van 151
Moses, Bob Parris 34–44, 49–50, 72–74, 106
Moss, Annie Lee 21
"Mother's Little Helper" 102
The Motorcycle Diaries 146
Murphy, Walter 164
Murrow, Edward R. 20–21
Murtagh, John M. 161
"My Back Pages" 105
"My Eyes Adored You" 163
"My Son John" 30
"My Uncle" 111
Mystery Trend 130

Nashville Skyline 140, 147
National Association for the Advancement of Colored People (NAACP) 37–38, 53
National Coordinating Committee to End the War in Vietnam 111
National Day of Protest 84–85
Nazareth 78

Index

Neil, Fred 32, 78
Nelson, Paul 90
New Christy Minstrels 27
New Faces of 1964 44
New Left 11-12, 22, 24-25, 33, 78-79, 84, 86, 88, 95, 101-102, 105, 114, 116-117, 121-122, 127-132, 141-143, 146, 154, 158, 165-166, 168, 170, 173-174
New World Singers 49-50
New York Civil Liberties Union 120
Newport Folk Festival 42, 55, 71, 88-90, 98
Newton, Huey P. 152
The Next President 60
Nicks, Stevie 155-156
Nietzsche, Friedrich 94-95
Nimitz, Adm. Chester A. 19
"The 1913 Massacre" 68
"Nineteenth Nervous Breakdown" 102
Nitty Gritty Dirt Band 151
Nixon, Richard 118, 128-129, 141-142, 146, 160, 167
"No More Auction Block for Me" 29
Novak, Michael 95-96
Nyro, Laura 149, 151

Obama, Barack 3, 175
Ochs, Jacob "Jack" 40
Ochs, Phil 1-3, 27-29, 31, 40-45, 54, 57, 63, 69, 88-89, 102, 104-108, 111, 117-120, 122, 124-126, 140-141, 168, 171-172, 174
Odetta 29, 51, 57, 61, 66
"Oh Freedom" 29, 56, 66, 80
Okum, Milt 61
Old Left 11, 86, 94, 104, 108, 114
On the Road 76
On the Waterfront 9
"On Work" 101
"One More Parade" 108
O'Neil, Joseph 6
O'Neill, Eugene 47
"Only a Pawn in Their Game" 43, 65-66, 71, 87
Ono, Yoko 146
Oughton, Diana 161
"Outside a Small Circle of Friends" 172
"Oxford Town" 65, 70

Pat Garrett and Billy the Kid 174
"Paths of Victory" 105
"The Patriot Game" 65
Patterson, Annie 171
Paul, Cyril 171
Paul Butterfield Blues Band 91, 93
Paxton, Tom 30, 32, 63, 111, 147
"Peace Will Come (According to Plan)" 147
Pearson, Drew 20
"People Got to Be Free" 137
Perelman, S. J. 23

"Pet Sounds" 130
Peter and Gordon 148
Peter, Paul and Mary 3, 27-28, 30, 33, 43, 50, 55-57, 59-63, 66, 70, 71, 88-89, 106, 108-109, 112, 116, 140, 174
Petty, Norman 32, 46
Pickett, Clarence 105
The Pilgrim Travelers 78
Pink Floyd 131, 148
Plant, Robert 78
"Pleasant Valley Sunday" 102, 150
"Pleasures of the Harbor" 172
Pleasures of the Harbor 141
Plessy vs. Ferguson 36
Poitier, Sidney 52-53
Pollock, Jackson 137
Poole, Charlie 130
Porco, Mike 61
Port Huron Statement 11, 57, 77-78, 80-81, 134
Post, Jim 33, 137
Postman, Neil 100, 149
Power, Katherine Ann 146
"The Power and the Glory" 29, 88, 108
The Power Elite 18
Pozo Seco Singers 78
Prairie Fire Collective 162
Prairie Fire: The Politics of Revolutionary Anti-Imperialism 162
Presley, Elvis 29, 41, 67, 79
Progressive Labor Party 89, 113
Proust, Marcel 65
The Purification 47

"Rainy Day Man" 150
Rand, Sally 172
Rankin, John E. 21
The Rascals 137
Rawls, Lou 165
"Red Sails in the Sunset" 64
Redbone 163
Reed, Lou 147
Reich, Robert 2
Reiner, Rob 155
Reisman, David 18, 170
"A Report on Senator Joseph R. McCarthy" 20
The Resistance 113-114
Resource Center for Nonviolence 106
"Revolution" 137
Reynaldo and Claire 174
Reynolds, Malvina 78, 171
"Rhinestone Cowboy" 164
Richmond, David 6-7
Riley, Jeannie C. 102-103
Ritchie, Jean 89
Rivers, Joan 62
The Road to Miltown 23

194

Index

Robbins, Hargus "Pig" 149
Robbins, Mary 78
Robbins, Terry 161
Robeson, Paul 56–57
"Rocky Mountain High" 163
Rogers, Carl 81, 137
Rohmer, Sax 64–65
"Rollin' and Tumblin'" 64
Rolling Stone Revue 174
The Rolling Stones 102, 131, 147–148
Rolling Thunder Review 56
Ronstadt, Linda 151, 153
Rose, Tim 78
Rotolo, Suze 65, 71
Rubin, Jerry 84–85, 117–120, 122–124, 126
Rubyfruit Jungle 5
Rudd, Mark 142
Rumours 156
Rush, Tom 150, 159
Russell, Bertrand 101
Russell, Sonny 79
Ryder, Serena 172

Safka, Melanie 78
Saga, Dr. Junichi 64
Sahl, Mort 60
"Saigon Bride" 131
Sainte-Marie, Buffy 30, 32, 50, 131–132
Sanders, Ed 147
Sandperl, Ira 106
Santana, Carlos 146
Saturday Night Fever 164
Savio, Mario 84, 106
Saxe, William 146
Scaduto, Anthony 87
Scarlet Ribbons 46
Schwerner, Michael 44, 50, 73
Seale, Bobby 124
The Searchers 78
See It Now 20
Seeger, Pete 3, 22, 26–27, 41, 57, 59–61, 66, 86–87, 89–90, 98, 108, 172
The Seekers 78
The Serendipity Singers 27
Sgt. Pepper's Lonely Hearts Club Band 130
"Shadow Dancing" 165
Shakespeare, William 21
Shapiro, David 135
Shapiro, Peter 164
Shaw, George Bernard 10
Shelton, Robert 69
The Shirelles
Silent Majority 129
"Silly Love Songs" 163
Silver, Roy 62, 70
Simon & Garfunkel 30, 86, 163, 172
Simon, Carly 150
Simon, Paul 101, 151

Simone, Nina 131
"A Simple Song of Freedom" 147
Sinclair, John 152–153
The Singing Socialists 41
Sirhan, Sirhan 127
"Sixteen Tons" 25–26
Skinner, B.F. 81, 137
"Sky Pilot" 137
Sloan, P.F. 30, 32, 109
Smith, Fred 152
Smith, Warren 78
"So Far Away" 150
"So Long, Mom (a Song for World War III)" 86
"Something in the Way She Moves" 150
"Sometimes I Feel Like a Motherless Child" 29
Song Swappers 60
Songwriters Hall of Fame Lifetime Achievement Award 62
South, Bill 149
Souther, J.D. 151
Southern Christian Leadership Foundation (SCL) 38
Spencer, Jeremy 155
Spock, Dr. Benjamin 94, 105–106, 114
Springfield, Buffalo 110
Springsteen, Bruce 153
Stanley, H.M. 10
"The Star-Spangled Banner" 131
Starr, Edwin 130
States' Rights Democratic Party 80
Steinbeck, John 68
Steppenwolf 137, 147
Stevens, Cat 150
Stevenson, Robert Louis 65, 146
Stewart, John 117, 150, 155
Stewart, Ron 165
Stone, I.F. 106
Stookey, Noel Paul 60–62, 140
Stop the Draft week 113
"Street Fighting Man" 147
Student Afro Society (SAS) 135–136
Student Nonviolent Coordinating Council (SNCC) 34–38, 40, 43, 52–53, 71, 74, 77, 88, 105
Students for a Democratic Society (SDS) 11, 77, 79, 81–83, 88, 90, 105–106, 113, 133–136, 141–144, 159
"Stupid Cupid" 148
"Subterranean Homesick Blues" 102, 141
"Summertime" 47
"The Sun Is Burning" 86
"Sunshine on My Shoulders" 163–164
"Sunshine, Sunshine" 150
"Superbird" 85
"Suppose They Gave a War and Nobody Came" 131

Index

"Take It Easy" 154
Take Two 98
"Talkin' Birmingham Jail" 88
"Talkin' Vietnam Pot Luck Blues" 147
"Talkin' World War III Blues" 71, 78, 87
Tape from California 141
Tapestry 150
The Tarriers 32
A Taste of Honey 165
Taylor, James 150
Taylor, Johnny 164
Teaching as a Conservative Activity 149
"Thank God I'm a Country Boy" 164
Theatre of the Absurd 47
Their Greatest Hits 153
"There But for Fortune" 108
"Thirsty Boots" 102
Thirteenth Floor Elevator 130–131
"This Cold War with You" 79
This Is Spinal Tap 155
"This Land Is Your Land" 108
Thomas, Norman 106
Thompson, Dennis 152
Thompson, Robert V. 169
Thoreau, Henry David 101
Three Dog Night 163
Thurmond, Strom 79–80
"Time Has Come Today" 130
"The Times They Are A-Changin'" 65–66, 87, 105, 108
Tobacco Road 6
"Too Many Martyrs" 88
Trane, John *see* Ochs, Phil
Transcendental Meditation 146
Traum, Happy 49
Travers, Mary 60–61, 89, 112, 140, 174
Travis, Merle 25
The Troggs 148
Truman, Harry 20, 22, 79–80
Trump, Donald 1, 3, 10, 175
Turn the Beat Around: The Rise and Fall of Disco 164
Turner, Gil 49–50
Tusk 156
Twain, Mark 65
"21st Century Schizoid Man" 147
Twitty, Conway 67
Tyner, Rob 152
Tyson, Ian 59

United Auto Workers 77
"Universal Soldier" 30, 131–132
"The Unquiet Grave" 89
"Uranium Rock" 78
Ustinov, Peter 18

Valerie, Robert 146
Valli, Frankie 163

Vanguard Records 55
Van Ronk, Dave 45, 60, 171–172
van Vogt, A.E. 9–10, 13, 19
Vee, Bobby 67
Vietnam Day Committee 84–85, 106, 130
Village Folk Revival 60
The Village Gate 47
Village People 165
The Village Vanguard 47
Vonnegut, Kurt 137
Voting Rights Drive 53

Walter, Jesse 160
"The War Is Over" 1, 118
War Is Over Rally 118
War Resisters' League 86
"War: What Is It Good For?" 130
Warhol, Andy 137
Warner Brothers Records 61, 155
Washington, Jackie 43, 171
"Wasn't That a Time" 108
Waters, Muddy 64, 91–92, 112
Watson, Bruce 40
Watts, Alan 106
Wayne Fontana & the Mindbenders 148
"We Shall Not Be Moved" 28, 80, 136
"We Shall Overcome" 7, 54, 66, 71, 80, 84, 108
Weather Underground (aka The Weathermen) 141–147, 154, 156, 158–163, 166, 171, 173
Weather Underground Organization (WUO) 144, 147
The Weavers 3, 22, 41, 59–61, 108, 172
Wein, George 89
Weinberg, Jack 83
Weiner, Lee 124
Weisberg, Eric 91
Welch, Bob 155
Welch, Kevin 5
West Coast Pop Art Experimental Band 131
"We've Got to Get Out of This Place" 148
"What Are You Fighting For?" 108
"What Have They Done to the Rain" 78
"When Jesus Lived in Galilee" 33
"When the Deal Goes Down" 64
"When the Ship Comes In" 65–66, 87, 108
"When Will We Be Paid for the Work We've Done" 80
"Where Have All the Flowers Gone" 108
"Where Is Phil Ochs When We Really Need Him?" 2
"Where the Blue of the Night (Meets the Gold of the Day)" 64
"Where You Lead" 150
Whiskey Rebellion 26
White Citizens Council 38
White Collar 18
White Panthers 152

Index

"White Rabbit" 130
White, Josh 172
White, Josh, Jr. 173
The Who 30, 148
"Who's Next" 86
"Will You Love Me Tomorrow" 150
Williams, Hank 32, 67
Williams, Hank, Sr. 41
Wilson, Brian 131
Wilson, Colin 9
Winchester, Jesse 150
"Witchy Woman" 154
"With God on Our Side" 65, 87, 89, 107
The Witmark Demos 70
The Wobblies 25, 108
Wolf, Kate 50
"Wooden Ships" 78
The Word 88
Wright, Fielding L. 79–80

Yarrow, Peter 33, 60–62, 89–90, 109, 140
Yiannopoulis, Milo 1, 2
"YMCA" 165
Yogi, Maharishi 146
"You Make Me Feel Like a Natural Woman" 150
"You'll Never Find Another Love Like Mine" 165
Young, Neil 151–152
Young, Rob 2
Young Socialist Alliance 89
"You're Gonna Miss Me" 130
Youth International Party (Yippies) 104, 117–118, 120–122, 124–125, 127, 132
"You've Got a Friend" 150

Zimmerman, Robert Allen *see* Dylan, Bob

www.ingramcontent.com/pod-product-compliance
Lightning Source LLC
Chambersburg PA
CBHW032100300426
44116CB00007B/830